STREETWISE®

PROJECT MANAGEMENT

STREETWISE®

PROJECT MANAGEMENT

How to Manage People,
Processes, and Time
to Achieve the Results
You Need

by Michael S. Dobson

Adams Media Corporation
Avon, Massachusetts

A Streetwise® Publication.
Streetwise® is a registered trademark of F+W Publications, Inc.

Published by Adams Media, an F+W Publications Company
57 Littlefield Street, Avon, MA 02322 U.S.A
www.adamsmedia.com

ISBN: 1-58062-770-6
Printed in the United States of America.

J I H G F E D C B

Library of Congress Cataloging-in-Publication Data
Dobson, Michael Singer.
Streetwise® project management / Michael Dobson.
p.   cm. Includes index.
ISBN 1-58062-770-6
1. Project management. I. Title: Project management. II. Title.
HD69.P75 D633 2002
658.4'04–dc21
2002010126

Cover illustration by Eric Mueller.
This book is available at quantity discounts for bulk purchases.
For information, call 1-800-872-5627.

Acknowledgments

No matter whose name is inscribed on a book's cover, there are almost always many people whose knowledge, time, and effort contributed to it. I thank my colleagues at Management Concepts, especially Ted Leemann, Shelly Smith, and Ginger Levin, for advice, technical support, and ongoing kindnesses. For the project management knowledge I've been fortunate to gain over the years, I thank my friends and mentors, including (in alphabetical order) Bob Bapes, Walter J. Boyne, Bill Capstack, Marshall Dodd, Rosina Harter, Pat McWard, Kai Rambow, Richard Vail, Dain Zinn, and many more. The editorial and production people at Adams Media, including Jill Alexander (and others yet unknown) have put in yeoman's hours on this project. I thank my agents Elizabeth Pomada and Michael Larsen for their continued support, and thank Celia Rocks for bringing me to this project and for her ongoing support. And, of course, my thanks and love to my wife and partner Deborah Dobson and my son Jamie for encouragement and space during the writing of this book. Any remaining errors and omissions are my own.

I provide training and consulting services in project management for clients worldwide. You can contact me through my Web site at *www.dobson-books.com*.

Contents

CONTENTS

PART IV: MYSTERIES OF PLANNING REVEALED

PART V: RISK, QUALITY, AND OTHER PLANNING CONCERNS

CONTENTS

PART VI: EXECUTING, TRACKING, AND ADJUSTING THE PROJECT

PART VII: CLOSING OUT THE PROJECT

Introduction

Projects have been around since before the building of the pyramids, but the modern discipline known as project management experienced most of its development in the late 1950s and 1960s here in the United States. Operating project managers—people experiencing major challenges in managing some of the most complex projects ever attempted in the history of the human race—turned to the latest disciplines of operations research, systems engineering, statistics, and the new field of computers to build tools to cope with those challenges.

Today, we are the beneficiaries of a great body of practical and tested project management knowledge and techniques, enabling us to succeed regularly at the most complex of project endeavors. The discipline of project management enables us to do many things we could not previously attempt. Isaac Newton famously observed, "If I see further, it is because I stand on the shoulders of giants." We accomplish what we can accomplish today because we, too, stand on the shoulders of giants.

Almost everyone manages projects, at least in some sense, whether they follow formal project management or not. We all know that projects have challenges. With the tools and insights of project management firmly in hand, you can manage your own projects better—and achieve the goal at hand on time, on budget, and with proper performance.

You will learn several skills of being a streetwise project manager. You will learn what exactly makes up a project as well as strategies and tips to help you better manage the project. You will learn that understanding the goal—the reason why something is being undertaken—is crucial, and that other people have varying degrees of interest and power that can have an impact on you.

This book will also help you stand up to challenges that seem impossible to conquer. While facing these challenges will take quite a bit of hard work and time, you will see that not following through correctly may hurt your project, not just in one phase of it but

> Project management enables us to do many things we could not previously attempt.

throughout the life of the project. For example, getting assumptions, constraints, deliverables, requirements, and hidden requirements fully identified and measured can be a difficult and time-consuming stage of any project. However, there are several consequences of failure at this stage. If you fail to properly identify assumptions and constraints, if you miss identifying some project deliverables, if you don't identify all the measurable requirements, you'll normally discover them late in your project, where the cost and time to get back on track may be prohibitive.

There is certainly a lot to learn about project management. From defining a project to figuring out who is for and against you, from finding the hidden opportunities in every project to determining risk levels, from figuring out which tools to use to providing motivation to team members, this book will take you through the various steps and give you the information you need to become a successful project manager regardless of what type of project you are working on.

Some investigation and questioning is a good way to get started on the right track. What else do you need to know to be a successful project manager? Let's look a little more deeply.

> This book will give you the information you need to become a successful project manager.

PART I

Kick-Starting Project Management

- **How an understanding of key project management principles can spell the difference between success and failure**
- **How to "reality-check" your project and define "good enough" in practical terms**
- **How to separate the important projects from routine work, and how to balance one project against others**
- **How to use project management tools to discover hidden opportunities within every project**

Why Are Projects So Difficult?

Defining a Project

Projects are a very special area in the world of work. Most work is ongoing. That is, there's no planned point at which you stop having to do it. Let's say you're in telephone customer service. There's no point at which the calls stop coming in. That's work. On the other hand, let's say you're writing a handbook of answers for typical customer questions. There is a planned point at which you've got the handbook completed and there isn't anything else to do. That's a discrete project.

The project's end is an essential element of any project, from writing a report to building the International Space Station. At the end of a project, you have an output, which is some product, service, or answer. If it's a good project, then the product, service, or answer is something that satisfies the project's customer, who may be classified as internal or external.

Temporary and Unique

The official definition of "project" by the Project Management Institute has two essential characteristics: temporary and unique. We've talked about the temporary part, namely the project's end. And if it doesn't end—if you have what people call an "ongoing project," you have a problem. Either what you're doing is not really a project, or it is a project, but in trouble. Some projects get stuck at the 90 percent completion point and tend to stay there, which costs energy and focus and doesn't produce results. One thing you will quickly learn is to finish your projects or kill them; there is no middle ground.

Projects are unique in at least some essential elements, even when they're structurally similar. For example, you might be responsible for organizing your company's participation in several trade shows. Each trade show is a project—it ends. Even though each trade show has numerous elements in common with every other trade show, each will also have unique elements: different convention center rules, different audiences to reach, different cities, different team members to attend, different brochures and handouts—and above all, different problems. You may have done this a hundred times before, but there may still be a lot of surprises out there.

> Some projects get stuck at the 90 percent completion point, which costs energy and focus and doesn't produce results.

Because projects are temporary and unique, many of the normal standards and disciplines in the world of work don't quite apply. Often, there's a lot at stake, so the interest of top management may be much higher, and their involvement more active. Because there are no "cookie cutter" projects, it may well be that neither you nor anyone else in your organization fully understands what you're up against. Deadlines may be arbitrary and even arguably unfair.

Techniques and Tools

Project management is a discipline that was invented "in the trenches." Almost all the techniques and tools of project management, from the Gantt Chart to critical path theory, were originally invented by active project managers trying to cope with the special circumstances of their own projects. Some techniques turn out to be applicable and useful in a wide range of project circumstances, and they've been tested under battlefield conditions over many years.

Your projects are unique. But practicing project managers from different backgrounds have experienced similar problems and similar challenges and have risen to meet them. And when you master the practical tools and concepts of project management, you'll find that your ability to get your projects done the right way—on time, on budget, to the agreed-upon standard—is remarkably improved.

What You're Up Against

In the movie *Apollo 13*, there's a scene in which all the project engineers have been gathered into a conference room. The mission chief comes in, trailed by his assistant whose arms are filled with tubes, boxes, and strange gadgets. "This is everything that's available on the ship," announces the mission chief. "You have to build a carbon dioxide exchanger from these items that will purify the air onboard. The crew has exactly one hour of breathable air left. And I want to tell you: Failure is not an option."

Now that's a project assignment! There's a definite and planned end, and a product that will be the output. Clearly, this project qualifies as unique.

When you master the practical tools and concepts of project management, you'll find that your ability to get your projects done the right way—on time, on budget, is remarkably improved.

The Bottom Line

Your first mission on any project is to understand its bottom line: what do you have to do, and what are the constraints under which you have to do it? The streetwise project manager gets this part done first, by asking good questions and probing the project's circumstance and history. Your ability to negotiate (if any) is always strongest at the beginning of a project and decays steadily from that point on.

Every project operates in the universe of the Triple Constraints, which are time (how long you've got), cost (how much can you spend, either in money or in resources or both), and performance (what exactly has to be accomplished). And you've got the Triple Constraints clearly spelled out. Following the example, how long have you got? One hour. How much can you spend? No more than the loose items on the table. What exactly has to be accomplished? The gadget you build has to purify the air well enough so that the astronauts can continue to live.

Notice that under normal circumstances, a deadline of one hour to build the necessary gadget would be highly unreasonable. And the available resources are pretty pitiful, too. But circumstances often drive projects. It has to be done because it *has* to be done, fair or not, reasonable or not. And notice as well that there isn't even a guarantee that it's possible to achieve the goal, in spite of the statement "Failure is not an option." The problem is that failure has consequences, even if it turns out not to be the project team's fault. Those astronauts would still be dead. Now, we hope that most of your projects aren't nearly so dramatic. Still, project managers often come into some pretty tough challenges.

Short of Time and Resources

From the building of the pyramids right down to the current day, project managers have always found themselves challenged by limits. As part of this great tradition, there are some feelings you've probably already experienced.

Would you answer the following questions the way most project managers do?

1. Do you get all the money you need? Usually not.
2. Do you have a nice, relaxed schedule? Well, normally not that, either.
3. Do you have access to all the tools, resources, and people you need to get the job done? As Blanche DuBois points out, we "depend on the kindness of strangers." In fact, most of

the time we know that we can't possibly succeed without the essentially willing and voluntary cooperation of people over whom we have no direct authority or power whatsoever.

4. Do you have full authority to match your responsibility? There's an old management joke about the "Firing Line." You live below the Firing Line if you can be fired for failure to meet your objectives. You're above the Firing Line if you have a subordinate you can fire—for failure to meet your objectives. You've definitely got the responsibility. Getting the authority is another matter.

If your answers to these questions are the same as those of most project managers—that is, most or all of your answers are "no"—then you may sometimes have had a sneaking suspicion that senior management has been sitting up late looking for new ways to stick it to your projects.

You may be surprised to know that's not just paranoia. The answer is "yes," and that's not intended as management bashing. It's part of understanding the environment in which most project managers live.

In your organization—in every organization, in fact—there is an almost infinite list of useful, desirable, and positive work that needs to be accomplished. We're never going to run out of projects to do. On the other hand, resources are always finite. Therefore, every time we give you a dollar, a week, or a person in support of your project goal, notice that it's a dollar, a week, or a person that can't be assigned to another project, one that also has merit and desirability.

Opportunity Cost

"Opportunity cost" in projects means that senior management can't possibly support each project to its fullest extent without choosing instead to get fewer projects accomplished each year. So we try to give each project the minimum it needs, and rely on the project manager's creativity and skill to pull it off anyway, while using those extra resources to get more and more total projects accomplished. It's not just the Internet Age we're in, it's always been reality: We need to do it better, faster, and cheaper to stay ahead in a challenging business environment. You're not alone in the problems you face.

Understanding the Power Gap

The power gap for project managers is often a serious challenge. Power is always an important issue, but one that often makes us uncomfortable to discuss. We don't want to be perceived as power-hungry or as power-seekers, but we realize that we need a certain amount of power to get the job done, and we aren't always given that power.

We know that other people have power, too, and some of them don't seem to have any reservations or doubts about using it, not always in ways that support you or your project goal. If there's a gap between your power as a project manager and the power of the people around you, you can easily feel whipsawed and manipulated, and that's often a recipe for project disaster.

Power doesn't necessarily have to be the negative that many people perceive it to be. Here's an engineering definition of power that's nice and neutral: Power is energy that overcomes resistance to achieve work. To achieve any work, you need power. And the official granting of power that's given to you as part of your job assignment or title may not be nearly as much as you need to do the work.

If power is energy that overcomes resistance, then the amount of power you need is related to the level of resistance in your situation. Let's look at the power dynamic surrounding your project. Who has power, what kind of power is it, and how will it be used?

Customers and Stakeholders

Projects are done for customers, who can be either internal or external. And the customer, as we know, is by definition always right. The reason is that the customer has the money and often has a choice about where it's spent. If the customer isn't satisfied, the money goes somewhere else. That's a source of power.

In addition to the customer, there are numerous stakeholders surrounding a project. A stakeholder is someone whose interests are affected by either the work or the output of your project. Your manager, for example, clearly has an interest in both the work and the output of the project: the work, because it uses resources that could otherwise go somewhere else, and the output, because the customer's satisfaction (or lack of satisfaction) tends to have financial or operational consequences.

You are a stakeholder, too. Your reputation, your chances for promotion, and possibly even your job are at stake. The same goes for your team members as well, and they have their own career interests to consider.

> A stakeholder is someone whose interests are affected by either the work or the output of your project.

Limits and Challenges

Your manager has position power over you, and may have larger interests than just your project. To the extent that your project goal or process interferes with larger interests, you may find some of your manager's power being used in ways that are negative to your project. On the other hand, if your project goals are in synch with those of your manager, then that power is used alongside your own to achieve those goals.

Other project managers are stakeholders if their projects are affected by the work of your project. Perhaps you're taking some resources they also need, and so your success adds to their risk. You need to be aware of the impact you're having on those around you, and be prepared to negotiate so you can get your essential needs met in a way that does the least damage and causes the least resistance.

Stakeholders have different degrees of authority and power, which they tend to exercise in a way that meets their own best interest as they see it. This often explains why project managers see their projects become "political." Even good things can come into conflict with each other, and the way that conflict is managed is part of your political environment.

The ultimate conclusion you should draw from all these limits and challenges and constraints is that project managers need creativity and skill to succeed and prosper. There's an old slogan, "You knew the job was dangerous when you took it." This kind of challenge can be exhilarating as well as frightening. The streetwise project manager recognizes the reality of the situation, and learns the skills, tools, and behavior to survive and prosper.

> Project managers need creativity and skill to succeed and prosper.

Stakeholders, Power, and Projects

The project to build a new Denver International Airport (DIA) to replace Denver's Stapledon Airport was originally planned at $1.2 billion, but ended up costing $5 billion, opening late, and becoming legendary for project snafus, the most famous being its automated baggage handling system.

Why did this happen? One of the root causes of the problem involved stakeholder management. Many people had a stake in the project. The nation's air traffic control system wanted more capacity in Denver because Denver was rated among the top ten worst air traffic bottlenecks in the United States, causing over $100 million a year in lost revenue. Local residents had opposing interests. The airport was to be built in another county, a ways from the city center, and extensive negotiation had to take place before the annexation of the land. There was another airport with lower operating costs less than three miles away from the proposed DIA, with businesses that would be substantially affected. The city of Denver wanted an entry point with a strong visual design that would be easily identified by travelers.

Two project management companies worked together on the project, one managing design and construction and the other handling engineering, architecture, and airport planning. They conflicted about the balance between aesthetic design and ease of maintenance.

> Local politics and a new mayoral race brought in conflict from different parts of the city's voting population, with a significant group favoring cancellation or postponement.

The major airlines that would use the airport refrained from participating in the design because they preferred the project to be cancelled, fearing a rise in operating costs. Continental Airlines finally insisted on a substantial redesign of its terminal, driving up costs. United Airlines wanted concourse changes and the infamous automated baggage handling system to shorten turnaround times and increase efficiency. Later in the project, Southwest Airlines refused to serve the new airport because airport fees would be in the $15–$20 per passenger range, which far exceeded the $3 per passenger fee they were seeking. Local politics and a new mayoral race brought in conflict from different parts of the city's voting population, with a significant group favoring cancellation or postponement. Hotel developers were reluctant to build so far out of town unless they would be supported by industrial and office parks built near the airport. Cargo carriers wanted to move from DIA to the cheaper nearby airport. And construction and operational personnel became hard to get because of the long commute.

When your project becomes embroiled in complex political negotiations and power struggles, it shouldn't be surprising that you can find yourself whipsawed between opposing interests, driving up costs and delaying the schedule. It's critical to get hold of these issues at the beginning of your project. If you don't, all the technical knowledge in the world won't be enough to save you.

Deciphering the Secret Code

"Pay no attention to the man behind the curtain!" cried the humbug Wizard of Oz as his secret was finally discovered. Sometimes there's a man behind the curtain in your project, and it's vital that you discover who he is.

Projects are temporary and unique, and they're done for the benefit of customers. Unfortunately, customers don't always know exactly what they really want or need, and even worse, sometimes they're unwilling (or even unable) to admit it. The problem is, their needs are still their needs, no matter how nebulous they may be. And if you solve the wrong problem, even if you solve it brilliantly, it's still counted as a failure. So here's another common experience among project managers: You did exactly what you were told and still got into trouble for it.

Projects' Origins

Projects originate in needs or opportunities. Perhaps a competitor's product is eating into your market share. That's a problem. There are a number of potential responses: a new product, an upgrade or improvement to your existing product, a price cut, a new advertising strategy, opening a new channel of distribution, or taking it to the global marketplace. The decision on which strategy to follow is often made at a high level of the organization, and the eventual project manager is usually not part of the discussion. That's reasonable, of course—there isn't a project yet, and depending on the course of action, different people would likely be chosen as the project manager. A number of critical decisions are made even before the project is decided upon.

Is it normal for you to get a complete briefing on the entire decision-making process that led to selecting your project? Often, the answer is no. Do you need to know this information? Often, the answer is yes. Understanding the background may be essential for

> Is it normal for you to get a complete briefing on the entire decision-making process that led to selecting your project?

figuring out the right strategy or the right output to achieve the project goal. People may assume you know, or may assume you really don't need to know, but in fact you do.

> Before you buy a mainframe, make sure that you need what the mainframe will do.

A Means to an End

"We need a new mainframe." There's an old marketing saying, "Nobody in the world needs a power drill. What people need are holes." A project is a means to an end, and if you don't know the desired end, you truly have no idea what the right means happens to be. Before you buy a drill, make sure you need a hole. Before you buy a mainframe, make sure you need what the mainframe will do. Perhaps we do need a new mainframe, but the critical thing you have to discover is why someone thinks so. Because if you do get that new mainframe installed and up and running, but the underlying problem doesn't go away as a result, the project's failure to meet its goals may not actually be your fault—but you can bet you'll share in the blame.

For more information on this topic, visit our Web site at www.businesstown.com

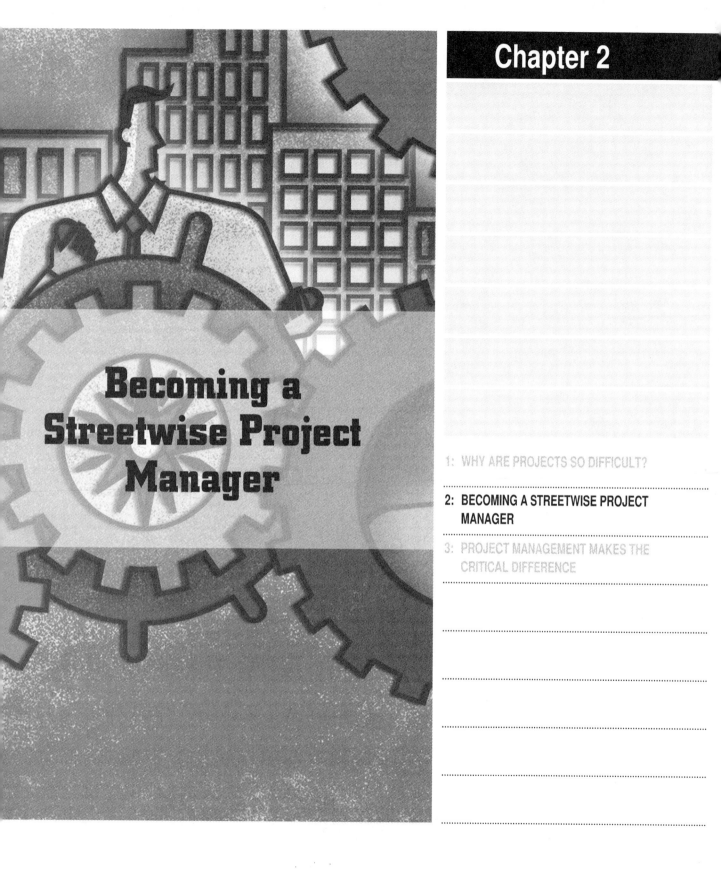

Becoming a Streetwise Project Manager

What Makes a Project Manager?

When people not familiar with the topic begin thinking about project management, they often believe the first step is to get some project management software. On the contrary, this should be a fairly late step in learning about project management. Not that the software isn't valuable, but its real value is only accessible when you understand the thinking that goes on behind it. In the same sense that a word processor won't improve your writing skills, or a spreadsheet program won't make you an accountant, project management software won't make you a streetwise project manager.

What will make you a good project manager? Having the right mindset, the right understanding, and—only then—the right tools.

Project Management—Just Software or More?

All the charts in the world won't help you if you don't know what you're doing. On a consulting visit to one company, I met a project manager who invited me to see his office. The walls were almost completely covered with printouts from his project management software package—every sort of Gantt Chart, Network Diagram, assignment list, and budget document imaginable, representing hundreds of hours of work.

Proudly, he indicated one point on the chart. "You see right here? That's how I can tell that we're exactly three weeks behind schedule."

"And?" I probed, waiting to hear his response strategy.

He shook his head firmly. "And, nothing. We're exactly three weeks behind schedule."

These days, novice project managers think the first step is to acquire the right software package. Instead, you need the right mindset, the right attitude, and the right wisdom. When your software tells you you're behind schedule, the proper question for the project manager is, "What can we do about it?" Your ultimate goal is to get the project done on time, within the budget, and to a satisfactory level of performance. Tools may give you insight and help identify places where action is possible, but tools alone do not constitute project management. If you don't get the job done, nobody cares why. And if you do get the job done, nobody cares why, either.

Your attitude and your understanding are the most important tools you possess.

It's Not Just a Job, It's an Attitude

Project managers are people who think like project managers. That may seem a bit obvious to you, but let's explore the idea.

We've started with a picture of the environment of a project: that it is a temporary activity, often started without full understanding of what the project will eventually entail, containing a certain inherent level of risk and uncertainty, and normally taking place alongside other work. What if you are the kind of person who is uncomfortable without a routine? What if you get more interested in the work process than in the goal? What if you don't completely agree with the people who are giving you the project assignment? As you can see, the wrong answers to any of these questions can leave you at a significant disadvantage when it comes to managing your way through the project.

Your attitude, your mindset, and your picture of what's going on have a substantial impact on you, on the members of your team, on your customers, and on those higher up in your organization. If you are confident, others around you will tend to be more confident. Alternatively, if you panic, don't be surprised when others around you fall into despair.

The Personality of the Perfect Project Manager

Project management is a hybrid occupation. One aspect of project management is technical: command of certain analytical tools that enable you to structure and analyze your project. The other aspect is human: the ability to manage people in a highly fluid and uncertain environment. Both are important to your success; both are worth cultivating.

How do we determine what the perfect project manager would look like? One way is to look at those who are already successful. When you survey the outstanding project managers in your own work environment, you are likely to encounter many of the following characteristics.

> Project management is a hybrid occupation.

Technical Competence

The perfect project manager has strong competence in technical matters as well as a commitment to personal self-development. Technical competence involves both those areas relevant to the subject matter of the project as well as project management in general. For example:

1. **The perfect project manager is analytical.** One of the most powerful tools available to the project manager is analysis: the process of breaking down a project into its components, determining the characteristics of those components, and using the knowledge and insight to create a solid plan.

2. **The perfect project manager is process-oriented.** The Project Management Institute (PMI) says that project management can best be described in terms of its component processes. The component processes are the methods by which a project—any project—can be broken down and organized.

3. **The perfect project manager knows the tools.** Much of this book will set forth the detailed tools specific to project management. Technical competence in these tools is important, but not sufficient. You have to understand why each tool is valuable, what it gives you as a project manager, and how to balance the work required to use the tool with the benefit you can receive.

4. **The perfect project manager knows the subject.** Projects involve specific subject areas, and your technical understanding of the relevant subject area is clearly important.

5. **The perfect project manager knows the system.** Projects take place inside organizations, and organizations have their own special dynamics. Managing projects in a government agency normally requires you to understand certain regulatory requirements and restrictions. Managing projects in retail often involves consideration of peak seasons and their impact on cash flow and ordering cycles. Your understanding of your own organization, industry, and environment is a crucial underpinning of your success.

> The perfect project manager knows the system.

The more unfamiliar you are with the project you're managing, the more complex it is, or the more important it is, the more you will find attention to process helpful in getting your mind wrapped around it.

People Skills

No matter how technically complex or sophisticated the project, project managers generally agree that it's the people and the politics that take most of your time and energy. Because project managers often are promoted from the technical ranks, they often find that they must work hard to supplement their technical skill base with improved skills on the people side. Let's look at some of the core competencies:

1. **The perfect project manager understands people.** Have you ever met an unmotivated person? Most people would immediately answer in the affirmative. But think about it: Have you ever met someone who spent more time and energy scheming to get out of the work than it would take to simply do it and get it over with? If so, would you classify that person as unmotivated—or highly motivated but in a different direction? As a project manager you need to know why people are behaving the way they are, especially if you hope to achieve change in that behavior.

2. **The perfect project manager understands politics.** Do you have office politics where you work? Try this simple test: Count the number of employees and if the number exceeds three, you've got politics. Politics, in a fundamental sense, is the unofficial way the organization makes decisions and allocates resources. It is a forum in which people exercise different types of power in order to achieve their goals. You ignore the political realities of your organization at your own peril. As a project manager, remember that you have limited direct authority to achieve your goals—the unofficial methods of gaining and using power are central to your success.

What If It Isn't Your Subject Matter Expertise?

It's not unusual for a project manager to be assigned to a project with major elements outside his or her subject expertise. You may manage a software project not because you're a software professional, but because you know the purpose to which the software will be put. Sometimes you get a project because you're there—the classic example is moving a company to a new building, coordinated by a staff member who has never run such a project. When you're not knowledgeable, you need to develop good sources of information by interviewing experts and paying special attention to the details so you can get it done correctly.

3. **The perfect project manager understands sales and negotiation.** Are you a professional salesperson or negotiator? Before you answer "no," think again. Do you have to sell your ideas, your vision, and your needs to an unsympathetic audience? Do you have to negotiate with others to get the resources, time, and tools you need to accomplish your projects? If you find that you are cast in the role of a salesperson or negotiator, then it's clearly a good idea to master the skills that the professionals use.

4. **The perfect project manager radiates confidence.** It's easy to be a manager on a good day. It's a lot tougher when everything seems to be falling apart all around you. That's when you discover that part of leadership is acting. The ability to look calm and confident when others around you are losing their heads is a powerful influencer. People look to the project manager for hope, cues, and clues of what behavior is appropriate. When you aren't confident, learn to project it anyway. That isn't lying, because when others also become calmer and more confident, the chance of success goes up tremendously.

5. **The perfect project manager works hard.** You'll frequently hear the time management slogan, "Work smart, not hard." It's clearly true that work that isn't smart often isn't relevant, and working hard on things that are useless and unproductive doesn't achieve good outcomes. But to conclude that hard work isn't part of the equation is rather naïve. The project manager normally needs to work smart *and* hard, not only to get the job done, but also to serve as a role model for others to emulate.

6. **The perfect manager keeps the goal in mind.** You may have seen the classic office cartoon with the caption, "When you're up to your ass in alligators, it's hard to remember that your original objective was to drain the swamp." If you take the statement at face value, there's truth in it. It is hard to stay focused on a long-term goal in the face of short-term catastrophe. Nevertheless, that's the challenge set before you.

> The perfect project manager radiates confidence.

Is this list of characteristics exhaustive? Not at all. But it's a good start to understanding the core competencies of project managers. To be a first-rate project manager, you need to be a first-rate manager— and even a first-rate human being. It's a lifelong challenge, and nobody does it perfectly. Set these as overall goals, and feel good about yourself when you make progress.

Why Better Is Better, and When "Good Enough" Really Is

It's easy to optimize a system to achieve a single goal, and it's often wrong as well. To achieve a world with no traffic fatalities, we could lower the speed limit to ten miles per hour and enforce it by banning cars capable of higher speeds. Add in cameras and radar detectors at every intersection, plus a beefed-up traffic enforcement operation, and the goal is achieved.

Such an approach would, of course, add substantial costs, both direct (enforcement) and indirect (economic damage from slowed transportation). Many foods could not be brought to grocery stores before decay set in. Clearly, this would be a very bad idea. We could reverse the approach and optimize in favor of the speediest transportation of people and goods, but it's likely that fatalities would increase dramatically. A goal of "no traffic fatalities" certainly has merit, but so does a goal of rapid movement of people and commodities. As a result, we try to balance these competing goals and strive for a reasonable tradeoff between them.

Don't Make Perfect the Enemy of Good

Project managers are very familiar with the need for tradeoffs, and another of the attitudes of the effective project manager is "not to make 'perfect' the enemy of 'good.'" Our project is seldom the only project going on. Therefore, maximizing the outcome of our project may create undesirable net results for the organization, if maximizing our project results in another project not being completed to at least a satisfactory level.

> Try to balance these competing goals and strive for a reasonable tradeoff between them.

Better Is Better

In an imperfect world, we must often work with incremental improvements. "Better is better" is a project manager's attitude, even if the outcome is less than ideal. If our project outcome cannot be perfect, then how good must it be? In other words, exactly how good is "good enough"? This is often a crucial question for the project manager.

Start each project by identifying what would be the ideal outcome, and then what would be an acceptable, or "good enough" outcome. To do this, remember that a project is a means to an end, rather than an end in itself. Focus on the goal to be achieved, and work backwards to find the satisfactory achievement level. We'll go into this method in more detail later.

The Godzilla Principle

Project management is also often about risk management, and there's a general rule of problem solving known as the Godzilla Principle.

In the archetypal Japanese monster movie, there's usually a scene early on in which the monster *du jour* is small and helpless. One prescient actor urges everyone to kill the baby monster, but no one else agrees. Later, usually after exposure to radiation or some exotic pollutant, the monster grows to giant size and begins to destroy Tokyo. Now, of course, everyone in the street is yelling, "What are we going to do?"

Project managers know the answer: to kill the monster while it's still an embryo, which embodies another important element of project management, the art of early detection and management of project risks. As a general rule, if you catch it early, it's easier to kill. That's the Godzilla Principle in project management.

The project management approach is to put more time into the initial phases of the project: determining what the project is and what approach will be taken (project initiation), and analyzing the project carefully to create a set of plans (project planning). These steps will almost invariably reduce the amount of firefighting and reactive behavior on the project. Do it right the first time (plan in advance) and then you won't have to find the time to do it over.

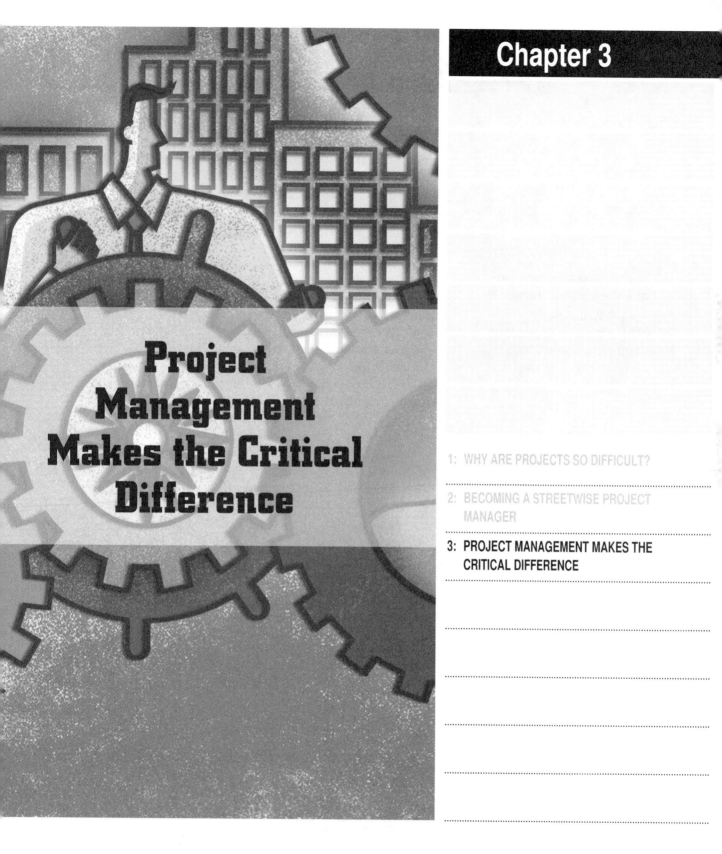

Chapter 3

Project Management Makes the Critical Difference

Modern Project Management

What we know as modern project management had its birth in the late 1950s and 1960s as government and private industry began tackling projects of hitherto unprecedented size and scope. Of course, projects have been managed since the dawn of civilization, and tools for planning and organizing projects are as old as projects themselves.

The best thing about project management is that most of the tools and concepts we use today were originally developed in response to real-world operational problems. They had their baptism under fire. Unlike some currently popular management ideas, they were not conceived academically, although they have subsequently been explored and formalized in an academic context.

Above all, project management is an increasingly popular toolset because it works. By following the reality-tested processes and using the analytical tools, you come to a deeper understanding of the nature of your project, the potential pitfalls, the hidden resources, the constraints and challenges, and the creative opportunities that empower you to get the job done. Project management can make the critical difference for you and your organization in facing the complex and difficult challenges ahead.

> Project management can make the critical difference for you and your organization in facing the complex and difficult challenges ahead.

Separating Projects from Work

As discussed earlier, projects have a distinct beginning and end rather than being ongoing job functions. The following are projects:

- Develop a new customer database.
- Move the company into a new building.
- Build a Web site.
- Create a marketing campaign for a new product launch.

The following are not projects:

- Manage the accounting department.
- Maintain a legacy computer system.

- Process benefit claims.
- Staff a help desk.

The important difference between the first group and the second group is that the first group is intended to be finished. At some point you will have a new database, or the company will be moved, or the Web site will be online, or the marketing campaign will be implemented.

The Question of Intent

However, there will be an accounting department as long as there is a company, the legacy computer system may stay in use for years, new benefit claims will arrive daily, and the help desk receives new calls every few minutes. Note that some of these *can* come to an end—the company can go out of business or the legacy computer system can be replaced—but there is no specific *intent* to complete them. Without an intent to finish, there is no project.

Projects Within Projects

So far, so good, but there are some special cases. Let's look at the marketing campaign for the new product launch. What exactly is the project? There's a marketing campaign, but for the product to launch, you have to have a product. The product must be manufactured, but before it can be manufactured, it must be designed. Perhaps it must be tested, or undergo regulatory approval. Before you know it, you end up with something like Figure 3-1.

If you're in charge of the overall new product development project, your responsibility is the top box on the chart, and all subordinate boxes are only project phases or project elements. But if you're in charge of one of the subordinate activities, such as designing the marketing campaign, that's a perfectly legitimate project as far as you're concerned. So to some extent, the answer to the question "what is a project" depends on your perspective. Where you stand often depends on where you sit.

> Without an intent to finish, there is no project.

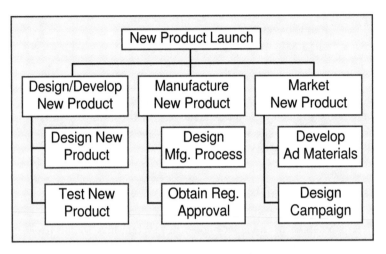

▲ FIGURE 3-1: *Hierarchy of projects.* **Each box is both a project and a subset of another project at the same time.**

It's important to know if your project is part of an *über*-project (meaning your project is one part of a greater objective), because it influences your understanding of the right way to go about it. Your individual choices as a project manager are constrained by the higher project. Your deadline and budget may be determined in reference to the higher project. How good is "good enough" is also determined by the higher project. Take testing, for example. If it's a matter of pass or fail, and you can make a minor adjustment to the product that will let it barely pass, it may not add value to make a major adjustment that would give it a perfect score.

Projects Within Work

Managing the accounting department is work, but closing the books at the end of the fiscal year can be considered a project. It has an intended finish, even if you're going to do it again next year. (That too would be a separate project.) Maintaining the legacy computer system is work, but when it had to undergo Y2K compliance checking a few years ago, that was a project. It will also be a project when you must import the old information into the new system that is being brought in to replace the old one. If regulatory changes must

> Closing the books at the end of the fiscal year can be considered a project.

alter the benefits claim processing, implementing those changes is also a project. If you decide that preparing an FAQ for your help desk would be a way to improve efficiency and speed of response, that's a project as well.

Even if your environment is work, projects often creep in. By the very nature of a project, work tends to be disrupted. Additional resources must be deployed. One of the challenges you will face as a project manager is that the work normally still has to go out even while the project is going forward. The balance of work versus project management must be carefully monitored and maintained.

Balancing Priorities among Multiple Projects

Not only is it challenging to manage a project when most resources must be devoted to work, but it is equally challenging to manage a project when other projects compete for the same resource pool. We might not be managing a single new product for release this year, but perhaps six or seven new products. Each requires design, each requires testing, each requires manufacturing, each requires approvals, each requires a marketing campaign, and so forth.

Throw It over the Wall

In a traditional organization in which specialists are grouped together (engineering, marketing, accounting, information technology), you can easily have a situation in which projects move sideways through the organization, worked on by specialists in individual departments before being "thrown over the wall" to the next stage.

Accountability is difficult in this situation. If you are the project manager for the entire project, you normally have a home in one of the departments, say, engineering or marketing. It would be highly unusual if you were expert in each of the numerous disciplines needed to get the project out. You must rely on people in the different departments to apply their special knowledge and skills. You're unlikely to be the direct supervisor of all the people you need—and possibly, some of the technical experts and specialists are higher in rank than you.

> You must rely on people in the different departments to apply their special knowledge and skills.

Technical experts have a tendency to elevate their own discipline and skill over others, and so each wants his or her piece to be as good as possible. Unfortunately, as we've seen, optimizing a project around a single good can create problems, so your project may find itself being thrown among different specialties, each trying to maximize itself at the cost of others.

You versus Other Projects

Now, even if everyone in the organization is committed to excellence and wants a great product to come out, notice that conflict is still inevitable because your product isn't the only one making its way through the system. Putting more effort or expense into Product A means that there is less available for Products B, C, and D. When your organization is managing multiple projects, the balancing act gets even more complex. You must not only balance projects versus work, one technical area versus another, but now projects versus other projects.

Managing in a Multiple-Project Environment

You're almost never the only game in town. The organization normally has multiple projects underway at any given time, and no matter how valuable your project, you aren't necessarily top dog, and even if you are, you still have to share resources.

Conflicts in multiple-project management are inevitable because it's not unusual that several projects need the same resource at the same time. No matter how carefully you put together your schedule, it's vulnerable to someone being late on another project, jeopardizing the moment when they can come to work on yours.

If you are working in a multiple-project environment, even if you're not the overall "portfolio manager," try to put together a list of all projects competing for the same resources. For each project, look for the factors that should elevate it or lower it in relative priority. Show your list to people in authority for modifications. If your project isn't on top of the list, make sure your plans and processes account for the likelihood that higher-priority projects will take extra resources, which will tend to delay or degrade your project.

If you are managing multiple projects, take control of resource scheduling from the top. In practice, managing priorities turns into managing resources—where you put your people and your money is the ultimate proof of what you find really important. If resources are allocated informally, based on politics and pleading, then you're not in control of your priorities. Take charge early and resolve conflicts quickly to get the best results possible.

The most important step in bringing this process under control is to make priorities clear. If one product is likely to bring in a lot more revenue than another, then it's reasonable that the project with higher potential takes priority in cases of conflict. The trouble is that reasons why one project trumps another are often ambiguous and sometimes political. Perhaps one of the products was the pet idea of one of the senior vice presidents. On a more positive note, perhaps a product with little first-year sales potential is seen as critical to the organization's long-range strategy. Maybe the sales potential of two products is close enough that it's unclear which should properly take priority. In these cases, the balancing act becomes increasingly delicate.

If people with the requisite authority or organizational position don't see the conflict clearly enough (and if they aren't experienced in the discipline of project management, they may not), then you find yourself in an environment of shifting priorities, which complicates any attempt at project scheduling.

Hidden Opportunities in Every Project

What you often want and need is more time, more money and resources, and more flexibility in acceptable results. Fortunately, project management tools will uncover some hidden opportunities in virtually any project, and that is one of the most important benefits available to you as you master these skills.

For example, the bleak picture of inter-project conflict we just discussed can be turned around into an opportunity if you look at it the right way. If your project is of lesser priority, then there are only three directions in which you can go:

1. You can extend the deadline if the resources you need must be assigned elsewhere.

2. You can obtain more resources (overtime, temporary help, second choice team members) if you can't extend the deadline.

3. You can lower the performance target of the project from "excellent" to "good enough."

> Project management tools will uncover some hidden opportunities in virtually any project.

**Setting Aside
Your Standards**

Who is demanding that the project achieve certain goals? Is it your boss or customer—or is it your own pride and ideas? As important as your own standards are, sometimes the right answer is for them to give way in favor of what the organization's needs happen to be.

Knowing how and when to exploit the flexibility in your project is an important skill.

Think you can't do any of these? Sometimes it seems as if your choices are constrained to the point of impossibility. However, since you can't do the impossible, something in your project is going to have to give. You're better off choosing than having fate choose for you, because the damage that will result is different depending on which way you go. Notice that if your project is of lower priority, senior management has already accepted the reality that damage to your project is more acceptable than damage to another, higher-priority one. So you need to determine which type of damage is most acceptable—or, alternately, least unacceptable.

By taking a close and careful look at the project's goal—the "why" behind the project—you can determine what to do. Why was the particular deadline chosen? Is it because of a fixed date, such as a trade show, or is it more general, such as being out in time for the back-to-school market? Or was the deadline simply picked because someone needed a date and that one looked reasonable? If you miss launching your new product at the trade show, it may result in a substantial competitive disadvantage. But if the date was fairly arbitrary, less harm will result if you miss it. (Notice that "less harm" is not the same thing as "you won't get into any trouble." Sometimes you're destined to get into trouble no matter what you do. In that case, pick the alternative that leads to less trouble, because while it may not be good, remember that "better is better.")

Managing Projects for Value

The value of projects is the reason we do projects. If we don't achieve the value, we haven't done it correctly. Here are five important concepts to bear in mind as you think about the "why" behind your project.

- ▶ **Concept 1:** Projects derive their value from goal achievement. You must understand the value you seek in order to realize it.

- ▶ **Concept 2:** Projects are investments made by management. The organization makes a commitment of money and resources in each project that could have been spent some-place else. The return on investment is why we want to do the project.

▶ **Concept 3**: The project investors and sponsors tolerate risk. Projects have an unavoidable risk of unsatisfactory outcomes, and your investors and sponsors accept this risk. It's their money on the line. You, on the other hand, manage the risk, taking steps to increase the likelihood of a good outcome.

▶ **Concept 4:** The investment equation becomes the project equation. You commit resources and take risk in order to achieve benefits, which is an investment-based understanding.

▶ **Concept 5:** Value is a balance of quality, resources, and risk. Determining this must ideally take place before we undertake the work, to understand the "why" and the "what" of the project we are to perform.

Adapted from *Managing Projects for Value* by John C. Goodpasture.

Project Management as a Set of Processes

Earlier, we discussed the idea that project management can be under-stood as a set of component processes. According to the Project Management Institute (PMI), there are five process groups and nine knowledge areas that make up the discipline of project management. Part II of this book will cover the five process areas (see Figure 3-2).

The most important lesson to derive from the five processes is that there is a flow to project management. By doing each process well in turn, you go into subsequent processes with much greater control and with lowered risk. If an early process is performed poorly or incorrectly, the damage may not become apparent until much later in the project, but the damage is done.

People without a background in project management have a tendency to get overeager in the beginning phases, and rush through them so they can jump right into the execution of the project. From

> The most important lesson to derive from the five processes is that there is a flow to project management.

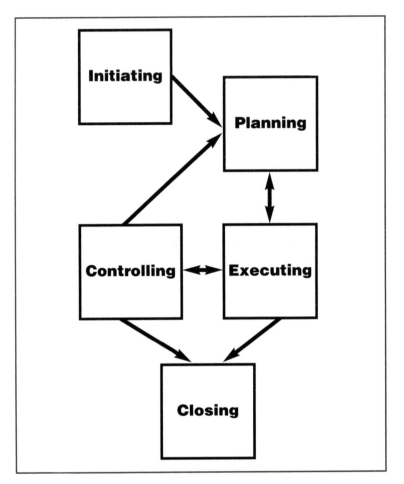

▲ FIGURE 3-2: *Five project management processes.*
The core process groups of project management describe the overall way in which a project is managed.

an outside perspective, that might look efficient, but it tends to generate more problems late in the project as well as more failures. Do it right the first time according to the processes, and you'll find yourself in better shape at the end.

PART II

The Life Cycle of a Project

- **How to break down, understand, and negotiate a project objective that can be achieved**
- **How to establish a scope management process for your project**
- **How to organize and manage a work team**
- **How to keep your project on time, on budget, and within specifications throughout the execution phase**
- **How to manage for risks and quality**
- **How to ensure that your project finishes successfully and delivers the desired results**

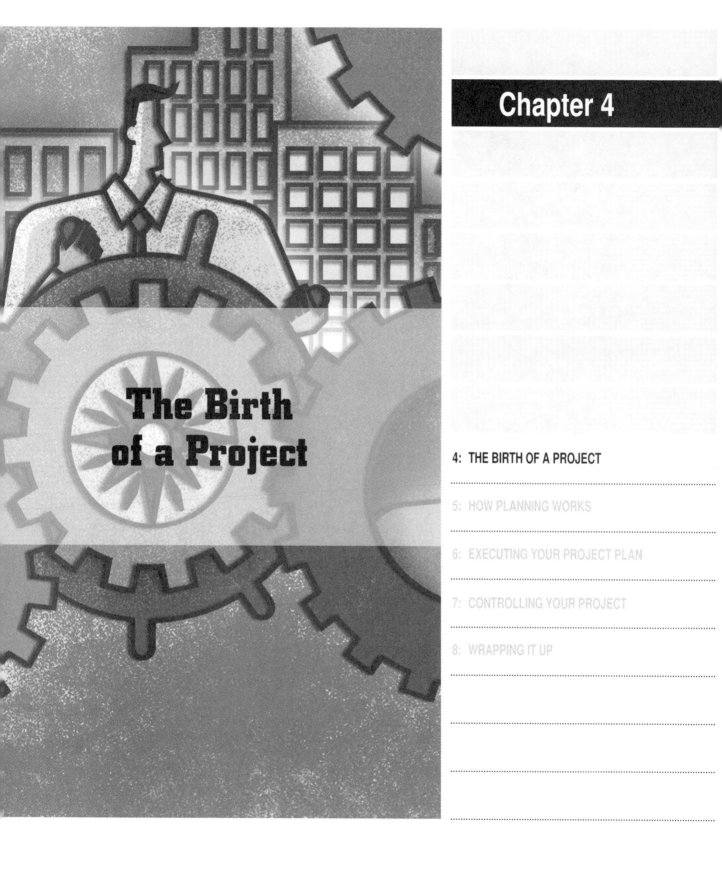

Chapter 4

The Birth of a Project

In the Beginning

In the beginning, there was a problem, and the world was without form and void. Then the customer said, "Let there be a project!" and there was a project. The actual part of getting started on a project is often a little more complex, but there is usually a mystery underlying the project, and you need to root it out in order to start on the right foot.

The first of the five PMI process groups (referred to in the previous chapter) is "Initiating," which involves all those activities that must be performed before the project becomes official within the organization. However, there are additional steps that normally take place in reaching the decision for a project to even exist at all, and if you don't know about them, you can start your project already in trouble.

From Problem to Solution

As we've mentioned, a project is not an end in itself, but a means to an end. If the project is to build a Web site, the first question that should concern you is "why." Why do we want a Web site? What problem will it solve? What opportunity are we attempting to exploit? Each possible answer results in a different approach to the project, and often generates questions of its own.

"We want to sell our product over the Internet." Okay, that's an answer, but it invites a follow-up "why." Why over the Internet? Why not through a catalog, a store, or possibly through someone else's Web site?

The purpose of this exercise is not to say that we shouldn't sell our product over the Web, but rather to help discover the hidden assumptions and agendas your customer may have.

Sometimes the reason given reveals the lack of thought behind the project. "We want to sell on the Internet because everyone else is!" "Because everyone else is doing it" is a reason to investigate further, but not a sufficient reason to make a commitment to e-commerce. Perhaps the correct next step would be to do a project study and make detailed recommendations.

There can be more thoughtful reasons underlying the reasons to undertake a project as well. "We are looking to reduce the turnaround time of reorders for our installed customer base by using the Internet." The goal of reducing turnaround time gives you the first clues about

Being a Project Consultant

Remember that doing the project you're told to do isn't always the right thing. People want their needs to be met, and if the project they ask for ultimately doesn't satisfy their needs, they will tend to blame you, not themselves. You should typically expect to act as a project consultant before you can move on to being a project manager.

the shape and nature of the site, and the criteria you can use to determine success or failure.

Compare this reason with the following: "We want to be able to offer our less-popular backlist items to customers but the cost of printing and mailing catalogs is too high for the potential volume of business. By using the Internet, we would like to have a low-cost way of offering a large number of items to our customers."

Would you produce the same Web site for these two customers? Almost certainly not. In the first case, a critical quality factor is speed; in the second case, the issue is cost. How, then, can you produce any Web site for a customer without a good understanding of the actual business problem or opportunity at hand?

Don't automatically expect your customer to supply this for you. Your customer, be it external or internal, may not have thought the problem through on a conscious level, or may not possess the expertise or insight to ask for the right things. It's a mark of an outstanding project manager to meet the needs that the customer isn't necessarily able to articulate!

Framing the Project

It's often the case that at least some of this process—answering the "why" behind a project—has taken place in discussions that led up to the decision to do a project in the first place. But it's not necessarily the case that you receive the complete story when the project lands in your lap. Figure 4-1 illustrates a typical process.

A well-run business operates from a long-term strategic plan, which is ideally encapsulated in the form of a mission or vision statement. Based on the strategic plan and the current business environment, the executive leadership determines objectives for a fiscal year, quarter, or other measurement period. At a departmental level, a variety of problems, opportunities, and threats are considered to see which ones would be most beneficial to attack, and from there come projects. The projects, to be effective, have to relate back up the chain to support the goals and objectives of the organizations.

With all of this, what is often overlooked is that the operational project manager who is responsible for the project is not necessarily a member of the senior leadership team, and isn't privy to all the

> A well-run business operates from a long-term strategic plan.

discussions and work that went into establishing the project in the first place. Without an understanding of the context of the project, you find yourself shooting in the dark, with the likelihood that you won't hit the target the organization needs you to hit.

Trace each project back to the goal or purpose it serves, because only with that knowledge can you begin to make smart decisions about how you will manage your project.

The Project Manager Arrives

> If there hasn't been a decision to *start* a project, obviously there's no need to have a project manager.

If there hasn't been a decision to *start* a project, obviously there's no need to have a project manager. Much of the pre-project phase is done without a formal assignment of a project manager.

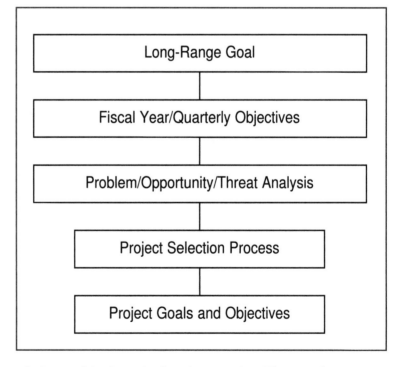

▲ FIGURE 4-1: *Steps in choosing a project.* **The typical project is the result of numerous steps, many of which take place well before a project manager is selected or assigned.**

Informed Consent

The most dangerous words that ever came out of a project manager's mouth are, "Yes, I'll do it," if said before you have a full understanding of what it is you're being asked to do.

Start with a positive attitude, of course, but understand that your initial objective is to find out the full story. And that means asking—and listening—to what people are requesting, even if you believe their ideas are wrong-headed and even destructive to the organization. The first goal of the project manager is to understand what is being asked of you. Then—and only then—are you in a position to give "informed consent" to the proposed project.

Questions to Start Your Project

Here is a list of questions to consider when discovering what your project is really about. Make sure in asking the questions that you don't come across as trying to give someone the "third degree." The purpose of these questions is discovery, not to challenge. You need to know what people are thinking, whether or not you end up agreeing with their thought processes.

Based on the answers you get, you may be ready to give a cheerful "Yes!" to the project, you may want to work at helping people understand why the project is a bad idea, or you may need to do some negotiation to end up with a workable project objective.

> You need to know what people are thinking, whether or not you end up agreeing with their thought processes.

- When the project is successfully completed, what will be different for the organization?
- Who helped in the decision to choose this project?
- What specific deliverables must be produced for this project?
- What resources will be available for the project?
- What other demands will be placed on those resources?
- Where does this particular project fit with other priorities of the organization?
- Who will decide how to measure whether the project succeeds or fails?
- What criteria will be used to measure success or failure?
- Why was the specific deadline chosen?
- What other options or choices were considered in choosing this project?

Negotiating the Objective

Often, project managers feel at an organizational disadvantage. As a general rule, the people who assign projects tend to outrank those who manage or perform projects. When you're given a direct order, you're pretty much stuck—aren't you?

Usually not as much as many project managers suppose. After all, you share one goal with those who assign the projects: You want to get it done. If it can't be done under the circumstances, do you really please your superiors by going ahead and failing? In most cases, the blame for failure ends up on your shoulders even if you knew from the beginning that the project was going to crash and burn.

Although it may seem unfair, it's justified, up to a point. After all, once you accept a project, even if you felt coerced, it is yours, for better or worse. The failure of the project doesn't meet the objectives of those who assigned the project to you. Therefore, everyone ends up better off if you negotiate a workable project objective in advance.

From a "power down" position in the hierarchy, it often appears that negotiation is out of the question, but that's not always the case. In our discussion of the "perfect project manager," we listed negotiation skills as one of the core competencies, and you need to use those skills from the beginning of the project all the way through. You do this not merely for your own self-protection (though of course that's perfectly legitimate), but also for the good of your customers, your superiors, and the organization. It benefits no one if the project fails, especially if you've spent all the money, resources, and time to achieve that failure.

> Your purpose in negotiating an objective isn't to make your life easier.

The First Step

The first step in negotiating an objective with those who outrank you is to make it clear that your goal is to achieve *their* goal, that you are planning to do your very best to ensure that the project succeeds. Your purpose in negotiating an objective isn't to make your life easier (though if that's an incidental benefit, so much the better), but to develop the most realistic objective in support of the most productive and worthwhile goal.

The Second Step

The second step is to understand (from your questioning) what is negotiable and what is not. In the *Apollo 13* carbon dioxide filter example, it isn't useful to argue that the time constraint is unrealistic and unfair. It's simply necessary.

What could be negotiated in a case like that? You have a table filled with spare parts. What if you need a part for your filter that isn't on the table but is on the spacecraft—it's needed in another step or another system. If you use the part to build the filter, it won't be available elsewhere, and might increase risk somewhere else on the project. Asking for that additional part is a form of negotiation—adding to your project something that was not part of the original picture. Both you and the mission director share the same goal—to get the astronauts home alive—so the negotiation becomes about risk balancing, which is part of numerous projects.

The Three Envelopes

The new project manager had inherited a project six months into the work and it had serious problems. The outgoing project manager was just clearing out the desk. "Listen, you've got some tough challenges ahead," the outgoing project manager said. "I've left you some help. In the drawer you'll find three envelopes. When you find yourself in trouble and you can't think of any way out, open the envelopes in order to find some help."

Soon enough, the new project manager was in trouble, and pulled out envelope number one. In it was a note that read, "Blame your predecessor." The project manager did so, and it worked, and the crisis blew over.

The second crisis came, and when the new project manager couldn't think of anything else, out came the second envelope. The note inside read, "Reorganize your department." And that made the project manager look proactive, and so the second crisis also blew over.

And then came the third crisis, and the third envelope. The new project manager couldn't wait to see what career-saving advice the outgoing project manager had this time. Out came the note, and the new project manager read it. It began, "Prepare three envelopes..."

Warning

Once you accept the project and dig into it more deeply, you'll often discover things you wish you'd known up front. That can't always be helped, and isn't necessarily a sign you've done something wrong. When you learn about something that threatens the project outcome, be prepared to go back and reopen the initiating phase. And if you find yourself going two steps forward and one step back on your project journey, at least you know that the net gain is real, and not illusory.

The Third Step

The third step is to keep yourself (and those with whom you are negotiating) focused on the shared goals: a successful project, a successful organization. The negotiation becomes about methods and options. When it moves onto this principled level, you become stronger in the negotiation, because it isn't any longer simply about hierarchical rank, but about the best way to get the job done.

Do remember that your power to negotiate is greater before the project has officially begun than it will be later on. Withhold the "yes" and focus on the "how" and "why" in your initial work on the project.

What You Should End Up With

The initiation phase of your project should end with a Project Charter, a statement of what the project is, the organization's commitment to go ahead and spend resources on it, and the project manager's authority to make decisions. We'll examine the charter in more detail later on. Right now, just know that your goal is to get it on paper for everyone's protection.

You should also end up with two lists: a list of constraints and a list of assumptions. Constraints are factors that limit your choices and options, such as an inflexible deadline, a limited budget, regulatory or legal requirements, or contractual terms. You must know what they are, because constraints are what make projects difficult. (After all, if you can take as long as you need, spend as much as necessary, and modify the objective as you go along, then nothing's impossible.)

Assumptions are things that people take for granted as true or certain. For example, you'll get a key resource whenever you're ready (conversely, something else may come up), there won't be any trouble ordering special parts (there's a backlog), and no other project will show up to compete for your resources (things happen). Discovering the assumptions that have been made about your project is vital. First, some assumptions can be tested, and then you'll know whether they're true or false. Second, assumptions are risks, since they might be false. When we discuss risk management on your project, your assumption list will come into play once again.

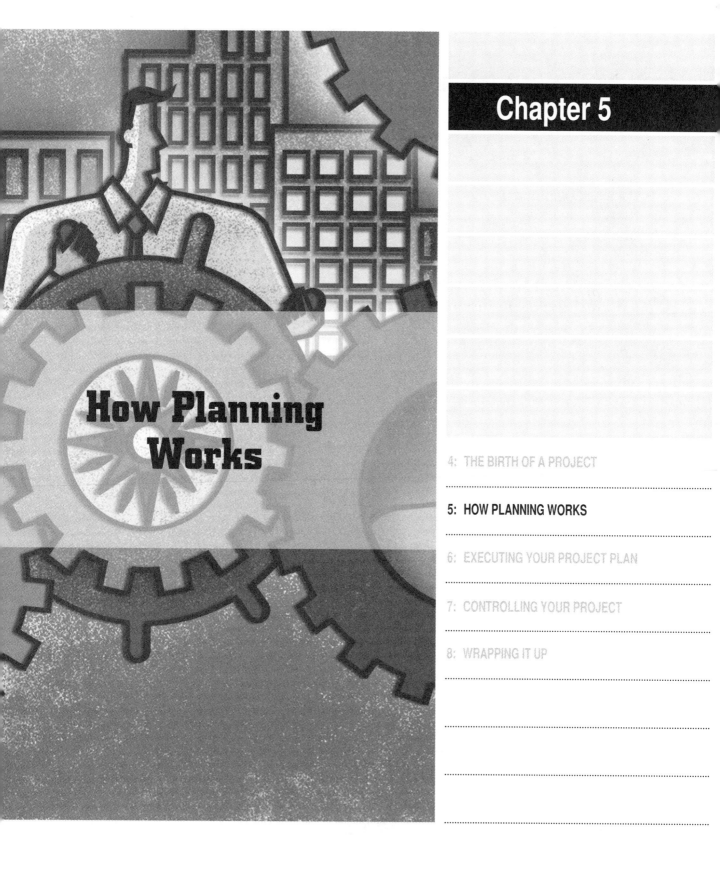

How Planning Works

Chapter 5

What Is Planning?

Planning is the second of the five process groups in project management. Because it involves the highest number of possibly unfamiliar skills, it takes up a large portion of this book–and of any other guide to project management. In this phase, you will encounter new tools and new ideas, all of which combine to put your project on the most solid footing possible.

The act of planning is often misunderstood.

Misunderstandings

The act of planning is often misunderstood. As a result, many who could get important benefits from planning fail to do so, either by not planning at all or planning in too superficial a sense.

One common misunderstanding is that planning is equal to scheduling. That is, a plan is simply a timeline of events. Certainly that's one part of a plan, but it's not all. We care about how long it will take, of course, but we also are interested in how much it will cost and what labor is required.

Another misunderstanding is that planning equates to certainty. That is, we start with an expectation that our plan describes what *will* happen on our project. While it's often desirable if our plan happens to play out exactly as scripted, in the real world of projects you often have such a degree of uncertainty that it's not a practical expectation. Should you bother to plan if you don't have knowledge or control of many key project elements?

Planning Examination

As we've said, planning is not about certainty, it's most often about risk management. A planning examination can help in this process. As our planning examination shows areas of risk, we can make contingency plans to help manage that risk. We can start our project with a reasonable appreciation of the likelihood of on-time, on-budget results. We can negotiate expectations based on our analysis.

Planning is about even more than that. You can plan for quality–how can we make sure the outcome is what we want and need? You can plan for communications–how do we keep people informed about progress? You can plan for change—how can we modify the project based on likely change requests?

Great skill in planning isn't the only talent of the successful project manager, but it's an essential one. Let's look at this in more detail.

Why Plans May Be Useless—But Essential

"In preparing for battle I have always found that plans are useless, but planning is indispensable," observed Dwight D. Eisenhower. That seems like an odd sort of paradox, but let's examine it.

Plans Are Useless

The military axiom, "No battle plan, no matter how well conceived, ever survives first contact with the enemy," has been variously attributed to Napoleon, von Moltke, von Clausewitz, and Murphy. Regardless of its origin, the saying strikes right at the heart of project planning.

First, the environment in which your project will take place is never completely knowable. There is inherent and unavoidable uncertainty in the business situation, resources, other demands and emergencies, and the attitude and focus of the people on whom you depend.

Second, the project itself carries inherent uncertainty. Does everyone really see the project in the same way? Do people seek the same outcomes? Will doing the project uncover problems unknowable in advance?

The upshot is that no matter how well or carefully you plan, you should never act on the assumption that you have thought of everything, and that nothing outside your carefully conceived universe will interfere.

> You should never act on the assumption that you have thought of everything.

Planning Is Essential

What, then, is the value of planning? The most important value of planning is the work itself. By systematically thinking through and analyzing your project, you gain valuable knowledge and insight.

Paying proper attention to planning equips your mind with the tools to handle inevitable project problems. Even if a schedule slips, the plan informs you that the schedule has slipped, allows you to calculate the consequences, and gives you the opportunity to look down the path to see where other alterations might be possible to bring you back on track.

Planning also helps you learn the terrain. Stakeholder analysis tells you who the key players are and what their interests and likely actions will be with respect to the project. Risk planning lets you exercise likely "what if" scenarios, and provides you with a tool to manage the Godzilla Principle, discussed earlier. Communications planning helps ensure that all those involved with a project are on the same page, and choose their actions with knowledge of their effect on the project. Quality planning tells you what customers value on your project, how to get there, and where the "good enough" point resides. Scope management planning helps you get agreement on what's included in the project and what's not, and implements processes and systems to control "scope creep" throughout your project.

The project manager who plans has power. The project manager who does not plan is at the mercy of uncertain events.

From Objective to Project Charter

A project has its roots in a problem, opportunity, or need, but doesn't become a project until it has been articulated as a goal statement. As we learned, it's not unusual for the initial stab at a goal statement to have problems. Perhaps the articulated objective won't satisfy the underlying need. Perhaps the first attempt is too vague and unmeasurable to be managed.

That's why the first mission of a project manager is to act in the role of project consultant, to help the customers (internal or external) specify a project that meets their needs.

It's considered a good practice in project management to write down the understanding in a document formally known as a Project Charter. The Project Charter has the following core elements.

1. It formally states the commitment of the organization to do the project.
2. It provides a high-level summary of project objectives and goals.
3. It assigns the project manager and states the authority the project manager has to make decisions and use resources in support of the project.
4. It is issued by (but not necessarily written by) a manager who is external to (and higher ranking than) the project. This authorizing person is often known as the project sponsor.

The goal is the purpose of the project, the benefit received from the project's successful completion. The objective is the description of the project itself, expressed in measurable terms.

While you can have an extremely formal and lengthy Project Charter, that's not necessarily beneficial. The length and detail of the Project Charter are often proportional to the size and scope of the project. It's also the case that sometimes you won't have a document formally labeled "Project Charter." For example, if the project is the result of a contract, the contract itself may serve as the Project Charter.

A Project Charter benefits the project manager and the customer as well. The benefit to the project manager is that the piece of paper is a way to protect oneself against an ever-shifting objective. The benefit to the customer is that the customer has a written statement of what has been promised and what it will look like when done.

> The goal is the purpose of the project, the benefit received from the project's successful completion.

Managing Project Scope

Whether or not there is a formal Project Charter, project scope—the statement of the products and services to be provided in and by the project—has a tendency to mutate during the life of a project.

This is true for a number of reasons. In doing the project, you may uncover things not known previously, and the project may have to change as a result. Outside circumstances may change, such as competitive moves, fluctuations in the economy, or new technology, which may require changes. Sometimes, the customer didn't know his or her own goals well enough, and seeing the project work helps the customer figure out that he or she needs something different. People see another project and pick up ideas that they now want you to incorporate. And, of course, people sometimes simply change their minds.

The Insidious Menace of Scope Creep

Any or all of these can result in changes to project scope. In fact, the insidious menace of "scope creep" is high up on the list of reasons projects fail. If you've managed projects for very long, you've probably encountered the problem of ever-escalating, ever-mutating project requirements. Although you can't have changes to the plan before you have a plan, the planning process includes a strategy for scope management. Let's look at a few common scope problems and their cures:

> The planning process includes a strategy of scope management.

- "This isn't a change in scope, it's what I always wanted from the beginning." Avoiding this kind of misunderstanding is one of the chief reasons you want a written Project Charter for your project. You may still need to make the scope change, but you are in a better position to negotiate extra time, resources, or the removal of other requirements in order to achieve the change.
- "I really can't tell you what I want, but do something and I'll tell you how close you came." The solution to this problem is known as "prototyping." Some customers are unable to visualize a final result from a rough outline, others are unable to articulate an understanding of what they want until they have something to look at. If you don't build this into the project, you find yourself redoing work. If instead you plan a prototype phase, you've already built the changes into your schedule and budget.
- "Surely the project includes these extra items, even if I didn't specify them up front." This may be a completely sincere statement, but it can cause enormous problems. It's worth spending time and effort to make an exhaustive list of project deliverables to avoid this situation. If you find yourself doing items not on the list because it's obvious to you that they

need to be done, you'll be in a weak position to protest when your customer asks for one thing more.

- "I understand that this is unforeseen, but this is your problem, not mine. I won't pay extra or allow you to move the deadline to deal with it." Who will pay for a necessary change is a big potential problem. Some changes are within scope, and they are your responsibility. You must indeed make those changes and swallow any associated costs. Other changes are outside scope and are properly the customer's responsibility. If scope has been properly defined at the beginning of the project, the potential for controversy is substantially reduced. If it's unclear, don't be surprised when people want to play hardball, especially if significant sums are at stake.

Scope Management Plan

The document that follows the Project Charter is a Scope Management Plan, a document that defines the agreed-upon scope in detail and sets forth the procedures that will be followed if changes in scope are required.

The basic procedure for scope changes should be:

1. All proposed scope changes must be in writing.
2. The project manager evaluates scope changes for impact.
3. The question of who is responsible for paying for changes is settled.
4. The scope change is accepted or rejected by the appropriate authority.
5. If the change is accepted, project scope is modified and the plan is changed.

Introducing the Work Breakdown Structure (WBS)

A scope management plan identifies the scope and deliverables. The next step in the planning process is to organize the project in terms of the work that must be performed to achieve the goal. This is

---

Delivering the Deliverables

The project deliverables are what you deliver: any measurable, tangible result that must be produced to complete a project. For a Web site, the deliverables include the site itself, but also specific components of the site, such as a shopping cart or tracking mechanism. In addition, deliverables might include documentation, a CD-ROM containing all the files, and a training program for users and operators.

The list of deliverables is not always obvious or clear, and one way to get into serious trouble on a project is to have an ambiguous list of deliverables. You may think you're completely done only to find a long list of additional items that must be completed. Getting a comprehensive and complete list of deliverables set up at the project's beginning is a critical requirement.

Make sure all deliverables are spelled out in the agreement to do the project, so you can ensure that each is actually done and turned over.

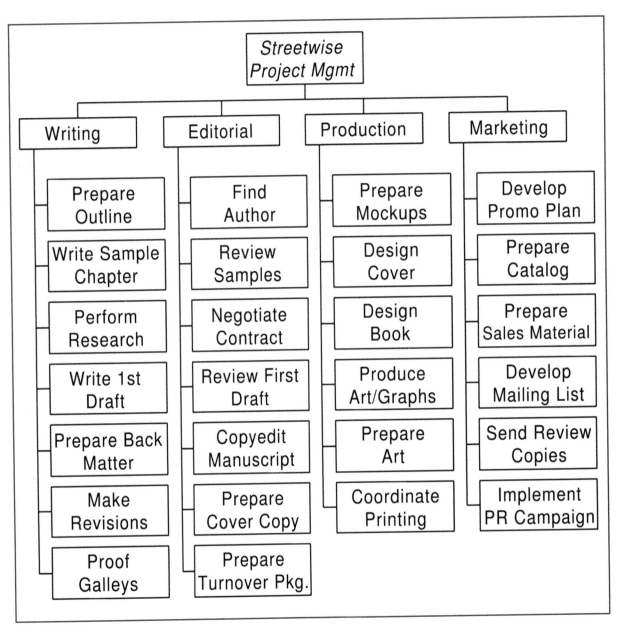

▲ FIGURE 5-1: *Work Breakdown Structure.* This WBS shows the production of the book you're holding, in terms of the tasks required, organized by department.

called a Work Breakdown Structure, or WBS, and it's the first of the formal tools of project planning. Because the WBS is fundamental to all subsequent steps in the planning process, it's extremely important to do a good job.

The WBS can resemble either an organizational chart or an outline, and, as the name suggests, displays a breakdown of the project into its component activities, or tasks. If it's done correctly, all the work necessary to accomplish the project is defined and shown. When all the WBS activities are completed, the project will be done.

Figures 5-1 and 5-2 give a look at this book as a project. The Work Breakdown Structures as shown here consist of three levels. That's minimum; you may have more. The first level, which would be the CEO in a traditional organizational chart, represents the project itself. The second level represents the departments or phases in the project. Here, the work is arranged according to which department is responsible, with a phased approach. You may arrange the work of your project in any organizational format that makes sense to you

I. *Streetwise® Project Management*
  A. Writing
    1. Prepare outline
    2. Write sample chapter
    3. Perform research
    4. Write first draft
    5. Prepare back matter
    6. Make revisions
    7. Proof galleys
  B. Editorial
    1. Find author
    2. Review samples
    3. Negotiate contract
    4. Review first draft
    5. Copyedit manuscript
    6. Prepare cover copy
    7. Prepare turnover package
  C. Production
    1. Prepare mockups
    2. Design cover
    3. Design book
    4. Produce art/graphs
    5. Prepare art
    6. Coordinate printing
  D. Marketing
    1. Develop promo plan
    2. Prepare catalog
    3. Prepare sales materials
    4. Develop mailing list
    5. Send review copies
    6. Implement PR campaign

▲ FIGURE 5-2: *Work Breakdown Structure.* This is the identical WBS presented in outline format. Either method is acceptable.

and meets your needs. The third level of the WBS consists of the actual work packages, known as activities or tasks. It is by doing these activities that the project gets accomplished.

Sequencing and the WBS

Notice that the WBS does not necessarily reflect the actual sequence in which the work will be performed. While the steps are listed more or less in sequence order within departments, the book will actually move back and forth among them. The Writer's task to "Make Revisions," for example, can be performed only after the Editorial task "Review First Draft," and "Review First Draft" can only take place after "Write First Draft."

Each activity in the WBS has the basic characteristic of a project—it ends. If the project is large enough, the WBS level three items will represent projects to the people responsible for doing them. They will break down the project into further levels until the work becomes manageable. There is no conceptual limit to the number of levels in a WBS, but micromanagement is seldom a beneficial strategy in project management. Once you've got a clear sense of a job, there is no value in breaking it down into smaller components.

Scope Management and the WBS

Among the many virtues of the WBS is that if it's done correctly, the scope of your project is set out clearly and unambiguously. The rule is, "If it's not in the WBS, it's not in the project." Of course, you'd better be careful not to leave anything out. If you leave work out of the WBS, you'll discover later that you need to do it, and you won't have budgeted money, people, or time to get it done.

As we get a clearer picture of the work involved in the project, we can add to the WBS. For each work package, we could develop an estimate of how long it will take to do it, assign a specific person to perform the work, identify budgeted costs to allocate for the activity, identify risks in the activity, and define performance specifications and quality measurements. All of this becomes possible using the WBS.

Break down the project into further levels until the work becomes manageable.

Sticky Notes Are a Precious Possession

The WBS is also the first activity we've encountered that can be performed with project management software. Most popular project management (PM) software packages will allow you to enter the WBS and display it in either org chart or outline form. However, it's not necessarily the case that you should bother.

Project Management Software and the WBS

Putting the WBS into your PM software package can speed up subsequent steps in your planning process, because you don't need to retype information. You can enter additional information (duration, resources, etc.) as you develop it, and then start the process of building your Network Diagram. If you do numerous projects that are structurally similar, you may turn your WBS into a template, which speeds up all subsequent similar projects because the information is already there waiting to be modified.

Sticky Note Planning

However, PM software is definitely not the tool of choice when it comes to constructing a WBS in the first place! You'll find that sticky notes provide a much better method.

Get the core project team together and start brainstorming the work packages necessary to accomplish the project. Don't worry that they will normally be listed out of sequence—in fact, that's an advantage. When someone calls out a task, others tend to call out the things that need to be done first. If you have a clear organizational format, you can start with the WBS level two already in place and assign the sticky notes to their owners as they are created.

Network Diagramming

The WBS contains the work, but sequence matters, too. If you're going to put a swimming pool in your backyard, you might include a task as "dig hole," and another task as "pour concrete," and it should be quite clear here that sequence matters.

Project Management Software of Choice

We're using Microsoft Project as our project management software tool in this book because it's a popular choice. Please don't take this either as an endorsement or a criticism of this package or any others. Individual project situations vary, and the best software choice (not to mention whether to use PM software at all!) can differ. Later, we'll look at ways to choose the tool that's right for you.

In project management lingo, we would say that to "pour concrete is dependent on dig hole," and present it in graphic form as shown in Figure 5-3:

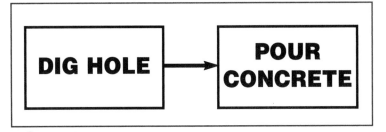

▲ FIGURE 5-3: *Dependency relationship.* **When one task cannot begin until a predecessor task is complete, the second task is dependent on the first.**

Notice from a scheduling perspective, if anything happens to make "dig hole" take longer than planned, the start of "pour concrete" will be delayed.

The Network Diagram (also known as PDM, or Precedence Diagramming Method) is a popular and easy way to sequence the tasks in your project. (You'll also see this referred to as a PERT Chart, which is technically incorrect, as we'll see later on.)

The easiest way to make your Network Diagram is to take the sticky notes from the WBS that you completed (after first copying the final version so you'll have it later on) and lay them out in sequence. For illustration purposes, we're showing here only the writing and editorial phases of the book (see Figure 5-4).

Now, we have a sequence of activities and durations for each activity, so we can now determine how long the project will take!

Critical Path

If you add up the task durations for each of the activities on the chart, you'll find they total 120 days. Is that the number of working days the project will take? Interestingly, the answer is "no." This project will take 108 working days. Why? Notice that some tasks are done in parallel; that is to say, in the same time frame as other activities. Look at the area from Task 3 to Task 7. There are two paths

> The Network Diagram (also known as PDM, or Precedence Diagramming Method) is a popular and easy way to sequence the tasks in your project.

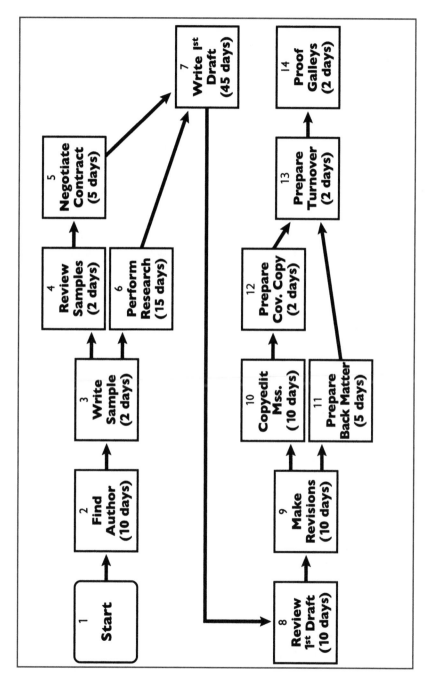

▲ FIGURE 5-4: *Network Diagram.* This diagram represents the activities from the WBS shown in the sequence they are to be completed. Note that time estimates have been added to each note. These time estimates represent Duration, or number of work periods, but not necessarily Level of Effort, because not all tasks are performed on a full-time basis.

Basic Concepts

We'll go into each of the tools in more detail in later chapters. As you can see, the basic concepts are fairly straightforward, even if they happen to be new to you. By following the steps in the process, you now have a list of tasks and a basic project schedule. You can analyze the schedule for risks, look at issues to ensure quality, assign people to the different activities, determine the budget, and much more now that the fundamentals are on paper.

you can take. The upper path consists of Tasks 4 and 5, which total seven days. The lower path consists of Task 6, which takes fifteen days. Only Task 6, therefore, counts toward total project duration, because it's longer. The other two tasks take place in the same time frame, adding no net days to project duration.

This concept is known as the *critical path*, and it's an important concept indeed. You can see an immediate advantage: If Tasks 4 and 5 take longer than expected, there's no consequence for the project deadline for up to six days of delay! On the other hand, any slippage in Task 6 immediately pushes out the project completion date.

Network Diagrams and PM Software

The Network Diagram can also be prepared using project management software. Again, sticky notes are the most useful tool for laying out the project in the first place, because they can be done in a team environment and allow for easy exploration of different ideas. The software will do the calculations for you automatically.

Meet Henry Gantt

The most popular project management tool is also the oldest: the Gantt Chart, named after Henry Gantt (1861–1919), one of the pioneers of scientific management at the turn of the century. Gantt worked for Frederick Taylor, the father of scientific management, and today he is best known for the scheduling tool that bears his name, the Gantt Chart. A Gantt Chart allows for the presentation of multiple overlapping tasks over a period of time. The easiest to read and understand for people not conversant with project management, Gantt Charts are most popular for small and medium-size projects. To make a Gantt Chart, all you need is graph paper, a list of the tasks, the duration of each, and either the start date or the dependency relationship of each of the tasks.

For more information on this topic, visit our Web site at **www.businesstown.com**

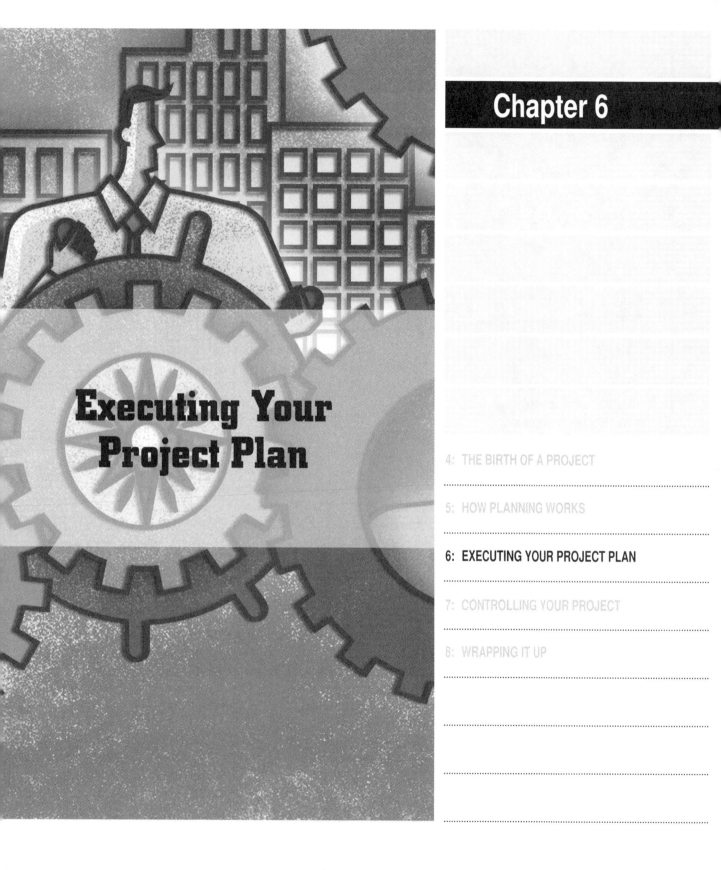

Executing Your Project Plan

The Executing Process Group

The Executing process group involves all the activities necessary to accomplish the work of the project. You assign project activities to team members, help the team work together effectively, manage and resolve problems, and coordinate with project stakeholders.

At the same time, you'll also be working on Controlling activities, which involve monitoring the status of project work against baselines, managing risks and quality, and handle changes to the original project. We'll cover those in the next chapter.

You're not completely finished with planning, even though you're now going about the business of getting the work accomplished. When a project involves a high level of unknowns, as is common in such areas as research and development and new product development, your initial plan may have gotten quite sketchy after the first few tasks, because the output of those tasks determines what will happen subsequently. As a result, you may find yourself continuing to develop and refine the plan by adding new information as you obtain it.

Executing the project is the part of project management that is most like regular management. You delegate work to team members, motivate them to perform well, lead the project in a specific direction, and build an environment that allows people to achieve their best results. We'll say less about the parts of management with which you're already familiar outside the project context, and focus on what makes projects unique and special.

> You're not completely finished with planning, even though you're now going about the business of getting the work accomplished.

Building the Project Team

The project team consists of the people whose work you need to get the project done. The team normally consists of a few people who are in the project pretty much from start to finish, and others who have specific technical roles to play. Once the roles have been satisfied, those people normally leave the project team. The team members may or may not be people who report to you in a traditional supervisory sense; some team members may have higher organizational rank than you.

Intact and Part-Time Work Teams

The project team can be either an intact work team or part time. An intact work team consists of people who are on the project full time, start to finish. Because they have little or no outside responsibilities during the life of the project, their time and effort are largely controllable by the project manager.

With a part-time work team, members of the work team have other projects and work responsibilities, and therefore work on the current project only on a part-time basis (with occasional spurts of full-time effort).

As you can see, it's much easier to build teamwork with an intact work team than with a part-time work team. Does that mean there is something wrong with the way this project is being conducted? No. The nature of the work in our example makes using intact work teams impractical.

This Book as a Project

Let's again look at the *Streetwise® Project Management* book as project. In most publishing situations, the editor is the project manager. Team members include, among others, the writer, art and production people, and someone from marketing. The editor supervises the writer, but the relationship is contractual (company to freelance as opposed to boss to employee) and the writer is typically in a geographically different location.

The art and production people typically don't report to the editorial group, and almost never to the editor directly. They have their own issues and deadlines, as well as numerous other projects to accomplish. Marketing normally doesn't report to editorial either, and in some organizations enjoys substantially more power than editorial. (In a "brand management" structure, the project manager can be the marketing brand manager, but notice that the relationships are still sideways across departments rather than primarily top-down.)

Here, we have a part-time work team, in which every member of the team is also responsible for other concurrent projects: The writer is simultaneously working on a second novel and delivering project management seminars. The editor is acquiring several *Streetwise®* titles during the same time period. The art, production, and marketing people also provide these services for all products, including backlist and reissued titles.

How can you manage a project under these circumstances? Very carefully is one answer. Read on for more answers.

When you are managing a project, it tends to be set up based on the practical nature of the work, not on the ideal circumstances for effective teamwork. Nevertheless, if you are the project manager, you must build a spirit of willing collaboration and cooperation or else the job is unlikely to be done, or done very well.

Teamwork in an Intact Work Team

Let's look at the easier situation first: building a team in an intact environment. First, the circumstances and nature of the work have to permit this choice. Second, you may or may not have significant power to choose the team members you prefer. Third, even if the majority of your team has an intact structure, it's common for at least some members to connect on a part-time basis.

Projects fail in the Executing stage for three basic reasons:

1. People on the team do not know the goals, the individual roles, or the performance expectations for the project.
2. People get bogged down in the act of working with one another because they do not possess the necessary skills.
3. Rivalries, politics, and personalities (and previous histories) generate conflict.

Teamwork and team building is frequently misunderstood, and you may have seen it presented in what is essentially a set of "feel-good" activities. Teams are necessary in organizations because they are a critical tool for getting the work done. As a project manager, you must understand fundamental team-building techniques and strategies in order to get your projects accomplished, such as the following:

1. *Goal setting.* To make your project team function effectively, the first thing you need to know is the GREAT model.

   Goals
   Roles
   Expectations/Performance
   Accountabilities/Abilities
   Timing

> You may or may not have significant power to choose the team members you prefer.

The GREAT model specifies what people must know before they can work together effectively.

Goals. What are the goals of the project? What is the goal of each individual activity? Why are we doing this?

Roles. What is my job as an individual team member? What do I do? What is the contribution I am expected to make? What expertise do I bring to the situation? What is everyone else's role and everyone else's expected contribution?

Expectations. How good is "good enough?" What is the level of performance that is desired? What level of performance is not desired? Why are the expectations set at this level as opposed to another?

Accountabilities/Abilities. Who is accountable for each phase of the work, especially on jobs that cut across functional lines or involve several people? What abilities do we possess that have a bearing on the individual job assignments?

Timing. When must this be done? At what pace am I to work? How does the timing of one piece of the work affect other pieces?

2. *Working together skills.* Some of the most important skills of working together are not systematically taught to people. To work together in a business setting, people must know how to run a meeting, how to conduct group decision-making and problem-solving, and other group processes. The traditional "seven basic tools of TQM" (Total Quality Management) are enormously valuable additions to any team member's skill set: flow charting, histogramming, Pareto charting, cause-and-effect diagramming, checklisting, scatter diagramming, and control charting. (See Chapter 22 for a complete list and examples.)

Delivering Information

Don't assume people have all the information they need or that they will figure it out on their own. Set a personal rule that you will deliver this information a minimum of four times: verbally to the group, in writing to the group, verbally to each individual, and in written form to each individual. See the later description of the *kanban* system for task communication for another idea. It's almost impossible to do this too much—and the more complex and longer the project, the more you must do it.

3. *Personality issues.* A good team involves people who bring disparate personality styles and sets of strengths/weaknesses to the situation. (Avoid the common problem of building a team of clones.) Use personality type systems to help each team member understand the others (numerous tools exist, ranging from the Myers-Briggs Type Indicator to books like *Exploring Personality Styles* [SkillPath, 1999]–use the tool that suits your purposes), and understand that the goal is to get people to operate with mutual respect, rather than necessarily to like each other or even enjoy working with each other.

4. *A final note on timing.* Even when you do everything right, know that teams naturally pass through a set of stages (known as the Tuchman Model): Forming, Storming, Norming, Performing, and Adjourning, each with predictable challenges. Don't mistake a natural developmental phase for an actual problem.

> The GREAT model is even more important for part-time teams.

Teamwork in a Part-Time Work Team

If all or some of the members of the team are not part of an intact work team structure, you still have to accomplish the same goals, but you have fewer tools to work with.

The GREAT model is even more important for part-time teams. When people have their attention divided among multiple projects, you simply cannot assume that they have enough focus on your project to know what the expectations are. Communicating expectations verbally a single time just doesn't cut it. Do tell them, but write them, e-mail them, and put it in your calendar that you have to remind them when it comes to the timing issues. Your firm persistence is the most valuable tool you have.

Personality conflicts are often less of an issue when people don't have to work closely with each other, but a long-standing rivalry or dislike can rear its ugly head in the middle of your project. Keep alert for these situations and show up to remind people what they have to do and when—remember, it's about the work, not about the personality. Know that you will often have to settle for minimum performance from people because your project simply doesn't have high enough priority, and if it does, it's still not always an absolute priority.

The better your own skills are at the disciplines of meeting management, conflict resolution, and so forth, the better you'll perform in this situation. One common complaint of project managers in the part-time team environment is, "I schedule a meeting, but key players just don't show up!" That's because meetings have an unfortunately deserved reputation as time-wasters, and busy people will attempt to dodge them if possible. When you do them right, you'll find that in time the word gets around and people are much more likely to be cooperative.

If you are in the common position of having to aid other people on their projects while managing your own, make sure you provide support to others on a timely basis if you expect to have enough influence to push them into completing your work on time. Keep good calendar records and practice effective time management.

Supervising People Who Don't Work for You

It's very common for a project manager to not be the official supervisor of the entire project team. This is true because projects are temporary, requiring a variety of people to be pulled under one roof for a limited amount of time. Because these people have "homes" to return to after the conclusion of the project, and because their expertise may be needed on a variety of projects, it makes little sense to reorganize the entire organization chart for this limited purpose.

The good news is that official supervisory authority isn't that great to begin with. While you may possess the technical power to fire somebody, in practice, you must get the cooperation and signoffs from people who outrank you in your own hierarchy and from outside groups (such as human resources or legal) to get it done. Supervisors quickly learn that official power is much less important

> It's very common for a project manager to not be the official supervisor of the entire project team.

than leadership—the ways we get people to choose to do what it is we want them to do.

The discipline of influence management, which is a practical and completely legitimate form of office politics, is another of the core competencies of good project managers. Influence management is, as the name suggests, the art and craft of gaining influence over others, which requires power. There are six sources of organizational power (see sidebar) that reinforce one another to give you expanded influence to get the work done.

Managing Tasks and Deliverables

While managing your team processes, you must ensure that the right tasks are completed in the right order. You'll find that your WBS,

The Six Sources of Power

Role Power. Your official role in the organization gives you certain influence. Even those who do not report to you in a formal sense normally have to show at least a minimum respect for your organizational role. Notice that this power is given to you by others and is capable of being countermanded.

Respect Power. A powerful source of influence management is the respect others have for you because of your track record, your special knowledge, your insight and intelligence, and your personal integrity and honesty. While respect power takes time to build, it's very powerful.

Rhetoric Power. Skill in the arts of communication is a source of influence and power. Your personal ability to negotiate, to sell, and sometimes even to plead are ways to influence others to get the work done.

Resources Power. You often have control of certain resources—your own time and priority list, if nothing else—that others require to get their work done. Go the extra mile for those who are willing to go the extra mile for you in return.

Relationship Power. Who you know and what kind of relationship you have with them is another traditional source of power. Good manners and a friendly smile are effective management tools.

Reason Power. Depending on the priority of your project, you may get additional power from it. Reason power comes from the "why" of your project. Under normal circumstances, you couldn't evict a vice president from his or her office, but if you're the acting fire marshal and there's a fire, your reason for giving orders is so high that everyone will tend to obey you. When your project has significant priority and legitimacy, it's completely appropriate to use that power in support of accomplishing your ends.

Network Diagram, Gantt Chart, and other traditional project management tools help you do this.

Don't forget to involve your customer in the process. If you complete some project deliverables before the project is completed, turn them over early and get written confirmation that they are acceptable—it puts you in good shape with the customer and adds to the customer's confidence in your performance as a project manager.

Give work assignments in writing and keep a log. Follow up at regular intervals. Insist that people tell you when they're completed *in writing*—it keeps people focused.

Keeping On Schedule, On Budget, and On Spec

There is a feedback loop between the Executing and Controlling project phases. By staying on top of the team process and ensuring that task assignments are given and received in written form, you are providing operational emphasis on the three project management goals: on time, on budget, and on spec.

Of course, there are reasons other than poor performance that result in missed deadlines, budgets, or performance targets. Perhaps the job had a high degree of inherent uncertainty, so the original estimate wasn't that solid. Perhaps unforeseen and even unforeseeable problems cropped up. Perhaps outside priorities interfered with your planned acquisition and utilization of project resources.

Whatever the reason, your monitoring and control systems will need to pick them up. Based on your analysis, you will then make performance changes that normally require work in the Executing phase, and so you can expect a steady stream of adjustments and modifications.

> There are reasons other than poor performance that result in missed deadlines, budgets, or performance targets.

Heading in the Right Direction

Everything else in project management is designed to help you with this most critical activity—*getting the work done*. Armed with strong advance analysis and negotiation of objectives, and a comprehensive plan, you approach the project and understand that your focus must now be primarily on the people side: teamwork, communications, and collaboration in support of task accomplishment. Remember the GREAT model and the stages of team development: Our goal is not necessarily to be friends, but to get a job done.

As the project manager, you'll find yourself going back and forth between this stage and the next, Controlling, so that you'll gain the earliest possible warning of potential difficulties on your project, empowering you to make the adjustments and keep yourself heading in the right direction.

> Our goal is not necessarily to be friends, but to get a job done.

For more information on this topic, visit our Web site at www.businesstown.com

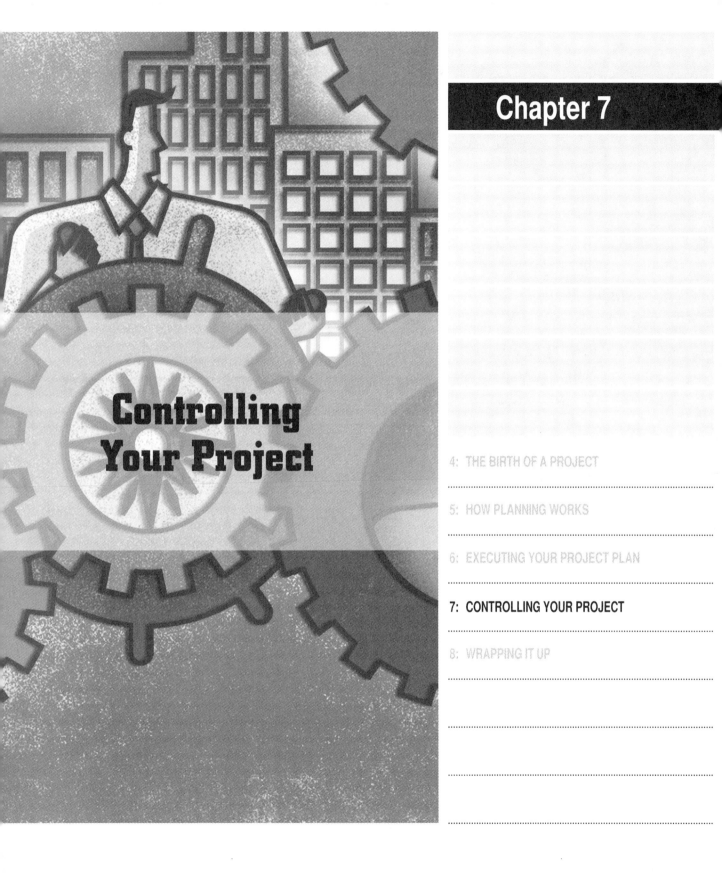

Controlling Your Project

The Controlling Phase

The other major activity of the project manager once the project has started is the Controlling phase of the project. In the Controlling phase, your mission is to monitor the project (as compared to the original plan) and to act to correct deviations. This means managing the scope of the project, including handling required project changes.

While the Executing process mostly involves the members of your team, the Controlling process tends to involve people outside your team—stakeholders, customers, managers, contractors—who have their own agendas and interests concerning your project. You'll find yourself using substantial negotiating skills during this phase as well.

How do you know how you're doing? By examining actual data compared to performance baselines.

> The Controlling process tends to involve people outside your team.

▶ THE TWELVE* IMMUTABLE LAWS OF PROJECT MANAGEMENT

1. No project is ever completed on time, within budget, and with the same staff that started it, and the project does not do what it is supposed to do.

2. One advantage of fuzzy project objectives is that they let you avoid embarrassment in estimating the corresponding costs.

3. The effort required to correct a project that is off course increases exponentially with time.

4. Everyone else understands the project purpose statement differently. If you explain the purpose so clearly no one could possibly misunderstand, they will.

5. Measurable benefits are real. Intangible benefits are not measurable; therefore, intangible benefits are not real (but are if you can find a way to measure them).

6. If you can be assigned to work on a project part time, you don't have enough to do.

7. A carelessly planned project will take three times longer to complete than expected. A carefully planned project will take only twice as long.

8. If the project is going well, something is about to go wrong.

9. Project teams detest progress reporting because it so vividly manifests the lack of progress.

10. Projects progress rapidly until they are 90 percent complete, then remain at 90 percent complete forever.

11. If project content is allowed to change, the rate of change will exceed the rate of progress.

   * Yes, there are only eleven. We're at 91.6 percent of specification.

Setting Up Performance Baselines

There are normally three performance baselines that you set for your project: the schedule baseline, the cost baseline, and the technical baseline.

Schedule Baseline

The first baseline is the schedule, normally displayed in the form of a Tracking Gantt Chart. On a Tracking Gantt Chart, you have one set of bars that represent the original plan, and a parallel set that record what has already happened on the project. By comparing the two, you can identify schedule discrepancies and identify their potential impact on the project.

Cost Baseline

The second performance baseline is the cost baseline. There isn't a standard tool like the Tracking Gantt to display this information. Normally, you'll use a spreadsheet showing the budget amounts for each task, enter the actual cost when it's determined, and monitor the variance, if any (see Figure 7-1).

We've priced this project with a planned outlay of $14,500, counting contracted and inside labor costs. To date, we've expended $5,600, so we've got plenty of money left. Or, do we? Task 2 took $500 more than anticipated, and Task 3 took $150 less, so we currently appear to

> There are normally three performance baselines that you set for your project.

be $350 over budget on this project. Again, we don't know our actual costs for tasks that haven't been completed yet, notably Task 7, our writing task, which is now 50 percent complete and as far as we can tell, proceeding on schedule. (We may not be able to tell at this stage whether the work will finish on time or not.)

Technical Baseline

The third baseline is the technical baseline, which normally involves monitoring of the tasks displayed in your WBS to ensure that each is satisfactorily completed (see Figure 7-2).

We've taken our WBS outline and turned it into a table. By recording when each activity is completed, we can look at performance by department, which is a different and often useful perspective, especially on large projects with numerous tasks. We can compare completion dates with targets, but the schedule baseline

▶ **FIGURE 7-1:** *Cost baseline.* **This spreadsheet shows the amounts budgeted for each task and the actual expenditures for those tasks that are completed to date, so you can identify any discrepancies.**

Streetwise PM Cost Baseline

Task	Name	Planned Cost	Actual Cost	Percent Done	Variance
1	Start	$0	$0	100%	$0
2	Find Author	$500	$1,000	100%	($500)
3	Write Sample Chapter	$750	$600	100%	$150
4	Review Samples	$250	$250	100%	$0
5	Perform Research	$1,000	$1,000	100%	$0
6	Negotiate Contract	$500	$500	100%	$0
7	Write 1st Draft	$4,500	$2,250	50%	$0
8	Review 1st Draft	$1,000			
9	Make Revisions	$2,500			
10	Copyedit Ms.	$1,000			
11	Prepare Back Matter	$1,000			
12	Prepare Cover Copy	$250			
13	Prepare Turnover	$250			
14	Proof Galleys	$1,000			
15	Finish	$0			
		$14,500	$5,600		($350)

has already given us that information. What we want to look at is the project from the perspective of work completed, and in this view we can also see any patterns that are developing within departments or subprojects in time to allow us to act.

Streetwise PM Technical Baseline	Complete Date
A. Writing	
1. Prepare Outline	1/13
2. Write Sample Chapter	1/14
3. Perform Research	1/26
4. Write First Draft	
5. Prepare Back Matter	
6. Make Revisions	
7. Proof Galleys	
B. Editorial	
1. Find Author	1/13
2. Review Samples	1/14
3. Negotiate Contract	2/7
4. Review First Draft	
5. Copyedit Manuscript	
6. Prepare Cover Copy	
7. Prepare Turnover Package	
C. Production	
1. Prepare Mockups	1/9
2. Design Cover	
3. Design Book	
4. Produce Art/Graphs	
5. Prepare Art	
6. Coordinate Printing	
D. Marketing	
1. Develop Promo Plan	1/5
2. Prepare Catalog	1/13
3. Prepare Sales Materials	
4. Develop Mailing List	
5. Send Review Copies	
6. Implement PR Campaign	

◄ FIGURE 7-2: *Technical baseline.* **By adapting the Work Breakdown Structure (WBS), FIGURE 5-2, we can record the technical completion status of the project. Although this example uses the outline format, the organizational chart format may be used as well.**

Managing Risks

A risk is not a problem. The difference? A risk is future tense; a problem is present tense. The Godzilla Principle tells us that the better job we do heading off our risks in advance, the fewer problems we'll have to wrestle with at the end of the day.

There are four parts to an overall risk management strategy, and they start in the Planning stage of your project. These are risk identification, risk quantification, risk response planning, and risk response control.

> A risk is future tense; a problem is present tense.

Risk Identification

The first step in risk management is risk identification, the process of identifying the potential risks on the project. There are a variety of strategies to use. Two strategies of particular relevance to project management are: analyzing tasks in the WBS for potential risks, and analyzing the Network Diagram (with particular attention to the critical path) for potential risks. Consider history with similar projects, expert opinion, and outside factors as well.

While risk identification starts with the planning stage of the project, it goes on throughout the project's life cycle. Some risks are not visible or detectable at a project's beginning, and must be added to the list. Other risks turn out to melt away in the light of reality and are removed.

Risk Quantification

A risk is normally described as Probability times Impact. If there is a risk to your project that is 50 percent likely to happen and will result in $1,000 worth of extra cost, the risk is considered to be 50 percent x $1,000, or $500. If the risk is only 10 percent likely to happen, the risk is now only $100.

You often cannot quantify probability or impact to this level of precision. Instead, you can group risks into rough "buckets" of high, medium, and low. The reason for this step is that not every risk can be addressed in a cost-effective manner. If the cost of eliminating the risk is lower than the risk itself, then it's usually wise to do so. But sometimes the cost of risk response is greater than the risk itself, and accepting the risk and its consequences may be smarter.

Throughout the project, you may find it wise to reassess probability periodically, because events on your project make some risks likelier or less likely.

Risk Response Planning

By narrowing your list of risks to those of significance, you can now start developing your responses. Let's imagine that you're planning a company picnic and the risk you are concerned with is rain. There are basically four things you can do with a risk:

Throughout the project, you may find it wise to reassess probability periodically.

1. *Acceptance.* You can accept the risk, which means proceed on your original course and take what comes. If it rains, it rains. We get wet.

2. *Avoidance.* You can modify your project plan so that the risk event either cannot happen or has no impact. We decide it won't be a picnic, but an indoor event. It may rain, but that doesn't affect us any longer.

3. *Mitigation.* You may be able to lower probability and/or impact, but not eliminate the risk. If we rent a tent, the rain still washes out certain activities, but others are okay—the impact is lessened. If we plan the picnic for a drought season, the probability of rain is lessened.

4. *Transfer.* You might buy insurance to reimburse your costs if it rains. In transfer, the risk probability and impact may be unchanged, but someone else assumes the liability for damage, usually for a fee of some kind.

For each risk that you select for a response strategy, you modify your original plan or plan a response strategy for when (or if) the risk even occurs. Have a written risk plan and revisit it throughout the project on a regular basis.

If you do similar projects, you can start with previous risk lists and with some quick modification, have a comprehensive risk management strategy with relatively little effort.

Maintaining Quality

Quality and performance are not synonymous. Quality is what you want; performance is what you do. If you want performance on your project to be of good quality, it takes effort in planning, execution, and control. Quality is never an accident, but a result of deliberate action, and the project manager is operationally responsible for quality.

Definitions of Quality

If quality is not defined, or thought of as some vague concept of "goodness," you can't very well pursue it methodically. In the discipline of Total Quality Management (TQM), there are several schools of thought, each with its own definition.

One well-known definition comes from W. Edwards Deming, who defined quality as "exceeding customer expectations." The value in this definition is that it relates to the behavior we are seeking. If a customer is dissatisfied, the customer goes somewhere else next time. If a customer was satisfied, but no more, he or she may seek a lower price or try someone else just to see what's out there. But if a customer has his or her expectations exceeded, then the customer will come back, and usually price is not the primary purchasing consideration.

The limit of this definition is that the project manager or project team doesn't always have direct access to the customer. If you don't know what the customer expectations happen to be, it's rather difficult to plan to exceed them.

Another popular definition of quality comes from the work of Philip Crosby, who defines quality as "conformance to requirements." Let's define precisely what you want, then we will deliver it precisely as you requested. The advantage of this definition is that operationally the project team is in a much better position to plan to achieve the requirements. The limit is that now you are the hostage of the person who specified the requirements. If that person didn't do a good job of working with the customer to develop the right requirements, you'll accurately deliver the wrong thing. And even though in one sense it isn't your fault—after all, you did what you were told—the negative customer consequences tend to fall on your head regardless of actual fault.

> The project manager or project team doesn't always have direct access to the customer.

Operational Quality

We've emphasized elsewhere the importance of defining "good enough," and that's not in opposition to quality. Both time and cost matter to customers, and in some circumstances trump the performance. If you're bleeding in the emergency room, you don't want to hear, "If you can wait until Tuesday, we can give you much finer quality." Adequate performance immediately is more valuable than technically superior performance several days later after you've already bled to death. Sometimes the use to which the customer will put a product is limited. An inexpensive product that does just enough is more desirable than a more expensive one full of bells and whistles of marginal value.

If your project runs into trouble, what should you cut? You can miss the deadline, exceed the budget, or aim lower on the performance requirements—the critical question is which does least damage to the customer's core needs. "Good enough" matters.

In your risk plan, consider risks to quality along with risks to schedule and budget. What could happen in this project that would lower our ability to deliver a top-quality product? Could we modify the project to lower either the probability or impact of the potential obstacles to quality?

If we have extra time or extra budget available, is it better to speed up the project or lower its cost, or is it better to invest any extra time, money, or resources in improving the performance? Answers vary from project to project.

If you begin your project with a focus on quality and build quality measurements into your planning process, you will have operational control of quality throughout the project execution phase. It's worth doing.

The Insidious Scope Creep—And How to Control It

Even with goodwill on the part of all project stakeholders, projects have a tendency to mutate. Change management is one of the critical functions of the Controlling process group. Changes can result

Measure and Test

Ideally, you want to work with both quality definitions in a feedback loop. The focus on the customer tells you with whom you must work, and a set of measurable, definable requirements you can integrate into your project is the output.

Look for opportunities to measure and test; you don't want a quality definition based on someone else's intuitive sense of whether what you've done is "good enough."

from plan slippage in the areas of schedule, budget, resources, or performance; from the discovery of previously unknown information; or because stakeholders want something different once the project has begun.

Preventive Action

Preventive action is taken with the goal of avoiding a problem by changing something in the way the project is managed. This could involve adding time to an activity, adding resources or money, or changing some aspect of performance or method. Preventive action can be designed into an initial plan or be added to a project underway based on your ongoing risk identification.

Corrective Action

Corrective action is reactive: There has been a problem and the corrective action is designed to mitigate or eliminate the damage. For example, when Task 2 ("Find Author") goes over schedule in our *Streetwise* project, we're looking at a delay in project completion. To overcome the problem, we might be able to shrink the time of one or more subsequent tasks to bring the project back on schedule.

Notice that if a delay is on a critical path activity, only reductions on other critical path activities will help return the project to schedule. If you reduce the length of time that a noncritical activity takes, you don't receive any schedule benefit.

Scope Creep

A change in project scope can be part of either preventive or corrective action, but other changes in project scope aren't an indication of project problems, but rather the result of a change requested by a project stakeholder, either the customer or someone else with an interest in the project. (Adding your objectives onto someone else's project is a traditional political technique, like attaching a rider to legislation already on the fast track.)

Scope creep isn't inherently wrong—it may be necessary, appropriate, even desirable—but it is troublesome because changes in scope normally affect other parts of the project. If someone wants you to do additional work, it's likely to take additional time, cost

> Preventive action is taken with the goal of avoiding a problem by changing something in the way the project is managed.

additional money, take additional resources, or affect your ability to do another part of the project. Therefore, you need to manage project scope actively in the Controlling phase of your project.

Change Orders

One important decision to make with respect to scope changes is who pays for them. In construction projects, for example, the question of who is financially responsible for each change is a matter of careful contractual negotiation. For each change, the question is whether it was within the original scope of the project. We are excavating for the foundation and discover that it is rockier than we thought, and will take longer as a result. Are we responsible for the condition of the ground, or did we exclude delays resulting from unknown subsurface conditions? In the first instance, we have to swallow the cost of overtime and extra equipment to stay on schedule; in the second case, our customer must pay.

One problem seen in many organizations is that project managers often feel unsure how to ask for additional money for out-of-scope change orders. They accept out-of-scope changes with the goal of creating goodwill for the customer.

It may be appropriate to eat costs that aren't really your responsibility based on the nature of the customer relationship, but you don't get the goodwill if the customer doesn't know the sacrifice you're making. Provide a "zero cost" change order at a minimum, showing the price you would normally charge, and then waiving it.

Re-Planning

There is an arrow going back to Planning in our process diagram (see Figure 3-2), which tells us that in some cases it is appropriate to reopen the planning process to deal with change. Because planning takes resources and time (and sometimes money), a comprehensive re-planning of the project is not something lightly undertaken.

Consider re-planning the project if the scope change is large, if you have to develop a new method to get from where you are back

Don't Shortcut the Process

Beware of the temptation to be nice and shortcut the process. This tends to get you in trouble later, especially because people requesting a scope change tend to verbally minimize what they are really asking for. Make sure the entire change is quantified so that the decision-making process will be meaningful.

to where you want to be, and if mapping actual progress against your benchmarks no longer gives you useful information.

Identifying Variances

To control your project, you need to have some measurements that reveal whether or not you're on track at any particular moment. The three measurements of schedule, cost, and technical performance form the baselines for your project. By measuring where you are compared to the baseline, you identify variances. Minor variances may be within acceptable limits for your project; major variances require corrective or preventive action.

Are You a Contract Manager?

You may not be officially a contract manager, and you might not even think of yourself as being a contract manager, but it's worth taking a second look. Even if contractual matters normally take place far above your organizational level, you may have much more involvement in contract matters than you suspect.

If you are participating on a project that has a contract, issues with the contract have a substantial bearing on your work. Are the deliverables specified? Are performance criteria clear? What about timing? How about scope? If the contract has not yet been drafted, remember that while your legal staff can handle the formal matters, the technical substance is something you know best. Your first and best opportunity to smooth problems out of the project is to get a good agreement done up front.

If that's not the case or if it's too late, your second best move is to read the contract and prepare your own written abstract of the technical specifications, scope, and deliverables. Circulate the draft to make sure everyone sees the issues and work in the same way. If they don't, it's possible to resolve it now.

It's not a sin or a crime to ask the other side for more money or more work if appropriate. One of the problems on a contract, especially a fixed price contract, is that with a weak description of deliverables, you can get stuck with a lot more scope for the dollar. Work toward a detailed description of scope so that when you're asked to do extra, you can figure out who should shoulder financial responsibility. Having a contract isn't very useful if you don't follow up and enforce its terms.

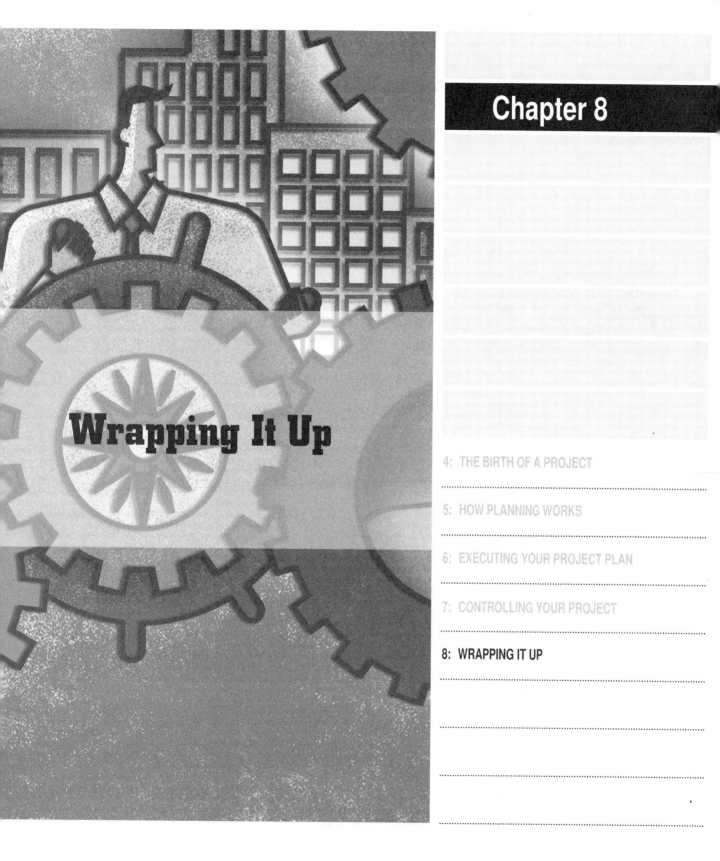

Chapter 8

Wrapping It Up

The Closing Process

We're almost at the end of the project life cycle, so this is a bad moment to lose focus on our sequence of processes. The final process is called Closing, and it involves the termination of the project and the delivery of the project output. If you've done everything right up until this point, you should have pretty smooth sailing from here on, but there are still a few potential danger areas through which you must navigate.

The "90 Percent" Project

There is a project management saying that goes, "The first ninety percent of the project takes ninety percent of the time and effort; the remaining ten percent takes the other ninety percent of the time and effort."

The place where a mistake is made is not necessarily the same place where the damage shows up. You can make a mistake early in the project and no immediate damage results. Often it stores itself up and makes itself manifest only at the very end. Here are some reasons why projects end up in failure:

> The place where a mistake is made is not necessarily the same place where the damage shows up.

- *Goal conflict.* Because there may be more than one customer for a project, goals can be in conflict. Sometimes, in the haste to get started on a project, we don't take the time to resolve goal conflicts. At the project end, we discover that key stakeholders are dissatisfied. Sometimes, stopping the project in its tracks seems a better alternative than bringing the missed requirements out into the open.
- *Needs change.* A project starts as a result of an identified need. Sometimes, during the life of the project, the need goes away. Finishing the project is no longer a way to solve a problem.
- *Over-optimism.* Sometimes, there was a belief (on the part of the project manager or on the part of senior management) that the project would be easier than it turned out to be. As reality sets in, the project begins to slip further and further behind.

Doing It Right the First Time

The best of all possible strategies is to spend more time up front in defining and planning so that you approach the project with a more realistic and informed knowledge base. The second best strategy (though it works well combined with the first) is to set up and maintain a good Controlling strategy throughout the project. The third strategy (not a "best" anything) is to be really creative in finding ways to dig yourself out of an ever-increasing hole.

Sometimes, you enter this stage of the project in difficult straits because of outside forces that are no particular indicator of fault on your part. Notice that at the end of the project, as throughout, there are only three things that can be modified: You can finish late and get it all done, spend more money or resources to get it all done on time, or finish by the deadline by eliminating some portions of the desired technical performance.

Bad News in Project Management

Of eighty U.S. Department of Energy major systems acquisitions in the period 1980–1996, thirty-one were terminated prior to completion after over $10 billion was spent. Only fifteen were completed, mostly behind schedule and over budget. Three of those have not yet been used for their intended purpose.

In a study of major private sector IT projects, it was found that 40 percent failed to meet business requirements, and 28 percent failed altogether. Of the ones that succeeded in meeting business requirements, 74 percent failed to meet the original budget or schedule.

In 1998, *Fortune* 500 company IT projects averaged $2.3 million, with only a 24 percent chance of success. The average cancelled IT project was scheduled for twenty-seven weeks but cancelled in week fourteen, with over $1 million lost for every IT project that failed to meet business needs. On average, eleven IT professionals contributed nothing of business value for at least six of the fourteen weeks.

U.S. business spends $250 billion a year on IT projects, with approximately $75 billion going to failed projects. Nearly half of all applications development projects have cost overruns of 70 percent more than originally budgeted.

In all projects, for every 100 major projects that start, ninety-four are restarts. Some projects have had more than one restart.

The Administrative Close

The two processes in Closing are known as administrative closure and contract closeout. Contract closeout is used when the project has been a contracted activity. You must verify that the terms of the contract have been satisfactorily completed and file final invoices.

Administrative closure is part of every project. It's sometimes not done well, and the biggest reason it is deficient is because—well, let's face it—it's pretty boring. Few people enjoy the final wrap-up paperwork, and some otherwise successful projects have become hung up in the final details and have ended badly.

As with most other stages in the project life cycle, begin thinking about closeout during the Planning phase. What will have to be done in order for the project to be considered completely finished? Who will do these various tasks? How long will it take?

Prepare a Closeout Checklist to verify that everything has been properly completed. Items on the checklist may include:

- Contractual obligations completed
- Project WBS reviewed
- Documentation completed
- Files archived
- Lessons learned report completed
- Customer satisfaction survey completed
- Personnel and resources reassigned
- Thank-yous sent

Learning Project Lessons

We traditionally associate age with wisdom, but that's a mistake. People grow older at the same rate (twenty-four hours per day), but we observe that they do not grow wiser with the same consistency. Wisdom is the act of learning from one's experience. Experience happens, but the learning part, alas, has always been optional. Project managers don't make it optional; they make it a mandatory part of the process, called "lessons learned."

Definition of Administrative Closure

Administrative closure is the process of verifying and documenting project results, formalizing acceptance of the product or service by the customer, collecting and reviewing project records, analyzing project effectiveness, and archiving information for future use. The process can also entail reassignment or return of personnel and equipment.

As you compile your final documentation, ask yourself whether the organization (or you personally) will ever do something similar to this in the future. If the answer is affirmative, make sure you keep a copy of the fundamental project documents to use as a template to aid the process of planning for the future. One reason why experienced project managers take less time to get a quality plan developed is that they are often able to draw on previous work.

Second, have a meeting with your core team to figure out what the act of doing the project has taught everyone. It's absolutely vital that everyone's attention be kept on the future, not on the past—this can't turn into a "blamestorming" session.

Compile the results from the evaluation process, distribute them to your internal project managers, and use them to form one of the foundations of your internal project management process improvement plan.

> Have a meeting with your core team to figure out what the act of doing the project has taught everyone.

▶ QUESTIONS FOR PROJECT EVALUATION

Here are six good questions to form the core of a project evaluation agenda:

1. What did we do right? (You want to do it again.)

2. What is imperative that we do right? (We may or may not have done all these right.)

3. What do we need to improve? (We did it right but we want to do it even better.)

4. What do we need to do differently next time? (Where should we change our approach?)

5. What are we not doing that we should continue to ensure we not do? (Knowing what not to do is often as important as knowing what to do.)

6. What new or different approaches are worth trying next time? (Experimentation may reveal new avenues for success.)

Now, It's Time to Celebrate

Do take some time at the end of the project to celebrate, even if you're by yourself. Pat yourself on the back. Say "thank you" to everyone who helped make the project a success—put it in writing for an even stronger effect. If it's possible, hand out mementos or souvenirs that recognize the shared experience. You'd be surprised at how powerful those can be.

Do this for two reasons. The first is that you owe people thanks for their contributions to your success. And the second is that we like working for people who appreciate us and who lead us to victory. One powerful way to steadily improve the quality of your project teams is to be the kind of person who does appreciate good work—you're much more likely to get it.

> If it's possible, hand out mementos or souvenirs that recognize the shared experience.

For more information on this topic, visit our Web site at www.businesstown.com

PART III

How to Launch a Project the Right Way

- Why "why" is the most overlooked question in project management, and why you can't afford to overlook it any more

- How Triple Constraints analysis provides you with powerful insights

- How to recognize and define the stakeholders of your project, and how to determine their interests and goals

- How to resolve conflicts when different customers and stakeholders have different objectives for your project

- How to prepare a Project Charter that serves as a written agreement for your project

The Principle of the Objective

Chapter 9

9: THE PRINCIPLE OF THE OBJECTIVE

Risk Levels

There are several "make or break" points in project management, and the first one comes in the Initiating phase of the project. Your risk is highest at the beginning of the project, but your opportunity is also boundless (see Figure 9-1). Don't let problems slip through the initial screen, because they will inevitably come back to haunt you before Closing.

What's the Assignment?

The question "What do you want?" is not synonymous with the question, "What can be done?" What people want and need is not always within the realm of possibility. Particularly when the project requestor is not expert in the same field as the project manager,

> What people want and need is not always within the realm of possibility.

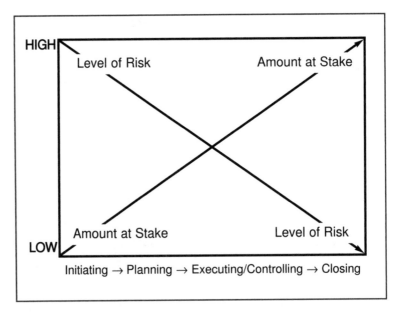

▲ FIGURE 9-1: *Risk levels.* At the beginning of the project, your risk is highest, but the amount at stake is relatively low. As the project nears its close, the remaining risk is low, but the amount at stake—the "sunk costs"—is very high.

there can be a significant discrepancy between what's wanted and what's possible.

You may find yourself shaking your head "no" as people are still in the process of describing their needs, because you can see clearly the cost, time, and technical hurdles between you and their goal. But that's often premature. As we've mentioned before, you often have to cast yourself in the role of project consultant before you can move into the role of project manager.

Take the time to find out what people want and need. You may find yourself in a much better position to recommend strategies to get there.

Filling in the Missing Pieces

There is no rule in project management that says the person with the need must also possess the knowledge or understanding. In fact, one reason we project managers have jobs is that often our customers don't have our knowledge and special skills. What must the customer have? Only two characteristics: a need and the money to pay for it.

Oddly, it's more difficult to work with a partially knowledgeable customer than one who is totally ignorant. The ignorant customer is often eager to find someone in whom to trust, and once you earn that trust, you're free to act as you see fit, as long as it's in that customer's best interest. The partially knowledgeable customer may be ruled by ego, by the need to seem more educated than he or she happens to be, and may frustrate your ability to deliver their goals and interests. (Never fear; this customer type will figure out a way to blame you for it in the end.)

You must start your work where the customer happens to be, but you don't necessarily finish there. Active listening starts the process, but you're not ready to move ahead until you have a good understanding of the customer's underlying need. Then you can start filling in the missing pieces to build the best possible picture of the project, one that you are certain will end up delivering the results the customer requires.

The Importance of Listening

The first thing a project manager needs to do is listen. It's too early to judge whether or not the project can be done—*listen* to make sure you understand fully what the customer wants and needs. This not only increases your knowledge, but also makes them more comfortable with you.

Don't worry if their request doesn't make sense or isn't feasible. You have to start somewhere, and finding out what's in the other person's mind is a necessary precondition to dealing with it if it's not workable. Only after you verify that you fully understand the request can you put on your critical hat and begin analyzing feasibility.

Listening has a number of advantages. It makes you appear smarter, according to experiments. It relaxes the other person and makes them more inclined to trust you. It gives you an opportunity to learn. It keeps you from putting your foot in your mouth—talking can get you into trouble a lot more easily than listening.

Start every project with your very best listening skills, and you'll end up better and smarter throughout.

The Most Overlooked Question in Project Management: "Why?"

A number of projects have gone astray because project managers unwisely confuse the "what" with the "why." You're not there to do what your customer *asks*, but what your customer *wants*. That's true whether the customer knows his or her wants in the first place.

In our earlier discussion about a project to build a Web site, we discovered that the underlying reason (whether to reduce turnaround time on reorders for our installed customer base or to offer our less-popular backlist items inexpensively) shaped the details of the project, and even serves to define our quality standards: "Speedy" is a quality indicator for the first site, but not particularly so for the second; "inexpensive" for the second but not particularly for the first.

This means that you cannot pretend you understand what it is you are supposed to do until you understand why the customer wants it.

Investigating the Big Picture

Projects also take place inside an overall context. It makes a difference if some competing company has just started offering online reordering. The urgency of the project has increased, for one thing, and the definition of quality now includes benchmarking.

Benchmarking is a powerful way to determine exactly how good is "good enough." If your goal is to be the best in your field, and you can figure out what is currently the best, you can establish that as a benchmark. If you're at least that good, you're tied for first place; if you're better, then you're the best. Of course, if the other side is smart, they'll be benchmarking against you.

It's difficult to achieve agreement on measurement points for your project, especially when you're working with customers with limited knowledge of your field. By establishing a benchmarking effort, you have the power to set an objective standard, eliminating ambiguity and confusion about whether you've hit the target.

Definition of Benchmarking

Benchmarking is a technique for identifying and measuring quality goals against an established reference point. Using benchmarking, you can compare conditions, processes, or results. By using benchmarks, you can identify potential improvements and quality goals.

For more information on this topic, visit our Web site at www.businesstown.com

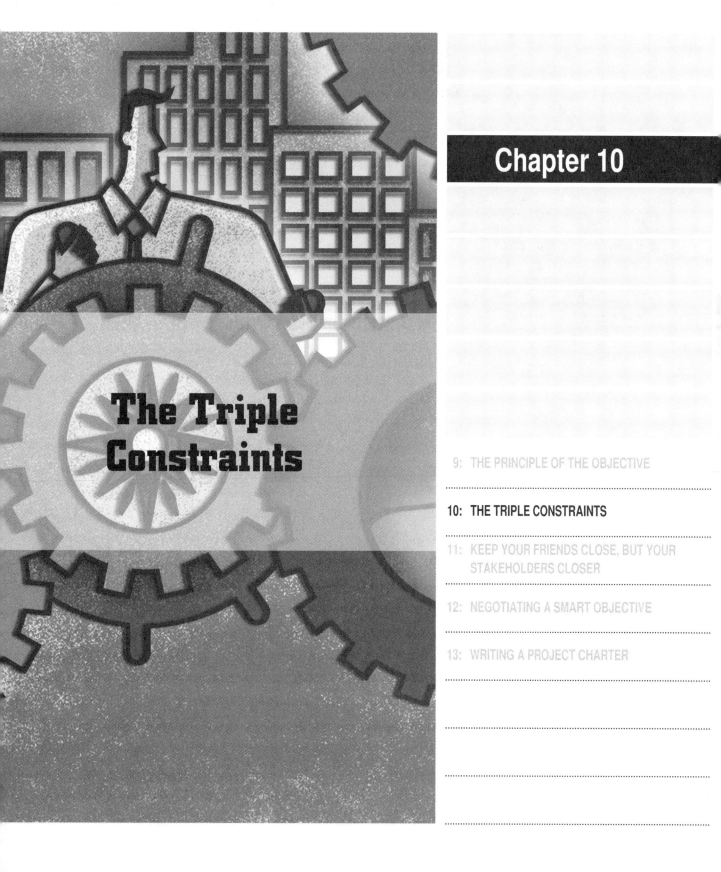

Chapter 10

The Triple Constraints

Time, Cost, and Performance

In project management, simple paradigms turn out to reveal deep truths. In no place is that truer than in our current topic, the Triple Constraints. At the heart of the Triple Constraints is a simple truism: Because a project is temporary, there is a time constraint (which is the deadline), there is a cost constraint (which includes dollars and resource expenditures), and a performance standard that you must meet. This is normally displayed as a graphic (see Figure 10-1).

> A constraint is a factor that limits the project team's options.

The Universe of Every Project

What makes a project easier or harder to accomplish are the specific constraints, or limitations, imposed on it. A constraint is a factor that limits the project team's options—restrictions that affect performance, cost, and/or scheduling of the project. A project always has the Triple Constraints of time, cost, and performance, but may have additional

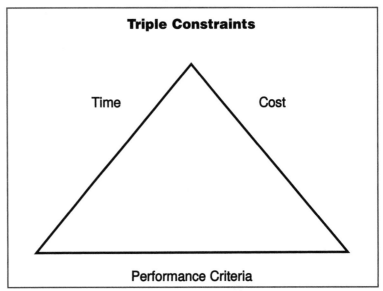

▲ FIGURE 10-1: *The Triple Constraints.* Every project is bounded by the Triple Constraints of time, cost, and performance. Tradeoffs and balancing of the Triple Constraints show you the path to optimum results.

constraints as well. The constraints are often what make a project possible or impossible, and discovering and analyzing the constraints, therefore, is also one of the first steps in project management.

Time Constraint

The time constraint may come in the form of an absolute deadline, or in a more general form, such as a plea for urgency. What makes a time constraint legitimate is that failing it has consequences. If you're designing a trade show exhibit, the opening day of the trade show is an absolute deadline. Fail to be ready, and the show goes on without you. Our *Apollo 13* emergency project had an absolute time constraint: Fail to design the filter in time and the astronauts die.

A time constraint can be absolute even if it's unknown! Let's say your project is getting the house ready for a new baby. The official due date provided by the doctor is, as we know, at best an approximation. The child may be born before or after the official due date. Therefore, you have a project with an absolute but unknown deadline—you'd better be ready. Normally, this turns into pressure to get the project done by the worst-case deadline, or to separate the project into essentials and optionals, and make sure the essentials are complete.

A statement like, "We'd like to have the project done in time for our annual meeting," represents a less-than-absolute time constraint. There may be some adverse consequences from failing to be ready in time for the annual meeting, but those consequences may be a lot less damaging than failing to meet the performance criteria or cost constraint.

> A time constraint can be absolute even if it's unknown!

Cost Constraint

The cost constraint limits what you can expend to meet your project goal. One category of expenditures, obviously, is money, and a project normally has a budget, often with consequences for exceeding it.

A person-hour is also an expenditure, and the cost constraint may be expressed not so much in terms of money, but in terms of human resource expenditures. You may have absolute limits on the number of person-hours available from a resource possessing unduplicated technical skills.

Finally, a cost constraint can be defined in terms of other scarce resources. Again, on the *Apollo 13* project, the available materials to build the filter are absolutely constrained by what is on the spacecraft. If you're one ten-cent bolt shy from a solution, and that bolt isn't aboard, you cannot finish.

Like the time constraint, elements of the cost constraint can be absolute or more general. If the money, people, or materials just aren't available, then the constraint is absolute. If the organization would prefer you not spend too much money on the project, that's more general, and you may have some flexibility.

Performance Criteria

The third leg of the Triple Constraints consists of the essential performance criteria for the project, or what the project is supposed to do or have to be considered successful.

You'll occasionally see someone define the Triple Constraints as consisting of time, cost, and quality. This is a serious misunderstanding. As we pointed out earlier, performance is what the project has and quality is what the customer wants. Quality, and the satisfied customer that results, is certainly a goal of the project. In the real world, however, we are frequently forced into tradeoffs—sometimes painful tradeoffs—among the Triple Constraints to get the project done, and that's why "good enough" is something you must recognize and define.

Misunderstandings about quality are also possible, and by developing a definition of performance criteria, you can check with the customer and confirm that this is the way to meet essential needs.

Remember that quality, for some customers, can represent factors more suited to the time constraint or the cost constraint. Speed equals quality for the *Apollo 13* project. Inexpensive equals quality for some secondary priorities.

By making the third leg of the Triple Constraints a definition of performance, it forces you to determine what is essential and what is optional; what is "good enough" and what is unsatisfactory.

> Quality, for some customers, can represent factors more suited to the time constraint or the cost constraint.

Other Constraints

The Triple Constraints hold true everywhere, but there can be many additional constraints on your project. If you're building a new factory, regulatory requirements such as building codes and zoning may limit your choices on the project. These requirements are constraints.

The state of today's technology can be a frustrating constraint for certain leading-edge projects. We might be able to accomplish it with ease five years from now, but at the moment, we can't get it to work with the tools we possess.

The macroeconomy can be a constraint. Are we in a recession? Has the business sector that employs us gone through a crash? Or are we in a period of such economic growth that we can't find enough skilled help because demand is so high?

The laws of physics can even be a constraint if you're sending up a spacecraft. So can the laws of governments if they prohibit or restrict certain actions in support of your project goals.

> **Listing Constraints**
>
> In an early meeting with your project team, try to develop a comprehensive list of constraints on your project. Test each to see if they are real. For those that remain real constraints, know that you will have to build your project around their limitations.

Why Triple Constraints Analysis Is Vital

If you don't know what your Triple Constraints are, you don't yet know enough to start on the project. Don't be surprised if your original project assignment was given to you in a form that left out one or more of them. People unfamiliar with project management may well not know the Triple Constraints.

If you don't get all three to begin with, another early-onset job you have as a project manager is to fill in the blanks, to determine any missing constraints and analyze their effect on your project.

While creativity and hard work will allow you to succeed on many projects in spite of constraints, you may run into a project where the constraints as defined make it clear that there is no possible way to complete the project. There may be consequences for calling this to the attention of your managers and customers, but compare that to the consequences of spending all the time and money and then failing. If you can't get it done within the Triple Constraints, there are two possibilities: Don't do the project, or get the constraints modified.

To the Moon (and Back Again) in Eight Steps

By analyzing a real project, we can get a better idea how this process plays out in practice. Imagine it's May 23, 1961, and you are administrator of the National Aeronautics and Space Administration. Your secretary buzzes you. "It's the president on line 1. He wants to talk to you about doing a small project for him."

> *"I believe this nation should commit itself to achieving the goal, before this decade is out, of landing a man on the Moon and returning him safely to earth."*
> –President John F. Kennedy, May 23, 1961

This is a project of high visibility, high complexity, and high cost, but not one of complete certainty. In 1961, you might think the odds are favorable, but the amount of uncertainty in this project is significant. The primary obstacle to completion would naturally be the Time Constraint–not only do we have to get it done, but get it done before the decade is out. If we didn't have the deadline, or had a more relaxed deadline, our odds of completing the project successfully would be higher.

But at the very beginning, we aren't yet interested in whether or not it can be done, but rather in gaining a full understanding of what our customer–the president–wants from us.

First-drafting the Triple Constraints

First, we write down a statement of the project.

> Project: Put a man on the Moon.

Why not add "return him safely to earth" to the statement of the project? Because that's a constraint. Note it would be faster and cheaper to make it a one-way trip. Requiring us to bring the astronaut back alive limits the choices we can make on the project. In fact, it would be better to think of "return him safely to earth" as part of our performance criteria.

> Performance Criteria: Return him safely to earth.

The primary obstacle to completion would naturally be the Time Constraint—not only do we have to get it done, but get it done before the decade is out.

There may be other performance criteria on the project, but for now this is all we have. The president hasn't asked for anything else.

We also have a statement of the time constraint: "before this decade is out." We're not sure yet whether this is an absolute statement or a general one, but we do see this as a source of pressure, a project constraint. We write it down, thus:

> Time Constraint: Before this decade is out

Always start your examination of the project by repeating the same language used by the customer. Refine it in subsequent steps, if necessary, until it's concrete and measurable.

Decoding Missing Constraints

There's only one more leg of the Triple Constraints to complete, but—uh, oh—we're in trouble. What is the cost constraint? The information is nowhere in Kennedy's request. We might conclude that there isn't a cost constraint, but the truth is there's always a cost constraint. At some point, if the bill is too high, we won't pay.

We need to determine what that cost constraint is. We might start by asking the president, "How much can we spend?" Unfortunately, his answer is likely to be, "I don't know. Whatever it takes, but don't spend any more than is necessary. You're the technical expert; come up with a number for me."

All right, we can do that. Notice that Kennedy's inability to answer the question specifically is not a negative reflection on him. After all, this isn't his job. It's your job.

The trouble is that you know full well that there is some secret limit to how much we're willing to spend to go to the Moon, and if you exceed that amount in your budget, you're in trouble. People aren't necessarily eager to give you that figure up front, because they may be afraid that you'll pad the project budget to use up whatever you can get. Withholding a budget figure can be a way of putting pressure on you.

You might yield to that pressure, and squeeze your budget request to the bone so you don't use a penny more than is absolutely necessary. The problem is that a tightly constrained budget will

> We need to determine what that cost constraint is.

probably put increased pressure on the time constraint and the performance criteria—it may take longer and increase the risk to the astronauts. So you really want to know the real number.

Getting an Answer

If you can't get the number from your customer, figure out who has the number. In a federal project, such as the one we're talking about, the funds you need will have to be appropriated by Congress, and you can have as much money as they allow, but no more. Since that's the case, and to be administrator of NASA you'd need to have a pretty solid Washington Rolodex, it might be wise for you to call up some key senators and members of Congress and sound them out informally on what they think a politically feasible number will be.

The limit is that the number you get this way will be a very rough approximation indeed, possibly several billion dollars off in either direction. Is there any use in a number that vague? Actually, quite a bit.

Remember that your initial need for the number is to do a rough feasibility analysis. If the political will exceeds the political wallet by too great a degree, then we're probably not going to the Moon after all. If that's the case, the earlier we deal with it, the better, for all concerned. But if it does look feasible, then we're on the way!

> Remember that your initial need for the number is to do a rough feasibility analysis.

Cost Constraint: Whatever Congress is willing to approve.

Refining the Information

Now, this is a very rough first draft of the project constraints, but we have to start somewhere, and given this information, we can certainly proceed to next steps. So, to summarize, we have:

Project: Put a man on the Moon.

Performance Criteria: Return him safely to earth.

Time Constraint: Before this decade is out.

Cost Constraint: Whatever Congress is willing to approve.

The Hierarchy of Constraints

Looking at this information, do you think that the Triple Constraints as written are equally constraining—that is, must they receive equal weight in your analysis of this project—or do you suspect that there is a hierarchy, that some are more central to the project than others?

If you think that there is a Hierarchy of Constraints, then you're right. On any project, the three legs of the Triple Constraints have different weights. Sometimes the time constraint is on top, sometimes the cost constraint, sometimes the performance criteria. Figuring out the right ranking for your project opens up a wide range of insights and even opportunities.

There are names for this hierarchy:

- *Driver.* The "driver" of the project is the constraint that must be met at all costs or else the project will be considered a failure.
- *Middle constraint.* The second level of the Triple Constraints hierarchy. The middle constraint has somewhat more flexibility than the driver, but less than the weak constraint.
- *Weak constraint.* The most flexible (but not necessarily least important) member of the Hierarchy of Constraints. Exploiting the weak constraint is a powerful technique for helping to accomplish your project goals.

Before we look at our man on the Moon project in light of the Hierarchy of Constraints, let's see how they function in some other projects.

Determining the Driver

How do we know which of the constraints is the driver? One way is to look at the consequences of failure. Imagine that you're General Norman Schwarzkopf in Desert Storm, and that you will fail one leg of the Triple Constraints. Which one would put you in the worst shape?

Time: "I won, but I'm two weeks behind schedule."

> Exploiting the weak constraint is a powerful technique for helping to accomplish your project goals.

Working in a Competitive Project Environment

Let's flip this picture around for a minute and put ourselves in Saddam Hussein's shoes. If General Schwarzkopf is forced to pick up and come home, what would Saddam call that? Frankly, that would be a victory for him. Given the imbalance in forces, that would probably be the best possible outcome as far as he was concerned.

From this, can we predict Saddam Hussein's likely strategy? If you think it's a strategy of delay, you're right—and that's actually the behavior we observed. It can be extremely useful if you're in a competitive situation to look at it from the other side's point of view—and our bet is that General Schwarzkopf did so regularly.

Cost: "I won, but I overspent the budget by ten percent."

Performance: "I know I lost, but at least I'm ahead of schedule and even under budget!"

The right answer is clear. In this project, performance is the driver. Now, let's look at the other two constraints. The order of the constraints is often influenced by the environment in which the project is taking place. Here, Schwarzkopf had two potential areas of concern: the stability of the international alliance and the level of domestic popular support for the war. It's fair to say that he would have to have known that the clock was ticking. If the conflict drags out too long (though we don't know exactly how long that is), he would probably be forced to pick up and come home. Time is the middle constraint.

Cost as the Weak Constraint

By the process of elimination, we're left with the cost constraint in third place, so cost is the weak constraint. What advantage does knowing this give us?

The first advantage of knowing the weak constraint is that it lowers pressure in at least one direction. If you have to fail to meet one of the constraints on this project, by all means go over budget in preference to either taking too long or losing the war outright. If you find yourself in trouble on the project, you might decide that spending money and resources to get yourself out of trouble would be an alternative worth considering.

You can go even further than that. You can deliberately exploit the weak constraint in order to improve your overall chances of project success. This isn't cheating; after all, the weak constraint is defined as having flexibility. Using that flexibility may be the smartest move you can make.

Identify the flexibility you have and apply it strategically to increase your odds of success. In this situation, you might (as Schwarzkopf did) bring over the largest force possible. During the buildup to the battle, there was a feeling that Saddam Hussein might choose to withdraw from Kuwait if it was made absolutely clear he would be ejected by force. While that didn't happen, it was a perfectly reasonable thing to try, and the size of the force lowered the intensity and destruction that would have occurred between forces more evenly matched.

What can you do with the flexibility in your weak constraint?

Time as the Weak Constraint

In 1791, Major Pierre L'Enfant drew up his master plans for a capital city for the newly founded United States of America. The plan included a site for a church, "intended for national purposes, such as public prayer, thanksgiving, funeral orations, etc., and assigned to the special use of no particular Sect or denomination, but equally open to all."

It was not until 1893 that Congress granted a charter to the Protestant Episcopal Cathedral Foundation of the District of Columbia for this purpose. Acquiring the land and planning took until 1907, when President Theodore Roosevelt and the Bishop of London laid the cornerstone. The first chapel opened in 1912, but it was not until 1964 that the central tower was completed. The nave was enclosed in 1972, and finally completed in 1976, but construction stopped in 1977 due to lack of funds. In 1980, construction began again, and in 1983 the final phase of the west tower was begun. In September 1990, after eighty-three years of construction, the Washington National Cathedral was finally completed.

Obviously, time was not the driver of this project—it was the weak constraint. Cost was a serious enough consideration that construction halted at one point because of lack of funds. In several phases of the project, lack of sufficient numbers of skilled stonecutters slowed the work. To resolve both sets of problems, construction was stopped or slowed accordingly—in other words, the flexibility of the time constraint was a way to keep the project on track.

This is an example of a performance-driven project. Building a Gothic-style cathedral is challenging under almost any set of circumstances. Here, they had to develop their own apprenticeship program to train workers in the stonecutting arts they required. No attention to

Back to the Persian Gulf

One of the interesting events of the Gulf War was that Iraqi soldiers surrendered at a great rate. Is that an argument that these soldiers were cowards? Not at all. People make rational decisions about their circumstances, and the Iraqis were facing overwhelming force. It's one thing to keep fighting when you have a chance, it's something else when you know you're going to be steamrollered regardless of what you do. Surrender is the rational move.

The fact that the Iraqis were facing overwhelming military superiority takes us back to the weak constraint. The project manager—General Schwarzkopf—had flexibility in the cost constraint. It was within his authority to choose a very large force. There is still a limit, however, even in the weak constraint. He could not have *all* the army forces; he had to leave some behind in Europe, Asia, and CONUS. He couldn't use nuclear weapons. But within those parameters he had a wide range of choices.

detail was too small. But that kind of performance doesn't come free. You can either spend a lot of money, or you can take a lot more time. In this project, the flexibility of the time constraint made it possible.

Performance as the Weak Constraint

Public Law 722, dated August 12, 1946, established a National Air Museum as part of the Smithsonian Institution "to memorialize the development of aviation; collect, preserve, and display aeronautical equipment; and provide educational material for study of aviation." Previously, aeronautics had been a small department in the overall Smithsonian structure. Its collections were displayed in the Arts and Industries Building next to the Smithsonian Castle, and in a Quonset hut behind the Castle that had originally been the shop where the World War I Liberty engine was designed.

In July 1966, Public Law 89-509 changed the name to National Air and Space Museum, added responsibility for memorializing the development of space flight, and authorized construction of a new building to house the collection. Unfortunately, they held off on providing the funds until the early 1970s.

Apollo 11 astronaut Michael Collins became director of the museum in 1971, and $40 million in funding became available. Inflation since 1966 had eroded the value of the $40 million, and the building that was originally planned was unaffordable. Architect Gyo Obata, of the firm Hellmuth, Obata, and Kassabaum modified the structure, and the project began in earnest.

The opening of the museum was planned for July 4, 1976, one of the major national events of the bicentennial celebration of American independence. Agreeing to this deadline was one of the ways funding was obtained. The project was notable in many ways, including being the first major government construction project in Washington completed on time and under budget in several years.

Time

Here, it's pretty obvious that time is the driver of this project. The Bicentennial tie-in is fixed, and the president of the United States is onboard to cut the ribbon. (In fact, later the president notified the

> The project was notable in many ways, including being the first major government construction project in Washington completed on time and under budget in several years.

museum that he had other plans for the Fourth of July, and the opening was moved to July 1, 1976. Circumstances can alter a fixed deadline and make it even tighter.)

Cost

The cost constraint consists of $40 million in federally appropriated funds. The $40 million is a round number, and should be understood that way. It's not as if someone did detailed brick-by-brick costing of the project and discovered that it all added up to exactly $40-million-and-no-cents. Imagine that the project had finished, say, $200,000 over budget. That turns out to be a budget variance of 0.5 percent. If you bring in a $40 million project within half a percent of the target, that's not considered being over budget—that's just rounding error. In fact, had the project ended up within a range of, say, 5 percent of the target, it would have been considered fully good enough. (Of course, you don't get the bragging rights for being under budget that way.) There's a small amount of flexibility in the cost constraint.

Performance Criteria

That leaves performance criteria. What criteria were used to measure performance on this project? One oft-repeated goal was that the final museum was to be "world-class." That's clearly important—but equally, it's not easily measured. There's a lot of potential flexibility in a statement like that; therefore, performance must be the weak constraint.

How do we exploit the weak constraint? Let's look at an example. The new museum needs to have aircraft hanging in it. How many do we need? Well, we need enough so that the building looks pretty full, and one of the airplanes had better be the Spirit of St. Louis! Notice that once we get past the top ten or so most famous historic aircraft in the collection, choices of which aircraft to display become more arbitrary. So we prefer aircraft that need little or no shop time for restoration before they can be put on display. Thus, the weak constraint has been exploited.

How many audiovisual exhibits do we need? Well, we definitely need some, but fancy AV pushes resources and time, so we need to

> Performance must be the weak constraint.

limit the total number and simplify where possible. And when some of them weren't fully functional in time for the opening, we didn't delay the opening, but rather removed the faulty audiovisual exhibits. They could always be put back in later on.

The core understanding of the team was that July 1, 1976, represented opening day, but we intended for the museum to be around long afterward. What we couldn't get done by the opening we simply left for later.

Is that any way to run a project? You know it is.

Return to the Moon

Finally, let's get back to our Moon project. What do you think the right order of constraints will be for this project? Let's review:

Project: Put a man on the Moon.

Performance Criteria: Return him safely to earth.

Time Constraint: Before this decade is out.

Cost Constraint: Whatever Congress is willing to approve.

> A performance-driven project will require different decisions than a time-driven project.

It's fairly obvious that cost has to be the weak constraint in this picture. It's much harder to choose between performance and time.

What is obvious is that whichever we choose will significantly change how we manage the project. A performance-driven project will require different decisions than a time-driven project. We must choose, and we have to be right. On what basis will we make this decision?

We could ask: "Mr. President, do you want us to do the job good, fast, or cheap? Pick two." Of course, we'd phrase it more diplomatically, but even so, we are likely to hear, "I pick all three. Now, get back to work."

Instead, let's go back to the most overlooked question in project management. You remember what it is: why? "Mr. President, all of us at NASA are eager to go to the Moon. But sir, let me ask—why are we going?"

The historical answer to this question is clear. "We've got to beat the Soviet Union in the Space Race." And if that's the reason we're going, then clearly time—not performance—has to be the driver.

Does that mean we're willing to risk astronaut lives in order to beat the Soviets? Yes, that's exactly what it means, and if you're going to lead the project, you need to be absolutely clear in your mind that this is your goal. (Alternatively, if you found that to be morally unacceptable, your other option is to resign.)

You might ask, "What if astronauts die? Won't that be a failure?" Not exactly. Astronauts did die in the Apollo project. Three of the deaths are famous: the capsule fire in Apollo 1. But there were other deaths as well, which got less coverage. The solution was to schedule multiple missions (a flexing of the cost constraint) in order to make sure at least one succeeded.

When you're the project manager, this is exactly the kind of thinking that is expected of you.

> The solution was to schedule multiple missions in order to make sure at least one succeeded.

For more information on this topic, visit our Web site at www.businesstown.com

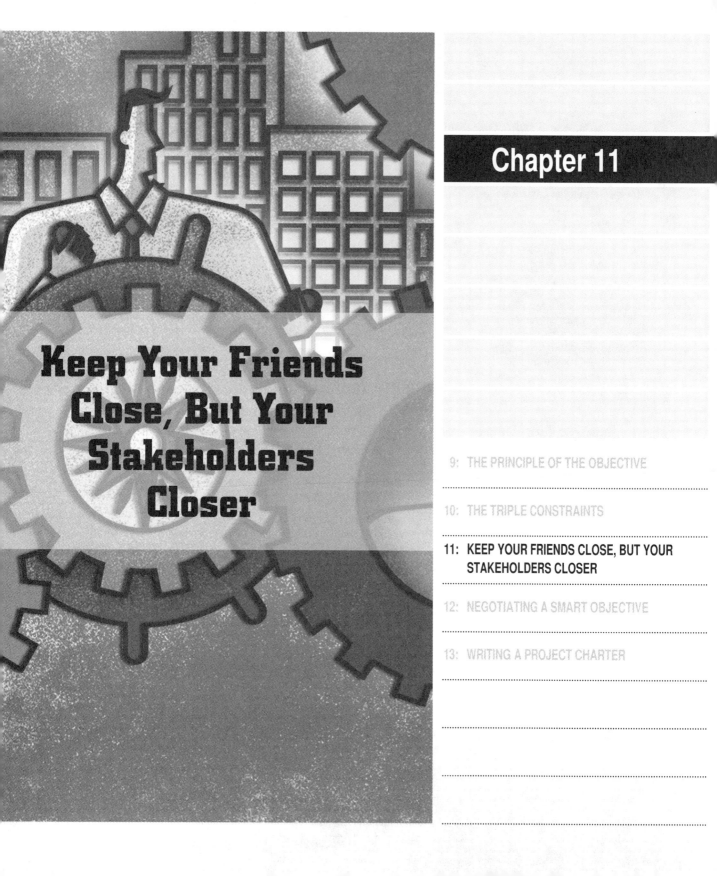

Keep Your Friends Close, But Your Stakeholders Closer

Chapter 11

List of Stakeholders

Make a written list of your stakeholders. Include name, organizational position, and the nature of their interest in your project. List whether the interest is positive or negative. Brainstorm ways you can gain better cooperation and support from positive stakeholders, and ways you can neutralize or turn around the interests of negative stakeholders. Consider doing this at home or someplace secure; you don't want an accidental copy of your notes to get around.

Managing Stakeholder Relationships

The chapter title is an adaptation of the saying "Keep your friends close, but your enemies closer." Michael Corleone said it in *The Godfather, Part II*, but it has been said before. This strategy has two purposes: It's harder to be blindsided, and it opens the opportunity for dialogue, which could possibly change an enemy into an ally—or at least into a neutral.

We don't mean to suggest that your project stakeholders are enemies (though it has been known to happen), but rather that actively managing stakeholder relationships from the very beginning of the project all the way through is another of the core success strategies in project management.

Who Are Your Stakeholders?

Stakeholders include a wide variety of people: customers, team members, sponsors, managers of other projects, competitors, public interest groups, regulatory organizations—anybody with an interest or stake in your project's processes or outcome.

A stakeholder can be a person or an organization that is involved in or may be affected by project activities, or someone with a vested interest in a specific outcome, or who exerts influence over a project. What makes someone a stakeholder is their stake—the interest they have in the outcome (what you deliver) or the process (how it's done, what resources it consumes, how it affects other projects or activities) of your project.

That tells you that there are two things you need to know: who all your stakeholders are, and what their specific stake happens to be.

Positive and Negative Stakeholders

The interest a stakeholder has in your project can be positive or negative from your point of view; that is, they may feel they benefit when your project succeeds, or they may feel they suffer a loss when your project succeeds. Since people often like to maximize their benefits and minimize their losses, you may expect positive stakeholders to support you and negative stakeholders to oppose you—but it can get a bit more complicated than that.

Positive Stakeholders

Positive stakeholders feel they benefit by the success of your project, or at least have the potential to benefit from it. They can benefit because the product of your project is useful or profitable for them. They can benefit when the product of your project moves their goals further along. They can benefit when the work done on your project is reusable for their purposes.

Positive stakeholders are often in a position to benefit most if they can slightly modify the scope of your project so that their objectives fall into your area of responsibility, sort of like attaching an unrelated rider to a bill before Congress. In that sense, positive stakeholders can be a sort of potential conflict and trouble—one person's "minor adjustment" is another person's major headache.

> Positive stakeholders feel they benefit by the success of your project, or at least have the potential to benefit from it.

Positive Stakeholders and Project Adjustments

Sometimes, the "minor adjustments" are indeed minor. If a small adjustment to your project can substantially increase the benefits from it, it may be very appropriate for you to accept the additional scope.

When President Kennedy set a national objective to go to the Moon, look at the wide range of collateral opportunities:

Science: Bring back Moon rocks and do basic science in space.

Medicine: Wire up the astronauts to gain lots of new medical data.

Economic Development: Bring jobs into a number of congressional districts. Provide contracts to major aerospace companies.

Media: Live coverage from the Moon; increased technological ability to put telecom satellites in orbit.

Technology: Exploitation of economic spinoffs, from Velcro to electronic miniaturization (and, of course, Tang).

The list goes on. While individuals may believe specific objectives on this list are more or less worthy, it's clear that many of these are desirable side benefits, and as long as they don't compromise the primary goal, should be added to the project. You will likely find this true of your own projects.

One way to increase the number of positive stakeholders on your project is to figure out ways in which slight modifications can expand the range of benefits to be obtained. Every person or organization that can benefit significantly is a source of support, extra funding in some instances, technical or political support, and much more. It's a win/win opportunity.

Negative Stakeholders

Of course, some people or organizations may see your project as a net loss to them, either in the product or in the process of your project. Here are some reasons people may be opposed to the product associated with your project. Perhaps your project will automate certain functions, allowing your company to lay off the people currently doing the work. Perhaps it may replace a comfortable, if old-fashioned, system with a modern, high-tech one. Perhaps the success of your project will be an ego blow to someone who has been loudly arguing that it cannot possibly work.

People can also object to the process itself. Perhaps your project is taking resources that they need to achieve their own goals. Perhaps your project is disrupting their everyday work. Perhaps someone was hoping he or she would be assigned as project manager, and is unhappy that you have taken that role.

Negative stakeholders can be inside or outside the organization. Outside negative stakeholders can include business competitors, for whom your success means fewer customers for their offerings. There may be public interest or watchdog groups who believe your project is bad—it causes environmental damage, involves weapons technology, produces morally offensive entertainment, or defames or damages a group of people, and should be stopped.

Regulatory and licensing organizations may be more neutral than negative, but their job is not to advance the success of your project, but to ensure that the interests they safeguard are protected. If you need FDA approval for your new drug, a UL seal for your new electrical product, or EPA clearance to build a chemical factory, you will need to recognize that their interests are not automatically in tune with your own and work with them accordingly.

Working with Negative Stakeholders

Here's where "keep your friends close, keep your enemies closer" turns into practical advice. It's tempting to make an equation of negative stakeholder equals the enemy, but that's not necessarily true at all. What makes someone a negative stakeholder is a different interest or goal. The first step, therefore, in working through any negative stakeholder situation is to identify who the person or organization is and what their goal in the matter happens to be. You can understand their goal without necessarily sharing it. What you must keep clear in your mind is that their interest is real and legitimate to them.

Do everything in your power to open up a dialogue and build a relationship with your negative stakeholders. First, you need to make absolutely sure you understand their goals. Paraphrase and double-check with them until they confirm your understanding. Second, you need to see if there's any way you can satisfy those goals short of sabotaging your own project. (Of course, if you discover through the process of listening to your negative stakeholders that your project is in fact harmful and destructive, you may need to be in the business of stopping your own project. It doesn't happen often, but it does happen.) If an acceptable modification to your project eliminates their objections, you can turn some negative stakeholders into neutrals or even positive stakeholders.

Third, you need to keep an open line of communication and negotiation open even if a win/win resolution doesn't seem to be in the cards. By keeping them apprised of your project in an honest and straightforward way, you give them an incentive to play straight with you in return. If they then choose dishonorable tactics, you are in a better position to confront them or to let third-party observers know who is playing fair and who is not.

> Do everything in your power to open up a dialogue and build a relationship with your negative stakeholders.

How to Use Your Project Sponsor

It's normally the case that project managers aren't the most senior managers in the organization. The operational responsibility falls a little lower in the hierarchy than those who are responsible for programs (collections of projects, a general mission) and those who are responsible for departments. (There are exceptions, of course.) This means that you normally don't have access to everyone you might need to work with. Therefore, you need to work on leverage with the higher-ups whose cooperation and support you often need to get the job done. The project sponsor is the manager in the performing organization who authorizes the project, allocates cash and other resources to perform it, and has executive responsibility for the project's successful completion.

You may or may not have a formal "project sponsor" identified by name, and sometimes this responsibility is parceled out among several managers (one provides cash, one controls certain key resources, one is in charge of the customer relationship), so you may have to do a little detective work to figure out who your key person is for the project.

You need the project sponsor because you need an ally of the appropriate management level to go where you can't go and make decisions outside your personal authority and scope. Operationally, the project sponsor is often the senior manager with the most active positive interest in having the project be a success. However, if that manager is not in your direct chain of command, you may find your access limited. Look in your own direct chain for the equivalent manager and work with that person as your project sponsor, but realize that it's sometimes the case that your own management chain of command is not very supportive of the project and can even be a negative stakeholder. (This is a very difficult position in which to find yourself, but do be aware that this situation can and does happen.)

Your project sponsor may have special interests of his or her own, and if you can accommodate those without destroying the project, it's often wise to do so because you need the help. Make sure to consider the situation from the sponsor's point of view.

More On the Way

Remember that in your role as project manager there's usually going to be more than one project. Peoples' positions and interests change, depending on what the project is. People who oppose you one day may be on your side the next, and if you have a reputation for trickiness and dishonesty, you may be buying yourself trouble on your next project.

How to Use Other Stakeholders

Because stakeholders have interests and goals concerning your project, they often find it in their own best interest to assist and advise you. This can be an extremely powerful opportunity for you as a project manager. Earlier, we've advised you to take the time to map out your stakeholders and their interests on paper (but don't leave the paper around your office or anywhere else it can get into the wrong hands).

Have up-front conversations with stakeholders as soon as you have identified them. Ask about their goals and objectives, and listen for clues to hidden agendas. As you prepare your plans, consider how stakeholders could be of support to the project, and specifically ask each stakeholder for the services you want. (You won't always get a "yes," but you'll frequently get at least some support.) Make sure that stakeholder's needs for information are satisfied as much as possible

Rules for Managing Project Sponsors

If your organization doesn't have a formal "project sponsor" role assigned, figure out who is doing the job.

Decide where in your project your sponsor needs to be involved. Cut across functional lines for communication? Open doors? Arrange specific approvals?

Not all project sponsors know they're project sponsors or what they are supposed to do. Talk to your sponsor and tell him or her the role you'd like him or her to play on the project.

Ask your project sponsor what his or her definition of excellence and "good enough" are for the project. Don't assume you know without asking.

If heavy political pressure is being put on you by someone else, let your sponsor know about it and ask for help and advice—don't wait until after the fact.

Figure out where your sponsor is in the formal hierarchy and in the political environment.

If your project sponsor is not your immediate supervisor, make sure your immediate supervisor is kept up-to-date so there's no opportunity for you to be seen as "going behind someone's back."

Ask for (and follow up on) a regular meeting with your project sponsor to talk about the project. Some sponsors want to be very much in the loop; others prefer sporadic briefings and a visit if there's trouble. Adjust the frequency of the meetings you request based on the sponsor's desires.

Keep sponsor dealings confidential (except for the updates you provide your own supervisor), especially if they involve the sponsor's candid political assessments of other managers.

Most supervisors and sponsors hate to be surprised. Problems happen; that's understood. Do all that is in your power to provide advance warning when possible.

without violating organizational confidences or policies. On areas of particular interest to specific stakeholders, make sure the stakeholders feel they have at least been asked for their input. If you must do something that is contrary to the interests and goals of one or more of your stakeholders, tell them about it in advance unless telling them violates organizational confidences or policies.

Take care of your negative stakeholder relationships as thoroughly and professionally as you do your positive stakeholder relationships. There are three reasons for this: First, you can win over some negative stakeholders and get them on your side. Second, you may have different projects in which your positive and negative stakeholders can change roles. And third, other people watch how you deal with those opposed to you; when you demonstrate honesty and professionalism in those relationships, you'll find that others have increased respect for you.

You may have different projects in which your positive and negative stakeholders can change roles.

The Rules of Effective Influence

Influencing others and being organizationally effective is something that can repay a lifelong study. Here are some rules and principles you will find effective in gaining cooperation and support from your stakeholders:

- For short-term gain, build common interests through negotiation. For long-term gain, work on building trust, confidence, and mutual respect, and demonstrate your own integrity and honesty.
- Have the courage to make necessary hard decisions, and the empathy to work with people who may be negatively affected by those decisions.
- Avoid making enemies. An opponent merely wants something different; an enemy is personal. To keep opponents from turning into enemies, make sure you show integrity and honesty in all dealings, and don't be seen as a double-crosser or manipulator.
- Be a worthwhile ally. Be careful about offering your whole-hearted and unreserved support, but do support people in

their worthwhile goals even if there is no direct benefit to you. Don't be a fair-weather friend; demonstrate that you care about your allies even if there is some political risk to you. In the long run, you'll earn respect.

- Be generous and do favors whenever possible. Don't tie favors to specific quid pro quo deals in the majority of cases, simply do favors when they are organizationally appropriate and within your power.

- Ask for favors when you need help. Don't remind people of previous favors; people of integrity will remember and act accordingly—if they are not people of integrity, you have learned something valuable about them.

- Keep lines of communication open across barriers and in times of conflict. Be open to diplomatic approaches and be prepared to negotiate on a principled foundation.

- Make it clear by your actions and choices that you do what's right and beneficial to the organization.

- Show respect for the opinions and goals of those with whom you disagree. Listen empathetically even if you cannot or will not adjust your position, and demonstrate that you understand contrary positions. Be willing to consider someone's arguments, even if you end up with the same decisions afterward.

- Be aware that others do not necessarily follow the same code of principles that you do. Act with integrity, but don't let yourself be blind to the reality of others' behavior.

- Remember that no matter how important today's project may be, there is a tomorrow as well. Unprincipled behavior may be a way to win a current fight, but other people notice and remember. A long-run perspective pays off over time.

> Keep lines of communication open across barriers and in times of conflict.

For more information on this topic, visit our Web site at www.businesstown.com

Chapter 12

Negotiating a SMART Objective

Is the Objective Negotiable?

The idea that your project objective is negotiable doesn't always jibe with the way project managers see their situations. Often, you may feel as if the decision has been made long before you come on the scene, and that it's another case of yours "not to reason why," yours "but to do and die."

It's certainly true that there are limits to what can be negotiated. In *Apollo 13*, for example, it would be fairly useless (if not downright inappropriate) to try to negotiate the time constraint. But look at it this way: If you ask the most overlooked question in project management (which, as we remember, is "why?"), the answer you get reveals whether negotiation is possible.

"Why do I only have an hour to come up with the filter?" "Because the astronauts will die if you take any longer than that." Compare that to "Why do I only have two members on my engineering team to come up with the filter?" "Because I don't feel like paying overtime."

If it's clear that the first Q&A is nonnegotiable, it should be equally clear that the second Q&A is absolutely negotiable. "If you don't want to stand in front of the press explaining why not paying overtime is worth three astronaut's lives, you'll get me every engineer you've got on-site within ten minutes." There is a not-so-veiled threat in this negotiation approach, and that's just fine. Decisions have consequences, and helping people understand those consequences is one of the influence management techniques project managers have to use.

Resolving Conflicts in Multiple Objectives

Many times, conflict about objectives is unavoidable because you have multiple stakeholders. Each stakeholder wants his or her objectives as part of the project, but it may not be possible to satisfy all stakeholders. How do you resolve conflicts concerning multiple objectives?

Identify Disparate Objectives

The first part of the process is to identify all the objectives, whether or not you will be able to achieve them. Just as in our initial approach to a single-objective project, we must understand what is being asked of us separately from whether the goals are feasible. And wouldn't it be a shame to deal with scope creep, unhappy customers, or failure because you didn't ask early enough what people wanted? Sometimes it *is* possible to do what everyone wants.

Negotiating Constraints

The second possibility is that you can do what everyone wants, but not within the constraints of time and/or cost. The good news is that you now have an opportunity to go back to your project sponsor or customer, explain the additional objectives and the value in achieving them, and try to get extra money and/or an extension to reach the revised goal. Again, sometimes this works quite well, and then you get it all done. And the worst they can say to you is "no."

Making Hard Choices

There are two scenarios left: 1) you can't get the extra time and money you need, and 2) some of the objectives people have are mutually exclusive. Either way, you can't do everything everybody wants, so someone's objectives won't be met. Negotiation is the only viable option.

In order, here are the steps to try to get an appropriate resolution to this kind of conflict:

1. Get the affected parties together and let them negotiate with each other and let you know the decision. If they can't or won't, then . . .
2. Rank the conflicting objectives by value to the customer or the performing organization, and select the highest value objective. If it isn't clear which has the highest value, then . . .
3. Identify the political clout and willingness to use it among the stakeholders with the competing objectives, and do what the person with the most power to help you/harm you wants. If there's a tie, then . . .
4. Look for people for whom one answer gives a benefit over another, and do what makes the greatest number happy. If it isn't clear, then . . .

> The worst they can say to you is "no."

5. Give it to your supervisor, manager, or project sponsor, and ask him or her to choose. If that doesn't work, then . . .
6. Prefer the faster to the slower, the easier to the harder, the simpler to the more complex. If there aren't significant differences, then . . .
7. You might as well flip a coin.

Getting Specific

It's not unusual for an objective to start in a vague and general state, because not much is known or has been thought through at the very beginning. That's not a problem, as long as it doesn't stay in that state. Through questions and answers, through negotiation, and through a preliminary investigation, your job is to put a detailed

Building Coalitions for Project Success

You can build a long-term support strategy for major projects, especially those involving issues of organizational change, by building a coalition of stakeholders in support of a shared goal. Because the project manager is often not a senior executive, you need the support of people with power if you're going to get a major project accomplished.

Recruit power. Not all stakeholders are created equal. Some have much wider influence than others. When you're leading a project where opposition is expected, you need power on your side. Not everyone who wishes to be your ally should be invited to join the team—some allies can weaken you. It's worth negotiating elements of your project objective in order to get the right people on your side.

Involve key players. The more your stakeholders get to participate in the project, the more they'll work to make it succeed. Interestingly, this is true independently of how much overall stake they have in your success. Personal involvement trumps almost every other consideration in getting support.

Showcase results. As portions of the project are done, do demonstrations and "dog and pony" shows to build excitement and support. Even a pilot demo can have a big impact.

Avoid surprises. People hate surprises more than they hate problems. Powerful people especially hate surprises, because their reputation often rests at least in part on them being "in the know." If they don't know, they lose status, and if they think you're responsible for their embarrassment, it won't do your reputation any good at all.

structure onto the objective so you have a clear, workable target at which to shoot.

The famous acronym SMART is a good test to determine when you're finished.

Specific

Measurable

Agreed to

Realistic

Time Constrained

Let's look at each letter in turn.

Specific

An objective must have enough specific detail so you and your project team know what the final product or service is supposed to look like. For the project to write this book, for example, both the writer and the editor had to agree in advance of the actual writing what the book would look like. How can this be done? Both editor and writer used samples to agree on specifics.

Other books in the series provided guidance to the writer on format, style, and approach, and based on that, the writer prepared an outline in the form of a detailed table of contents and a sample chapter in the desired style. Both the editor and writer were able to work out a specific agreement on what the book would be, which reduces surprises and problems on both sides.

> An objective must have enough specific detail so you and your project team know what the final product or service is supposed to look like.

Measurable

Look for ways the project can be quantified. Objective standards (where possible) reduce the opportunity for conflict. One objective measurement on this book was a minimum word count. There is no real room for argument about a word count; it is either sufficient or insufficient to meet the standard.

Sometimes you can't get to that level of precision. The editor must determine whether the manuscript is written in a satisfactory manner. While some part of that determination is subjective, not all is. Standards of quality and performance can include such things as proper English usage, technical accuracy, understandability to a lay audience, and conformance to standard format, all of which can be subjected to tests and measurements.

Reducing subjectivity in the process is to everyone's advantage. When the remaining subjectivity is limited in scope, negotiation and compromise can take you through to a satisfactory end. In the absence of any standards, both sides are deeply vulnerable.

Agreed To

Another important element in this process is that the standards of performance have been mutually negotiated and established before the project gets underway. If both sides have agreed upon what they want in advance, there is less chance that the final product will turn out to be disappointing.

If the project involves numerous stakeholders, reaching agreement becomes more complicated, but also more important to the success of the project. By following the process for getting consensus on objectives, you are able to start the project with a clear statement of agreement about what is to be done.

Realistic

Negotiation is crucial if the initial request is not realistic. Sometimes a project has unavoidably high risk, as with the *Apollo 13* example. We don't know if the goal is achievable; all we know is that we must do our absolute best. The realism in such a goal has to be the knowledge that there is unavoidable risk.

One way to improve the chance of achieving a project goal is to exploit flexibility and tradeoffs in the Triple Constraints. What makes a project difficult or impossible is often the constraints placed on it. If the constraints are not subject to negotiation, we must live with them and their associated risk. If the constraints are negotiable, then the likelihood of success can often be improved.

> The standards of performance have been mutually negotiated and established before the project gets underway.

Time Constrained

There isn't always a deadline, but there's always a time constraint. Everything else being equal, getting a project done more quickly is almost always desirable for two reasons: The benefit of the project is realized earlier, and the resources the project takes are now free to take on new work.

Time is often a motivator. When there is no urgency, people tend to procrastinate, even if the work is important and valuable. Imposing some time pressure on a project can be a useful supervisory tool for you to use as a team leader. (Sometimes you'll discover that others are using deadlines to motivate you.)

When your objective meets the SMART test, it tells you that you've got a statement clear enough to allow the work to take place.

Why Your Objective Must Be Measurable

Most of us don't know how to do the "Vulcan mind meld," though it would be an undeniably useful project management skill. Yet it seems that some of our customers have just that expectation of us. Sometimes people have very specific mental pictures of what they want, and either don't know how to communicate them or believe they are so obvious and universal that they need no explanation. Sometimes, the customer is playing a power game and your failure is the goal of the scenario.

In a case like the above scenario, when you make the necessary effort and it seems to go nowhere, the best thing you can do is call in your project sponsor and senior managers on your team early. They may have leverage to pin down the customer on his or her needs and wants that you do not have. And if they can't get a straight answer either, at least the level of blame for failure that might otherwise land on you is somewhat neutralized.

Moving Toward Agreement

You can expect that the process of achieving a workable SMART objective will take more than one round, especially when multiple customers are involved. Don't worry if this takes some time; you will

"Bring Me a Rock"

Ever been in this scenario?

Customer: "Bring me a rock."

Project manager: "Okay. Here's the rock."

Customer: "That's not the rock I want."

Project manager: "How about this one?"

Customer: "That's not it, either."

Project manager: "Well, tell me in detail what kind of rock you want."

Customer (getting irritated): "A rock. R-O-C-K. How hard is that? Just bring me a rock."

Project manager: "How about this one?"

Customer: "Can't you do anything right? That's not it, either. All I wanted was a simple rock and you couldn't deliver. I'm going to take my business somewhere else!"

Project sponsor (to project manager): "We've just lost our biggest account because you failed. You're fired."

Moral: Unclear objectives are fatal. It's vital that you get early agreement on what the project is before you ever agree to do the project.

No matter why, the "bring me a rock" syndrome will always cause problems, and conflict is generally unavoidable. As usual, facing the conflict up front beats the alternative.

likely save so much time in the rework that will otherwise be necessary that you'll come out ahead.

Follow this process:

1. Make sure you meet with all stakeholders in each round of the process. Stakeholders who feel left out and unable to make a contribution tend to put pressure elsewhere on your project. This is true even after a particular stakeholder's objective has been cut out of the project. By meeting with them you protect their self-esteem and sense of participation.

2. Summarize and paraphrase what each participant asks for in each round until he or she agrees that you understand. This is true even if your answer will end up being "no."

3. As you complete a round, prepare a draft objective statement in writing, and give it to each stakeholder in turn as you begin the subsequent round. Invite feedback and discussion.

4. You are finished when the objective is SMART and accepted by all stakeholders. (A stakeholder whose objective has been cut doesn't have to like the final decision, but has to acknowledge that he or she understands that the objective will not be in the final project.)

> Make sure you meet with all stakeholders in each round of the process.

Chapter 13

Writing a
Project Charter

Setting Forth an Agreement

The output of the Initiating phase of the project is a document known as a Project Charter. It's unimportant whether you use the exact name or produce a document in the identical format we show here—what is important is that you end up with a piece of paper (or occasionally papers) that sets forth the agreement to do the project and the desired destination. Without paper, you start your project in a state of vulnerability. As with most failures in the Initiating phase, the damage may not show up until much, much later.

Protecting Both You and Your Project

Have you ever seen a project come into existence with no official decision to commit to it? This happens for many reasons: Someone took a general verbal discussion to be an actual commitment, a project manager really wants to do this but management isn't sold on it, a senior manager wants to sink so much money into a particular project that it will be impossible later on for the organization not to finish it, or the organization simply has no formal process for project approval.

When this happens, everybody gets hurt. First, the leaders of the organization aren't aware what commitments have actually been placed on staff members. New work gets added on based on the "official" level of work already assigned—but because the other work isn't noticed, people get overburdened. When unofficial projects get into trouble, the lack of organizational commitment means that repairing the problems may be impossible. When projects are being run "under the radar," a level of structural dishonesty permeates the organization, and trust vanishes.

What's in a Project Charter?

Figure 13-1 is a sample Project Charter for a new product development project, a videogame called "Tiger Dojo." Notice that the organization as a whole, the project manager and team, and the departments in the organization all start with a clean, clear understanding of what they are to do.

MEMORANDUM

To: See Distribution
From: Spiro Shiplap, Vice President, New Products
Subject: Project Charter
Date: 5 January 2003
Version: 1.0 INITIAL

Tiger Dojo Videogame

The executive committee has selected the "Tiger Dojo" proposal to be our lead videogame release for the Christmas 2005 season. Aloysius Snodgrass is appointed Project Manager for "Tiger Dojo" and will report to me.

<u>Objectives</u>: "Tiger Dojo" is our lead entry into the martial arts videogame market, a market in which we currently have no entrants. Accordingly, this is considered a top priority project.

<u>Product Description and Objectives</u>

A preliminary design brief was completed for this project, and approval of the project is based on the design brief submitted. Significant changes to the design brief may be required during project execution, but all such changes will be submitted to and approved by the executive committee. The following guidelines have been approved:

- The game is set in a dojo environment where martial arts students face a series of higher and higher combat challenges. At higher levels, the dojo environment changes from realistic to more fantastic.
- It will be aimed at younger players, and must receive an ESRB rating of "E" or at the most "T." Because of the target rating, graphic violence (including gore and blood) are to be avoided.
- Initial levels will be playable by six-year-olds, and the most difficult levels will be within reach of skilled twelve- to thirteen-year-olds.
- The game will feature character personalities that have trademark and licensing potential in action figures, cartoon shows, and other arenas. Characters are to be teenage humans with recognizable special abilities and costumes. Opponents may include fantasy characters, who should also be designed with licensing potential in mind

▲ FIGURE 13-1: *Project Charter.* A Project Charter establishes the project, authorizes the project manager to do the work, and confirms management approval of the project.

- The game will be released in multiple formats, including PlayStation 2, Xbox, and GameBoy Advance. A PC Windows version may be added at a later date. Core visuals and routines will be coded with standard protocols to speed conversion from one system to another.

Major Milestones

To be in-store for the Christmas 2005 sales season, the following milestones must be met:

Character art completed	1 Mar 03
Initial system designed	1 Jun 03
Animations completed	1 Aug 03
Level construction toolkit completed	1 Oct 03
Initial playable prototype to playtest	1 May 04
Playtest round completed	1 Sep 04
Revisions and bug fixes complete	1 Dec 04
Second playtesting complete	1 Feb 05
Final product ready	1 Apr 05
Box art and packaging done	1 Dec 04
Marketing plan completed	1 Dec 04
Marketing kickoff	1 Sep 05
Product ships	15 Oct 05

Project Management

This project is a cross-departmental activity that requires cooperation from multiple sources in support of the overall goal. It has been given a top priority by the executive committee. Therefore, requests for support from the Project Manager will be considered to be issued by the executive committee. Conflicts with other critical items will be negotiated if possible, and will be settled by the executive committee if staff-level agreement is not reached.

The Project Manager will prepare detailed plans for the project bearing in mind the above milestones, with particular attention on defining workload burdens for the operating departments. As much as possible, conflicts should be identified and resolved in the initial plans.

▲ FIGURE 13-1 (continued)

Reporting and Change Control

The Project Manager is responsible for ensuring adequate information flow and documentation with the executive committee and department heads, and will submit a reporting plan for approval alongside the detailed execution plans.

All significant proposed changes to scope on this project must be submitted in writing to the Project Manager, who will evaluate them for project impact and submit them through me to the executive committee for final disposition.

Significant project alterations will involve a modification to this project charter and to planning documents. This charter and all plan documents will contain a Version Number; when changes are made, the next Version Number will be assigned and placed on all documents. Each manager and employee on the distribution list is responsible for ensuring that he or she is working with the most current version of charter and plans by checking version numbers and release dates. The Project Manager shall maintain a complete set of revisions and will supply current versions to all authorized staff upon request.

Approved

_____/signature/_____
Spiro Shiplap, Vice President, New Products

_____/signature/_____
Zebediah Rolston, President
(for the Executive Committee)

▲ FIGURE 13-1 (continued)

In order to write this charter, it's clear that a number of meetings have been held and a number of decisions have been reached. That's why the charter is the output of the Initiating process. It takes all the work we've done up to this point, and puts it down on a piece of paper we can use from here on to plan and manage the project. Let's look at some elements of the charter.

> The fundamental time constraint is cited here, along with a reason.

- *Version control.* Project Charters, along with other planning documents, may evolve during the process. For paper that may be modified, use version control numbers to ensure everyone is working with the most recent update. (Toward the end of the charter, you'll notice a responsibility statement specifically addressing this.)
- *Decision.* There must be a formal decision to do this project. Notice it's clear (if not explicitly stated) that other projects were considered and rejected.
- *Triple Constraints.* The fundamental time constraint is cited here, along with a reason—it's a Christmas release, which has significant sales implications. We don't yet have detailed information on resource/cost constraints—planning will establish those—but assigning the project "top priority" reflects likely flexibility there. The importance of performance is also clear from the priority statement and the fact that we don't have an entry in this category. It's clear that cost is the weak constraint; we aren't yet sure about the driver. Because the competition is already in the market and Christmas sales are crucial to companies in this market, we suspect the Hierarchy of Constraints will end up being time–performance–cost, but aren't yet sure.
- *Change control.* We know that scope creep is a danger on this project (it threatens deadline), so the Project Charter sets forth specific and measurable design objectives that have been agreed to (that's S-M-A from our SMART acronym) for the project, and establishes a change management process.
- *Milestones.* Key milestones are checkpoint and approval dates for the project. They encompass both product development and marketing issues. The planning must be done around those milestones. If milestones have to be adjusted based on

the planning work that is yet to be done, the executive committee will have to review and approve those changes.

- *Priority and consequences.* When a project cuts across functional department lines, there's always a predictable risk of conflict and lack of cooperation. Notice that the Project Charter makes it clear that a request for help isn't just from the project manager, but from the executive committee itself.
- *Duties and responsibilities.* Certain critical responsibilities and expectations have been established for the project manager, for other departments who will need to cooperate, and for the executive committee. That's enough for a preliminary document like this. More detailed guidance will be in the plan.
- *Approvals.* We discussed the role of the project sponsor in our discussion of stakeholders. Here, it's clear who the sponsor is and clear that the sponsor plans to be a participant in

Documenting the Project Manager's Authority

A critical part of the project charter is getting a clear definition of your authority and responsibility for the project. Even if you don't like the answers to the following questions, you need to ask the questions—and with luck, you can negotiate the additional power you need.

- What is the functional level of the project manager in the organization (manager, director, vice-president, senior technical staff)?
- What authority does the project manager have to spend money without someone else's signature? At what point does the project manager have to get a written approval?
- In case of conflict between the functional manager and the project manager, how will the conflict be resolved?
- What authority does the project manager have to require other departments or activities to perform work on the project?
- What decisions are to be made at the project management level?
- Who decides on the selection of vendors and subcontractors, the project manager or someone higher?
- What role does the project manager play in developing and approving the project plan?
- What access does the project manager have to the customer? At what level is the contact? At what level must others in the organization be involved?
- What issues does the project manager have the authority to resolve directly with the customer?

the project and exercise certain control authority. The twin signatures of the vice president of new products and the president of the company give weight to the document.

Depending on the nature of your project, you may not find a complete match between this format and your situation. Different projects require different information. Other information that may be part of your project charter include a review of competitive projects, key stakeholders and their interests, a historical description of the problem, more detail about technical roles on the project and who will fulfill them, authorization to issue contracts, descriptions of other constraints and limitations, and more.

Other Forms the Project Charter Can Take

If you are doing a project under contract for another organization, the contract itself may contain enough information to serve as the Project Charter. Preparing another document would be redundant. Sometimes other memos, reports, forms, or legal documents contain enough of the relevant information to serve the purpose. What's important about the Project Charter is the purpose, not the form.

In some organizations, the Project Charter can turn into something much more detailed and comprehensive, including a scope statement/statement of work, a Work Breakdown Structure (WBS) to at least the third level, a spending plan, resource requirements, résumés of key personnel, responsibility assignments, organizational structure, policies, and more—when done to that level, it actually functions as the project plan.

Now, if you have to do all this work in order to bid on a contract job in the first place, you might as well go with the comprehensive project charter approach, but otherwise we don't recommend it. While each of these elements must eventually be prepared to make your project plan, you normally want to see if you can get approvals at each stage. Having to do it all before you find out that it's not what the customer wants means a lot of wasted work. And if someone needs a fifty-page document before a project is approved, the incentive to do a project in the first place is lessened rather drastically.

> If you are doing a project under contract for another organization, the contract itself may contain enough information to serve as the Project Charter.

PART IV

Mysteries of Planning Revealed

- **How to develop a scope statement of project requirements, and discover unstated requirements for which you are accountable**

- **How to construct a Work Breakdown Structure at the necessary level of breakdown, and how to display the results**

- **How to construct a Network Diagram from the WBS**

- **Practical tools for estimating in cases of uncertainty or unfamiliarity**

- **How to develop a formal Gantt Chart both manually and in software from information in your Network Diagram, WBS, and project estimates**

- **How project management software can help you manage your projects**

Chapter 14

The Devil Is in the Details

Scope Statement

As important as a good Project Charter is to your project, it's only the beginning of what you need to manage your project in the most effective manner. By its nature, the Project Charter gathers and organizes high-level information about the project, and does not delve deeply into details. Unfortunately, the details *are* the project, and it's not infrequent that even with the best of intentions, important unknown details can drastically mutate or even destroy the project. In areas like R&D, where outcomes are necessarily uncertain, the Project Charter is a license to get started, but no one should be surprised when you need to revisit the initial understanding based on the information you've gathered in the planning process.

At the first level of detail in the Planning phase of our project, we are trying to develop another document, this one known as the Scope Statement or Statement of Work. "Scope Statement" is the term used by the Project Management Institute (PMI). "Statement of Work" is used in one of the standard academic references in project management, Dr. Harold Kerzner's *Project Management: A Systems Approach to Planning, Scheduling, and Controlling* (see Bibliography). There are some differences in the two forms, but they are aimed at achieving the same overall goal. Whichever term you use (we'll use Scope Statement from now on), this is a more detailed description of the work and how it is to be completed. As in our discussion of the Project Charter, the format is less important than the substance.

> The Project Charter is a license to get started, but no one should be surprised when you need to revisit the initial understanding based on the information you've gathered in the planning process.

Analyzing Project Scope

Getting something done may require a project, or it may require multiple projects, depending on its size and complexity. Sometimes, all the work necessary to accomplish the goal belongs to the project, but other times only part of the work is in the project; the rest is done by or supplied by someone else. The first part is the project scope, the second part is out of scope, even if it's very important. Scope is all of the products and services that are to be provided within the project.

Your operational responsibility is for the scope of the project. Others are responsible for out-of-scope activities. If they don't provide their work on a timely basis, it can have an impact on your ability to get your project done. If something crops up on the project that has not been anticipated, the question of whether it is in scope determines whether fixing it is your problem or not.

The scope of the project includes a list of requirements that must be met, deliverables that must be completed, and responsibilities that are owned by the project. If you don't define scope completely and in detail, you may find others attempting to shift their scope onto your project—one of the fundamental conditions leading to "scope creep." Make sure initial project scope is well defined; it's critical to your ability to manage scope creep later on.

Scope of "Tiger Dojo"

In our "Tiger Dojo" project, one important realization from the Project Charter is that you, the project manager, are responsible for both the product development and marketing functions. That's part of a Scope Statement, because it's not necessarily the case that it has to be that way. New product development and marketing for the game could be considered two separate projects, each with its own project manager and project team.

If we take that approach to the project, notice how the scope definition changes. The product development project manager is responsible for the technical work, but not for things like box-cover art and a television commercial. The marketing project manager is responsible for those items, but not for the visual design of the characters. Getting a successful game into the stores, however, requires both projects to be successful. Each project manager must understand his or her specific scope, but some decisions in one area influence choices in another. In addition, parts of the project must involve collaboration. The project sponsor must be aware of the potential for conflict between project managers, and be ready to facilitate teamwork and decision-making from the perspective of the overall goal.

Assumptions and Constraints

Some aspects of project scope may not be known or understood at the beginning of the project. To help uncover hidden scope issues, develop a list of project assumptions and constraints. To review, assumption is something taken for granted as being true or certain without a factual basis. Constraint is a factor that limits the project manager's options on a project, a restriction that affects the performance of the project, or a factor that affects when an activity can be scheduled.

Assumptions

In the absence of full knowledge or understanding of the project, it's common for project customers, sponsors, or stakeholders to make various assumptions. Typical assumptions might be that the technology exists to perform a certain action, or that the specialized resources you need will be available when you're ready, or that there is little or no risk in a particular activity. Develop a list of assumptions being made by project stakeholders and test as many as you can to see if they are really true or false. The ones you can't determine in advance get added to the project risk list.

One of the most powerful analytical things you can do is develop a list of the assumptions that people are making about the project. Unfortunately, some of the most problematic assumptions are formed and held on a subconscious level. The person making the assumption has made it on such a deep level that he or she is actually unaware that it is an assumption.

You can hold subconscious assumptions about the project as easily as anyone else, and it's very difficult to uncover one's own assumptions. Nevertheless, it's worth some self-examination to try to uncover them.

Once you have a list of assumptions, inspect them. Some can actually be confirmed as really true; others can, upon examination, be determined as false. Not all assumptions, unfortunately, can be checked out in advance of doing the work. Those get added onto your list of risks, which we'll develop further in later chapters.

If you find out some important assumptions are false, it's time to reopen dialogue with your stakeholders. If you have a long list of

> One of the most powerful analytical things you can do is develop a list of the assumptions that people are making about the project.

unverifiable assumptions, it's a good idea to let your project sponsor know that the project has a significant risk attached to it. Avoid surprising your management and customers whenever possible.

Constraints

Our initial work has uncovered some of the constraints on the project, but further examination may find other obstacles. Not all constraints, as we've pointed out, are part of the Triple Constraints, but they can limit your options and sometimes mean that the project cannot be completed as initially intended.

Note that you can assume something is a constraint—not all assumptions are positive ones. You may believe that there is a big barrier to your success, but maybe it's just an illusion.

On "Tiger Dojo," we have a final deadline of October 15, 2005, which is 34½ months after the memorandum. There are a number of

Assumptions in "Tiger Dojo"

What are some assumptions in the "Tiger Dojo" project? First, that there's room for another martial arts game. The company obviously expects to make a lot of money, and if the game flops, the project manager may be held responsible. But if there's no room in the market for a new entrant, failure is inevitable. If you're the project manager, you might like to satisfy yourself that a good game will, in fact, have a market.

A second assumption is that the stated platforms (for instance, PlayStation 2, Xbox, and GameBoy Advance) will be popular by Christmas 2005. That may be the case, but it's possible that the platform environment could change drastically. What warning signals might suggest to you that the platform decision needs to be revisited? How could you design the project to minimize reliance on the platform?

A third assumption is that the timeline (January 5, 2003–October 15, 2005) is adequate to get the work done. Until we do some detailed planning, we don't know yet if we can fit the work into the schedule. As a rough measure, we could look at how long it's taken us to produce games in the past. Is this time about average, is it luxuriously long, or are we already in "deadline doom" mode? Of course, it's also an assumption that this game will take an average amount of time to do—some projects go quickly, but if you're pushing the technological envelope, schedule and cost overruns often come with the territory.

interim milestones, some of which have flexibility, others of which are pretty firm. A high company priority normally suggests that we will have reasonable access to resources and money, but one technical constraint is that the pool of talented artists and designers is limited. We have a constraint in terms of target age and rating. When we design the characters and setting, we have to create something suitable for a game environment and also suitable for toy licensing, which involve different dynamics. We also have an approval process involving senior managers, which means necessarily that there will be some approval-related delays in the schedule.

Identifying Deliverables

People want you to do a project so you can satisfy a need or solve a problem. You want to give them a product or service that achieves the goal—but what exactly is that? The physical things or acts that you turn over to the customer are known as "deliverables," because, well, you deliver them. Deliverables are what you must produce to complete a project—any measurable, definable, verifiable outcome, item, action, or result from your project. External deliverables are deliverables that must be approved by the project sponsor or customer.

For our "Tiger Dojo" videogame, what are the deliverables? There may be more than initially meets the eye. To complete the project, you will have to produce all the items you see in this list. Can you think of more?

- A computer program
- Various pieces of art (all of which need to be put on another list)
- A CD-ROM containing the program for each format in which the game is to be distributed
- A label or graphic for the CD-ROM
- A plastic box to hold the CD-ROM for each format
- An instructional brochure
- Documentation for the computer program
- A full-page magazine ad/poster
- A television commercial

> Deliverables are what you must produce to complete a project.

- A press release/press kit
- Character licensing packages
- A backstory document on the world and environments of the game
- And more!

Each deliverable on this project will require the use of resources (staff time) and may involve the expenditure of money as well. As you can see, it's vital that you start your project with a comprehensive list of the deliverables. These in turn will be integrated into the plan, and you can verify that the work is done and the turnover is made for each deliverable in the process. You'll see the deliverables list show up next in producing the Work Breakdown Structure (WBS).

Determining Project Requirements

In our earlier discussion of quality, we identified Philip Crosby's definition: "Quality is conformance to requirements." In other words, we first establish in detail what someone wants, and specify these items as a list of requirements. As we accomplish the deliverables, we ensure that each deliverable satisfies the requirements placed on it. If we've done that successfully, at the end of the project, quality should be a measurable fact.

From our list of deliverables and our understanding of the project, we must produce a set of requirements and make sure those requirements are agreed to by our customers, internal or external.

Requirements management is a life-of-the-project process, and it's one of the measurable, verifiable ways you can build quality into the project. People also play games with requirements; they can be a way to sneak scope creep into a project. You need to be concerned, therefore, not only with what the requirements of the project are, but also from whom the requested requirement comes. In the same way that you can be blindsided (either deliberately or inadvertently) by a deliverable you didn't know you had, you can also be blindsided by requirements that show themselves only after you've completed the work in question.

> **Definitions**
>
> A requirement is a need, function, feature, or attribute wanted by the customer. Also, it is a condition or capability required by contract, specification, or other formal document. Requirements analysis is the process of determining the formal or actual requirements, creating detailed specifications, and confirming understanding with the customer or users. Requirements allocation and tracing is the process of linking requirements to the deliverables, actions, or processes where they are to be satisfied, and verifying that requirements have been achieved.

Requirements

On "Tiger Dojo," one set of requirements is specified in the Project Charter.

The game must be set in a dojo.

It must receive an ESRB rating of "E" or "T" (the ESRB is analogous to the MPAA movie rating system).

It must be playable by six-year-olds and the hardest levels playable by a skilled twelve- to thirteen-year-old.

Characters in the game must be suitable for trademarking and licensing.

Characters are to be teenage humans, though opponents may be fantasy characters.

The game will be released in multiple formats, including PlayStation 2, Xbox, and GameBoy Advance, with a PC Windows version as a later option.

The programming will use standard protocols to speed conversion to multiple systems.

Discovering Requirements

It's highly unusual on a project of even medium complexity for you to be presented with a perfect and complete requirements list at the beginning of your project. Many requirements are yet to be determined, and unfortunately some are assumed, and therefore not spelled out. Expect to do some digging to figure out your initial set of requirements, then circulate them around your stakeholders a couple of times to find out what you've missed. In the first round, you simply want input. Afterwards, you may want to inspect and weed out some requirements that may not belong.

By using requirements management, you take a lot of the ambiguity out of the final determination: Is the product satisfactory?

Requirements can be located in many places: the Project Charter, the contract, applicable rules and regulations (we can get a copy of ESRB standards in advance, for example), systems engineering documentation, and more. Some requirements are interpolated—a consequence that the game must run on these various platforms may generate requirements for how certain parts of the game actually work.

Analyzing Requirements

A requirement may be either functional (about how it works or what it does) or technical (an engineering description of a standard it must meet). Technical requirements should be rooted in functional ones—how does this technical requirement affect the customer?

Requirements need to be analyzed for assumptions and constraints, for technical issues and interpolated requirements, and for source and legitimacy.

Not everything labeled as a requirement is legitimately binding on you. Someone elsewhere in the organization may show up and say, "You know, this has to also work for online play." Maybe that's correct, and needs to be on your requirements list. On the other hand, maybe online gaming wasn't part of the project, and this request is an attempt to make an end-run around the management decision-making system. Before accepting (or rejecting) this proposed project requirement, you need to escalate this to either the project sponsor or the executive committee. If they say "yes," then it's a requirement. But if they say "no," then it isn't. If you don't check, you run a big risk by doing it (and finding out later you shouldn't have) or by not doing it (and finding out later that it was completely legitimate).

Requirements Allocation and Tracking

At the conclusion of this process, you want to have a detailed and written requirements list that has been approved by the key stakeholders for your project. This now becomes a measurable set of objectives for you and your team to meet.

Will requirements change? It's likely they will, and that becomes part of your change management system. Remember to ask for all changes in writing and always identify the consequences of making the change. If you've done this correctly, changes with big consequences for your project (like risking missing Christmas 2005) are easier to resist.

> You want to have a detailed and written requirements list that has been approved by the key stakeholders for your project.

On the Hook

By handling this process correctly, you want to put yourself in a position in which you are following an agreed-upon set of standards for your project that has objective measurements. If you achieve the standards, you have succeeded. If this process has not been performed well, then you may find yourself taken by surprise when you've done exactly what you think you're supposed to have done, and yet people are unhappy with the result. This usually means that there were some requirements or goals that you didn't know about.

Sometimes, that's your problem even if your customers or managers never told you about it! Returning to the "Man on the Moon" project, notice that the underlying goal of the project is to win the Space Race—to beat the Soviet Union. So, what's the time constraint? You were told officially that the time constraint was "the end of the decade," but now you realize that isn't actually correct. The *real* time constraint derives from the "why" of the project, and it's, "Get there before the Soviet Union, or by the end of the decade . . . whichever comes first!"

Can you be held responsible and accountable for a project requirement you were never told about? Absolutely you can. Imagine you're scuffing your feet on the Oval Office carpet while you're being dressed down by the president because the Hammer and Sickle is flying over Tranquility Base. "But you never *said* I had to beat the Soviets," you complain. Doesn't work, does it? At this level, you're expected to understand the project well enough to figure this one out for yourself. You are on the hook, and that's another reason to analyze assumptions.

There are some objectives and requirements for which you are expected to have the judgment and knowledge to figure out on your own. In those cases, you are fully responsible whether you actually figured it out or not. To avoid this kind of problem, steep yourself in the context and circumstances of your project, as well as the organizational environment in which it takes place.

Consequences of Poor Scope Definition

A construction executive in Chicago bid on a new building project a few years ago. In an interview, he said, "When I put together my proposal, something nagged at me that I'd forgotten something very important. But I couldn't think of anything I missed, so finally I sent in the proposal, and I won the contract. It wasn't until I was sitting in my trailer at the construction site looking out the window one day that I suddenly remembered what I'd forgotten to put in my bid: site preparation. And preparing the site set me back two million dollars." That's the kind of cost involved when you forget something important at this stage of the project.

Make sure you get extra eyes on your initial work, because mistakes can easily spiral out of control at this stage. Put your development materials in writing and get them signed. Use your "lessons learned" file and the wisdom of those who've done it before to keep you from overlooking anything.

Commercial pilots with thousands of hours of flight time still use checklists to make sure they don't forget anything when taking off. It's not that they don't know what to do, it's that mistakes can be made by anybody, even experts. Be self-confident, but avoid the kind of overconfidence that leads to this kind of error and omission.

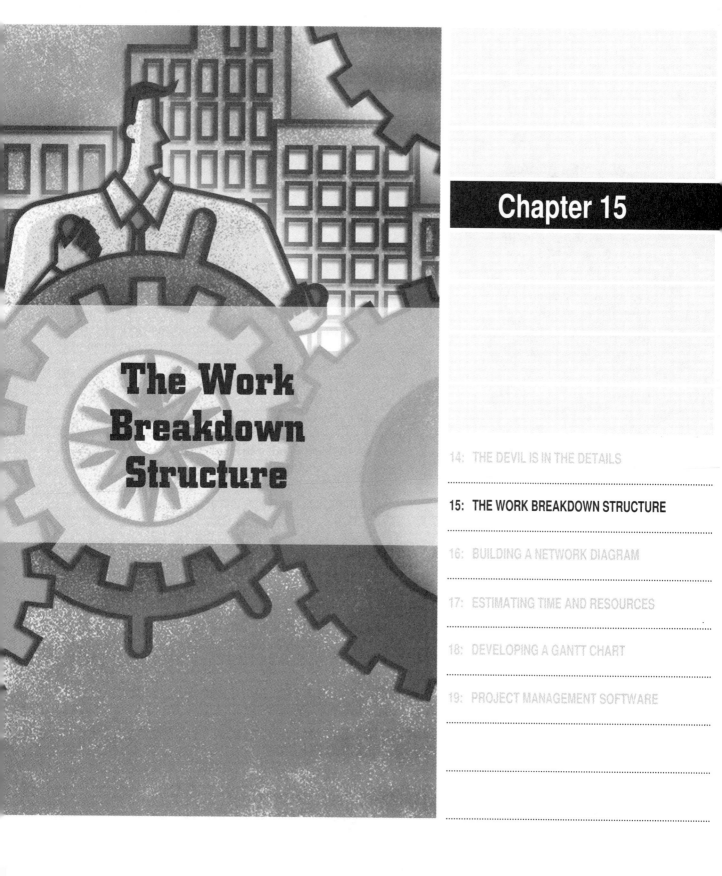

The Work Breakdown Structure

Chapter 15

Why the WBS Underlies All Steps in Planning

The Work Breakdown Structure (WBS) can be thought of as an organizational chart for the work, or a family tree for the project. Especially when displayed in "org chart" format, the WBS gives a clear, graphic display of all the tasks and activities necessary to complete the project.

What's challenging about the WBS is not so much the theory—it's pretty straightforward, as we've seen—but rather the importance of getting it right on the fine details. The work we did in the previous two chapters is all preparatory work for this stage. We can't afford to miss anything, and we can't afford to get confused about scope issues. Once we've done a WBS and had it reviewed by key stakeholders, we can move into the construction of schedules, budgets, and operating plans to get the project's work accomplished.

The WBS is used for project scheduling, estimating, risk management, change management, and communications with the customer and team member. What do the project manager and the project team need to know in order to accomplish a project? They need the following:

1. A list of all the work packages and activities necessary to accomplish the project. What exactly must be done?
2. A list of assigned responsibilities and accountabilities for each of the work packages and activities, grouped together for each organizational unit that will be working on the project. Who will do each job, and how will jobs be grouped together?
3. A match of the project's requirements to the specific tasks and activities in which the requirements must be satisfied. How good does each task have to be to accomplish the overall project?
4. A sequence in which the work is to be done. What comes first, and what comes next?
5. What problems could we anticipate? Where will those problems occur in the project?

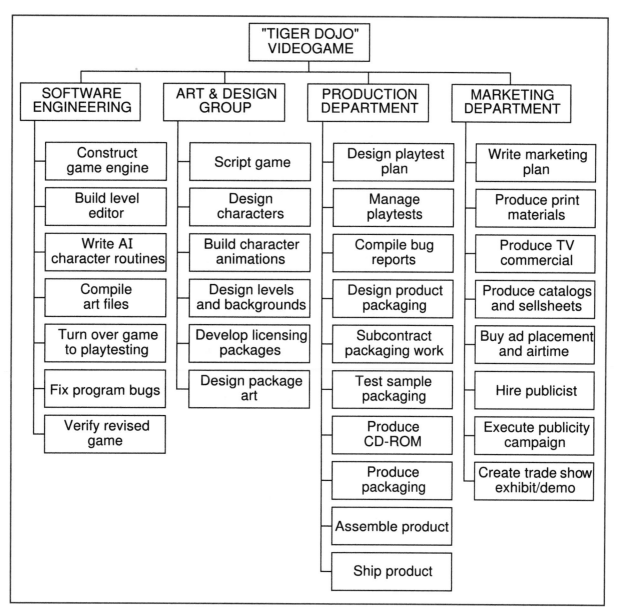

▲ FIGURE 15-1: *Work Breakdown Structure (WBS).* This "high-level" WBS describes the major work packages and departments necessary to accomplish this project. Work groups may subdivide their tasks into smaller units in their own WBS.

The WBS either accomplishes or serves as a foundation for accomplishing each of the objectives. It then serves as the technical or performance baseline for the project, allowing you to measure the amount of work accomplished.

Because the WBS is so crucial, let's look at the construction process of putting one together. We'll use our "Tiger Dojo" project once more (see Figure 15-1).

A Task? Project? Program?

One thing you'll notice about the "Tiger Dojo" WBS is that some of the tasks—"Construct Game Engine," for example—can take a tremendous amount of effort, time, and money. If this task is assigned to a team, the team might well consider the assignment to be a project in its own right!

That's a perfectly legitimate way to look at the situation. The difference between a task, a project, and a program has some arbitrary elements to it, and you can use whichever term seems reasonable and appropriate to define *your* relationship to the work.

The same work can be considered to be all three—task, project, and program—depending on your relationship to the work. Looking at the "Man on the Moon" project, the highest-level breakdown in that project would look something like Figure 15-2:

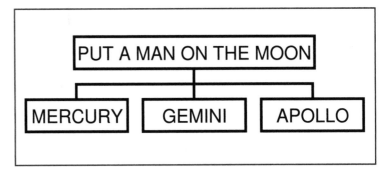

▲ FIGURE 15-2: *Project, program, or task?* In this WBS, the subprojects within the program are clearly projects—or even programs—in their own right.

"Put a Man on the Moon" is a project—it's a temporary endeavor to create a unique result. It's also a program—a group of comanaged projects. It includes some elements of ongoing work—the administration of a federal agency.

The three major phases of "Man on the Moon" are projects—temporary endeavors to create unique results—and each is also a program of comanaged projects (see Figure 15-3).

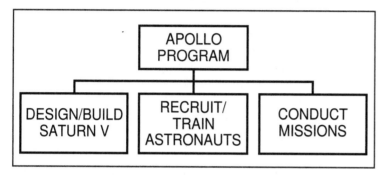

▲ FIGURE 15-3: *A subproject becomes a project/program.* Within the Apollo program, there are major subdivisions that can be considered projects (or programs). The three items below APOLLO PROGRAM are at the third level of this project WBS.

Werner von Braun and the team at Marshall Space Flight Center in Huntsville, Alabama, clearly regarded "Design/Build Saturn V" as a project, even though it's at the third WBS level. They might subdivide it again (see Figure 15-4).

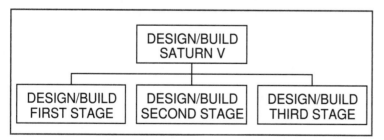

▲ FIGURE 15-4: *Additional subdivision.* The Saturn V was a three-stage rocket, each stage posing unique engineering issues. How many more levels of subdivision are required?

Delving Into Deeper Levels

Now, we're at Level 4 of this WBS, and it's clear that we aren't nearly finished. Within "Design/Build First Stage" there might be tasks for the rocket design and for the engine design as separate activities. Within rocket design, there's:

- Developing the design itself
- Preparing engineering drawings
- Building a prototype
- Testing the prototype
- Integrating the engine into the rocket, integrating the first stage into the other two stages
- More testing
- Planning the actual manufacturing process
- Developing and issuing contracts

And many of those activities are large and complex enough to justify breaking them down into smaller and smaller units. Of course, this is a very large project, and smaller projects can likely be resolved in fewer WBS levels. What's right for your project?

There isn't any official standard for how far down your WBS should be divided. There are a variety of different standards available—in one, tasks should be no more than eighty hours of effort; in another, tasks should represent from 0.5 to 2.5 percent of the total project. You have to do what makes sense for your own project. The WBS is a more flexible tool than some others in project management because it must allow you to handle projects of any size and dimension.

The answer to whether you've broken your project down deeply enough has to do with whether you and the team that will be doing the work find that the job is manageable: that you can get your mind comfortably around it and that your team can get it done. If you see your work as a program and assign projects to subordinates, if your boss sees your work as a task and your divisions as subtasks, it doesn't matter. If the choice of perspective helps you manage the work for which you are responsible, you've done the right thing.

There isn't any official standard for how far down your WBS should be divided.

Displaying the WBS Graphically and in Text

The size of the project and the number of levels of the WBS influence the decision whether to display it as an org chart (as we have been doing so far in this chapter) or as an outline (see Figure 5-2). If you're going to try to keep track of all the tasks in "Man on the Moon," you'll quickly find that the org chart approach is so graphically unwieldy as not to work. You'll likely display a project like this as an outline (see Figure 15-5).

```
1.0    Put a Man on the Moon
       1.1    Mercury
       1.2    Gemini
       1.3    Apollo
              1.3.1   Design/Build Saturn V
                      1.3.1.1       Design/Build First Stage
                                    1.3.1.1.1    Develop Design
                                    1.3.1.1.2    Prepare  Engr. Drawings
                                    1.3.1.1.3    Build Prototype
                                    1.3.1.1.4    Test Prototype
                      1.3.1.2       Design/Build Second Stage
                      1.3.1.3       Design/Build Third Stage
              1.3.2   Recruit and Train Astronauts
              1.3.3   Conduct Missions
                      1.3.3.1       Apollo 1
                      1.3.3.2       Apollo 2
                      ..........
                      1.3.3.11      Apollo 11
                      1.3.3.12      Apollo 12
                      1.3.3.13      Apollo 13
```

▲ FIGURE 15-5: *Outline format WBS.* **Because of the complexity and number of tasks, the organization chart format becomes impractical for a very large project.**

Because of the control potential of project management software, more large projects have a comprehensive task list and schedule maintained at a headquarters level.

Because of the control potential of project management software, more large projects have a comprehensive task list and schedule maintained at a headquarters level. Historically, because of the cost and complexity of tracking, it was more common for each level of management to focus on their own areas of responsibility. At NASA Headquarters, for example, you might have the high-level WBS for the project, and in Huntsville, Alabama, Dr. von Braun's crew has their own WBS for their own project. There is no fundamental requirement that all WBS levels be maintained at a central control level. If the WBS levels are being separately maintained, notice that each group may use an "org chart" approach if desired because the individual work areas are small enough to work with that kind of visual display.

If you're going to go to the work and effort of maintaining a comprehensive single file of all tasks on a mammoth project, you need to have a benefit in mind that will repay the significant expense involved in building and maintaining it.

One of the values of a WBS is that it provides a method for cost accounting on a project. If you want to aggregate costs by cost centers, you can develop your WBS with that in mind. Each category in Level 2 can be a major cost account, so when you expend money, it will flow directly to the appropriate budget category, allowing for detailed financial control of the project.

> One of the values of a WBS is that it provides a method for cost accounting on a project.

Divisions and Groupings of the WBS

There are several levels of the WBS to consider.

WBS Level 1

The first level of a WBS is the project level, and there's only one box in it: the project itself. It's the top of the chart, and all underneath it supports the achievement of that goal. You need this level because you may be doing multiple projects at the same time.

WBS Level 2

The second level of the WBS tends to vary. It's sometimes called the cost account level, because if you are organizing your project for the goal of improved financial control, you'll divide the project into accounting areas. (Engineering, marketing, acquisition could all be cost codes allowing charging of expenses to them.)

Sometimes, the second level of the WBS is referred to as the subproject level. That implies that each of the major divisions of the overall project/program can be considered projects, with a specific defined goal for each. ("Build Industrial Complex" could be divided into "Build Warehouse," "Build Offices," and "Build Assembly Plant," describing the component projects.)

The second level is also known as the phase level. This means that the divisions are being done in order, with each phase ending and providing input to the next phase of the project. (For "Man on the Moon," the chronology of phases "Mercury," "Gemini," "Apollo" provides a sequence to the work.)

And the second level is sometimes called the department level. When you have existing functional departments and all the work will be assigned to one or another of those departments, then you would use the department names as your second level categories. (Engineering, marketing, and manufacturing are the departments that will perform project work.)

Use the format that makes most sense to you based on the circumstances of your project.

WBS Level 3

The third level of the WBS represents work packages, or tasks. This is where the work necessary to do the project is placed. A task, as we've noted, must have a specific end or output to be achieved—it's finite, not ongoing. (Certain ongoing activities like project management and systems engineering are indeed ongoing throughout a project, and do not always get reflected in the WBS. If you want to have them there, you can; we'll show you how and where to place them shortly.)

Always describe a task with both a verb and a noun. The task in excavating a swimming pool should be written "Dig Hole," not just "Hole." If you have a task labeled "Hole," people can be unsure whether to dig it, measure it, or fill it. The verb specifies the necessary action for a task.

A WBS Level 2 does not have to have a verb unless it's a subproject. "Construction" can contain all the tasks that are part of construction, but "Construction" can be an ongoing department or program rather than a project.

WBS Levels 4+

When the project is large and complex, your WBS Level 3 tasks are often too big to manage effectively. You can subdivide them into smaller units until you've reached the desired level of control.

Ways to Organize WBS Categories

Components of the product or service—the program, the packaging, the licensing package.

Subsystems—programming, art, writing, marketing

Projects within a program—Games: "Tiger Dojo," "Pirate Joe," "Spaceman Spiff"

Processes—story, art, code

Time phases—initial story design, game engine, levels

Geographic areas/offices—Lake Geneva, San Mateo, Bethesda

Organizational units—systems group, marketing department, art department

Love Your Sticky Notes

As we said earlier, sticky notes may be your best friend for building a WBS. Make building a WBS a team activity. Using a whiteboard or flip chart, have the group brainstorm activities. Write each activity on a sticky note and put it up. Prepare additional sticky notes for WBS Levels 1 and 2, and organize your WBS that way. The big advantage of this technique is early flexibility. It's easy to move notes around; add, subtract, or edit notes; or consider alternate strategies for structuring the project.

In breaking them down, think of each WBS Level 3 activity as a project. WBS Level 4, then, would be the equivalent of WBS Level 2—a subproject/phase/department categorization of the work. WBS Level 5 would be the equivalent of WBS Level 3-tasks. If you have to subdivide again, then WBS Level 6 is another subproject/phase/ department level, WBS Level 7 are more tasks, and onward.

Developing the Task List

There are two basic processes for building a WBS, known as the "top down" method and the "bottom up" method. The circumstances of your project will normally influence the choice you make; both are equally legitimate and effective.

Top Down Method

In the "top down" method of building a WBS, you normally start with the first two levels of your WBS already complete. Sometimes the initial project organizational structure is established by your company or by your customer; sometimes there's just one sensible way to set things up.

You start at the highest level and break down large pieces of the project into components. On "Tiger Dojo," for example, we work in a company where game projects cut across functional divisions: software engineering, art and design, production, and marketing. Starting with software engineering, we ask ourselves, "What tasks have to be done by software engineering to accomplish this project?" We know immediately they will have to write a lot of code, but "Write a lot of code" is a little too general to serve as a good task description. We need further breakdown to make it manageable.

The program for our game will have several major modules. One of them is the overall game engine, and then there is an editor program that allows rapid design of the various levels of the game. We identify both those as WBS Level 3 tasks on our project, "Construct Game Engine" and "Build Level Editor."

From an executive perspective, maybe that's what we want to know—is the game engine finished, and does the level editor work?

But within the software engineering department, perhaps the team wants a bit more detail. As the overview of the system is developed, the team will identify numerous components of the system, which in turn will be assigned to individual programmers or small teams. That constitutes WBS Levels 4 and onward.

You won't necessarily have all the information to complete a top-to-bottom WBS for the project in a single meeting. Sometimes the executive summary level of the WBS gets done early by the senior team, and then the individual work groups go away to develop their detail lists. In a subsequent meeting, the details get combined back into a master project WBS.

Bottom Up

On other projects, you don't start with a WBS Level 2 completed. A project may be so new that we don't have an organizational structure to handle it. You may want to consider a variety of approaches to the project.

Accordingly, in the "bottom up" technique, you and the team brainstorm as many different tasks as possible. Arguments and discussions are welcome, as this is a brainstorming event. Once you're satisfied that you have a comprehensive task list, then look for logical groupings and build your WBS Level 2 backwards.

Don't Forget Anything

Don't forget anything . . . and don't put down what shouldn't be there. One important rule in constructing a WBS is that it is—by definition—the sum total of the project. The rule is: "If it's not in the WBS, it's not in the project!"

Because all subsequent planning is based on the WBS, what if you've forgotten a task that is required? Unfortunately, the answer is that when you discover—too late—that the task is required, you've budgeted neither money, nor resources or time, to get it done. This can be a project killer.

And because the WBS is a complete statement of project scope, if your WBS contains work you are not supposed to do, you're wasting money and time and may be treading on someone else's toes by doing it.

> **Breakdown Variances**
>
> Different WBS categories may need different levels of breakdown; it doesn't have to be the same for each Level 2 category. One area may be broken down in very fine detail and another consisting of one or two large activities, and that's okay. As long as each area is something you and your team understand well, you've done a fine job.

How can you be sure, then, that your WBS is complete and correct? Try these ideas:

1. *Deliverables.* Each deliverable for your project requires at least one task to get it done. (Some require more.) Take your list of deliverables and make sure the WBS contains all the work to get each deliverable completed.
2. *Scope.* Read the other project documents you've developed–Project Charter, Scope Statement, etc.–looking for indications that there is specific work required.
3. *Reviews.* Get others to review your WBS looking for what you may have missed. If you can, set aside your draft WBS for a few days. You can make it a game, offering a soda and candy bar to each person who catches a serious WBS omission.
4. *Dual brainstorming teams.* Divide your project team in two and have each one develop the project WBS separately. Compare the two for anything one team thought of that the other team missed.
5. *Customer/sponsor approval.* Have your WBS reviewed and approved by the customer and sponsor. They may not catch everything, but it's a little better for you if they missed it too.

When—And If—to Use Software

You can enter your final WBS in most project management software programs (see Figure 15-6). The advantages are that you have a file copy, you can build a template from it, and you don't have to re-enter the task information in subsequent steps. You can also use the WBS as your technical baseline. That being said, not everyone who uses project management software enters the WBS. On smaller projects, it's not as important.

Templating

If you do similar projects, you may find a substantial time-saving advantage in building templates for your projects. Although we've established that projects are not only temporary but also unique in at least some areas, the similarity in projects means that

ID	Name	Predecessor	Resource Name
1	Software Engineering		
1.1	Construct Game Engine		
1.2	Build Level Editor		
1.3	Write AI Character Routines		
1.4	Compile Art Files		
1.5	Turnover Game to Playtest		
1.6	Fix Program Bugs		
1.7	Verify Revised Game		
2	Art & Design		
2.1	Script Game		
2.2	Design Characters		
2.3	Build Character Animations		
2.4	Design Levels and Backgrounds		
2.5	Develop Licensing Packages		
2.6	Design Package Art		
3	Production Department		
3.1	Design Playtest Plan		
3.2	Manage Playtests		
3.3	Compile Bug Reports		
3.4	Design Product Packaging		
3.5	Subcontract Packaging Work		
3.6	Test Sample Packaging		
3.7	Produce CD-ROM		
3.8	Produce Packaging		
3.9	Assemble Product		
3.10	Ship Product		
4	Marketing Department		
4.1	Write Marketing Plan		
4.2	Produce Print Materials		
4.3	Produce TV Commercial		
4.4	Produce Catalogs/Sellsheets		
4.5	Buy Ad Placement/Airtime		
4.6	Hire Publicist		
4.7	Execute Publicity Campaign		
4.8	Create Trade Show Exhibit/Demo		

◀ FIGURE 15-6:
WBS software view.
The project management software added WBS numbers based on the task entry. All indented tasks are subactivities and carry a decimal number. Notice this view does not have durations or dependencies; they will be added in later steps.

you can start from a common WBS and make modifications necessary for the individual project. If we acquire and publish multiple books, if we make numerous videogames, if we build swimming pools for a living, we have the opportunity to use a template.

Using templates is a great opportunity to improve planning and project quality by recycling already completed work. It's a very good idea.

WBS Numbering

At a certain complexity level of project management, you'll find people who believe that it's important to set up a standard WBS numbering system. Figure 15-5 shows how you can set up a numbering system for your WBS; other systems look more like traditional outlines (e.g., I. A. (1); a. *(1) a.*; and so forth). We hold no preference for one numbering system over another, but consistency is important if you use WBS numbering.

If you've selected a project management software package and plan to enter your WBS into it, the software's internal numbering protocols are probably the best ones for you to choose. (Depending on the package, you may be able to modify their defaults.) If you're using the WBS for cost accounting, you may want to use codes developed by your accounting department.

If you're managing multiple projects, you'll need to number each project. Our first project is 1.0 TIGER DOJO, but 2.0 CHARIOT RACE is also in production. Because each of these videogames probably includes constructing a game engine, the different codes help avoid confusion about which project we're working on at any given moment.

When you finish your WBS, you, your team, and your stakeholders can visually appreciate what is involved in doing the project. There may be more work than you thought, or sometimes you find now that it's up where you can see it, it's not nearly so troublesome as you feared. Don't be in a hurry to lock down the WBS; make sure you've got it straight before you move on.

There's seldom only "one right way" to build a WBS. Different skilled project managers can take the same project and end up with different structures, and it can easily be the case that all of them work just fine.

> There's seldom only "one right way" to build a WBS.

Chapter 16

Building a Network Diagram

The Next Step

Our Work Breakdown Structure (WBS) gives us the tasks and a sense of who will do what, but we don't yet know the order in which the work will be done, or how long we should allow for each activity. That's why the next step in our process is to build a Network Diagram. You'll be glad you used sticky notes in building the WBS, because you can use them again to lay out your network. (Remember to save your WBS, either in software or on paper, because you'll need it later in developing the technical baseline of your project.)

Understanding Dependencies

In Chapter 5, we gave an initial example of a dependency relationship. This is actually only one kind of dependency relationship, a Finish-to-Start (FS) dependency: You need to finish Task 1 before you can start Task 2 (see Figure 16-1). It is the most common type of dependency, and it's normally assumed as the default dependency, especially in project management software.

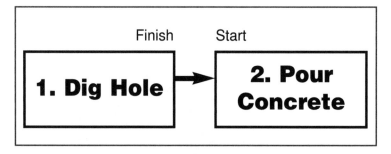

▲ FIGURE 16-1: *Finish-to-Start (FS) dependency.* The start of Task 2 cannot occur until the finish of Task 1.

Start-to-Start

Imagine that you plan to manufacture 1,000 widgets and then put them in boxes. Do you have to wait until all 1,000 widgets are done to put the first in a box? No, certainly not. There's probably some minimum number of widgets that need to be completed before it makes sense to start the boxing process, and the final widget can't be put into a box until it has been manufactured. But you can drastically shorten the calendar time if you use a Start-to-Start (SS) dependency: The start of Task 2 depends on the start of Task 1, with a slight lag to allow the first 100 widgets to be completed before boxing starts (see Figure 16-2).

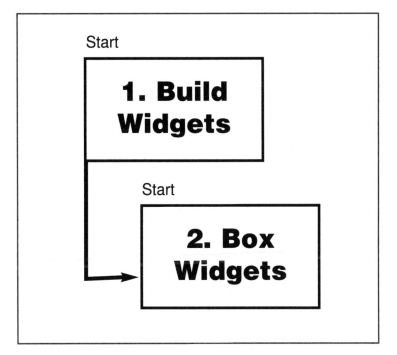

▲ FIGURE 16-2: *Start-to-Start (SS) dependency.* **The start of Task 2 cannot occur until the start of Task 1, in this case with a slight lag.**

Definitions

"Lag" is a planned delay until you start the next activity. After we pour the concrete for the swimming pool, we need lag time for the concrete to set before we can paint it.

"Lead" is overlapping one task so it starts before something else is finished. If we want the appliances to install in our new kitchen, we can order them with enough lead time so they will be here when we're ready to install.

Finish-to-Finish

In cooking Thanksgiving dinner, you normally work backwards from the scheduled mealtime, and figure out when to start each dish so that they will all finish at the same time, and be hot when brought to the table. That's an example of a Finish-to-Finish (FF) type dependency, in which the finish of Task 2 is dependent on the finish of Task 1, with or without lag or lead times (see Figure 16-3).

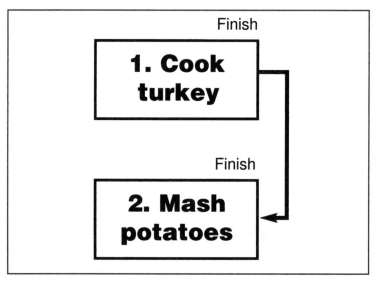

▲ FIGURE 16-3: *Finish-to-Finish (FF) dependency.* **The finish of Task 2 cannot occur until the finish of Task 1, in this case with no lead or lag.**

Start-to-Finish

There is a fourth type of dependency that is very rare—hardly ever seen outside the classroom. But in the interests of completeness, we'll list it here. It's called a Start-to-Finish (SF) dependency, in which the start of Task 1 depends on the finish of Task 2. In other words, Task 2 goes ahead of Task 1! How can that be?

You may be familiar with a management concept known as Just-in-Time (JIT) inventory management. To keep inventories low and manufacturing productive, people using inventory have cards (*kanban*, in Japanese) that they send to the supply department as they consume the inventory at their workstation. The cards "purchase" more inventory, drawing it through the system at close to the exact rate it's being consumed. (There's quite a lot to this concept, most of it outside the scope of this book. If you're interested, consider starting with Maasaki Imai's *Kaizen*, listed in the Bibliography.)

The goal is for you to acquire inventory just in time to use it, so you would set the start date for ordering based on your forecast of the finish time for using, with enough lead time so you'll have the

> The goal is for you to acquire inventory just in time to use it.

goods when you need them. This means the start of reordering inventory (Task 1) would be dependent on the finish of when you consume inventory (Task 2) (see Figure 16-4).

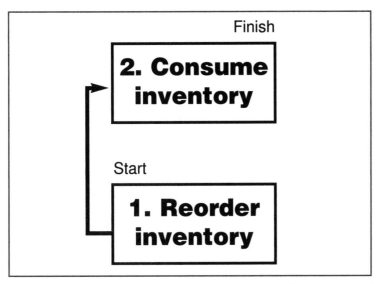

▲ FIGURE 16-4: *Start-to-Finish (SF) dependency.* The start of Task 1 depends on the finish of Task 2, in this case with no lead or lag.

You want to have all four kinds of dependencies in your project planning toolkit because these tools give you a range of options. If you can't seem to fit in all the work before you hit the deadline, can you start some tasks without waiting for the entire completion of their predecessors?

> You don't always have a choice about the order in which the tasks of your project must be done.

Strategic Choices in Task Relationships

You don't always have a choice about the order in which the tasks of your project must be done. In the sequence "Dig Hole–Pour Concrete," there's only one feasible way to do it.

Other times, there are a lot of possible choices. When that's the case, explore them all. Each will affect your project in different ways, and you can choose the answer that suits your needs best. Here are the different combinations you can use (see Figure 16-5).

Task B is dependent on Task A

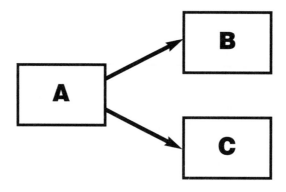

Task B and C are dependent on Task A.
Task B and C are parallel to each other.

▶ FIGURE 16-5:
Task layout choices.
**You have numerous
options in how to lay out
tasks in your project.**

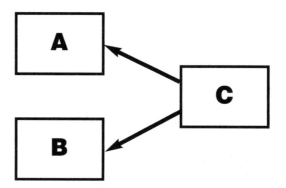

Task C is dependent on Task A and B.
Task A and B are parallel to each other.

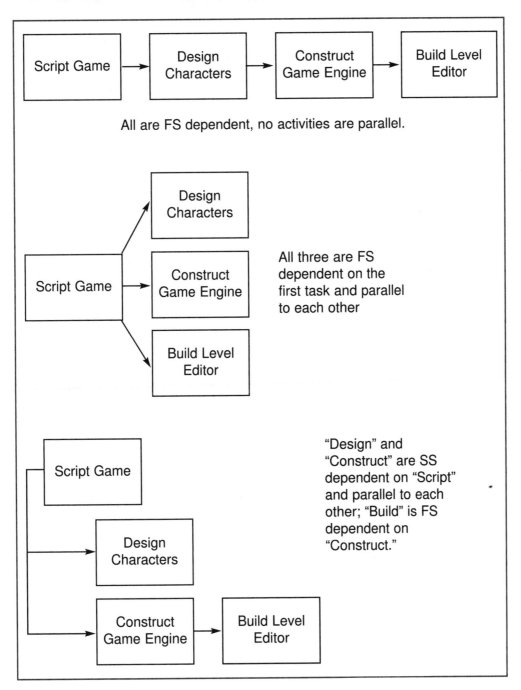

All are FS dependent, no activities are parallel.

All three are FS dependent on the first task and parallel to each other

"Design" and "Construct" are SS dependent on "Script" and parallel to each other; "Build" is FS dependent on "Construct."

◀ FIGURE 16-6:
Task layout choices.
You have numerous options in how to lay out tasks in your project. Each choice tends to create a different outcome.

Let's look at four of the tasks from the "Tiger Dojo" project WBS (Figure 15-1): "Construct Game Engine," "Build Level Editor," "Script Game," and "Design Characters."

Depending on how we choose to define the activity, we might have to have all of "Script Game" done before we can start on "Construct Game Engine." It's also possible for us to define the work so some parts of "Construct Game Engine" can start at the same time as "Script Game." (We'd have to have a pretty good idea of what we were doing so that people could go off and act independently.)

We'd likely have to have some part of "Construct Game Engine" completed before we could meaningfully start on "Build Level Editor," but we don't necessarily need every single aspect of "Construct Game Engine" to do that. Similarly, we might get started before "Script Game," but may not need all of that activity complete.

Similarly, we could start "Build Characters" at the same time as "Script Game," or wait for "Script Game" to be complete, and our relationships with "Construct Game Engine" and "Build Level Editor" are subject to negotiation.

This suggests to us that we can consider using the various types of dependency relationships, not only the Finish-to-Start (FS) type. We might do that to save time (if we think our schedule is very tight); we might make the choice because we think one answer will give us better quality than another; we may be influenced by availability and scheduling of specific resources.

Here are a few different layout options (see Figure 16-6)—you can develop more, if you want to.

Remember, we built our original WBS using sticky notes, and one advantage of this is that we can reuse the sticky notes for this stage of the project. Here, there's a lot of flexibility and numerous choices about how you can assemble these four tasks. For each choice in Figure 16-6, consider pros and cons for your project.

> We may be influenced by availability and scheduling of specific resources.

- *Option 1*. Each task is finished before the next one starts. Control is at the highest level, the fewest number of resources are working at any one moment, but the total time to get the work done is highest.
- *Option 2*. Everyone starts from a complete script, which is the primary control process. Need for communication among

parallel activities is high, coordination is likely difficult, uses the most resources at a single time, and time to complete the sequence is low.

- *Option 3.* Neither the character designer nor the game engine constructor has a complete script at the start. Because of the overlap, time to complete is very low, coordination needs are very high, and the likelihood of having to redo work is increased.
- *Option 4.* Creative work is compressed, but focus on character design (needed for licensing) is substantial, and rework potential in "Script" and "Design" is high. Difficult technical work is spread out and technical people have complete script documentation from which to work. Time required is moderate, and resource consumption is also moderate.
- *Option 5.* Creative work is completely done before technical work begins. Script and character design have room in which to work, you have the ability to focus resources heavily in that area. Technical work, which probably takes the longest, is shortened by making the activities parallel, but coordination needed in technical work is high. Resource consumption is moderate.

The decision to choose one of these options (or look for additional choices) is a value-based decision. Your knowledge and understanding of your own project, the constraints under which you work, preference and style issues of you and your staff, and organizational customs and norms will all influence your decision. Even when you think you're sure which choice is right, brainstorm different options before you finalize. You might be surprised what you find.

Every once in a while there will be a single option so much better than any other that it's obvious what you should choose. More often, every choice contains some drawbacks, so it's your balance of advantages versus drawbacks that leads you to make the decision.

Putting the Diagram Together

Start by making a new sticky note and labeling it "START." Put it up on your whiteboard or flip chart. Make a second new sticky note, label

> Even when you think you're sure which choice is right, brainstorm different options before you finalize.

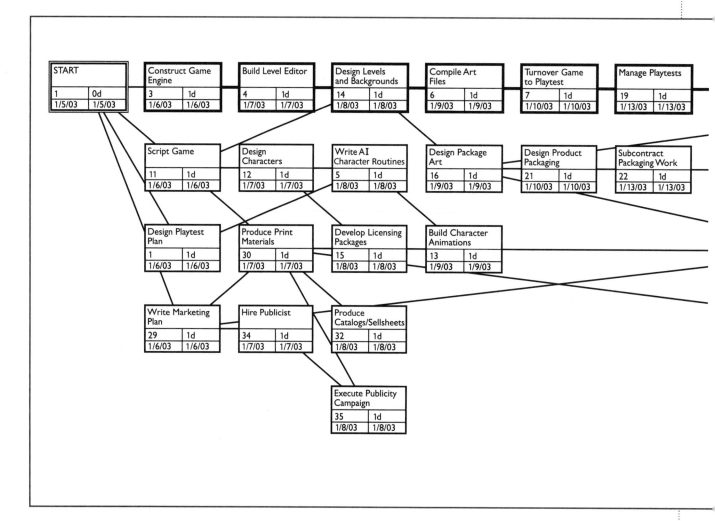

▲ FIGURE 16-7: *Completed Network Diagram.* This is what a Network Diagram looks like when produced by project management software. Note that other ways to sequence this project are possible.

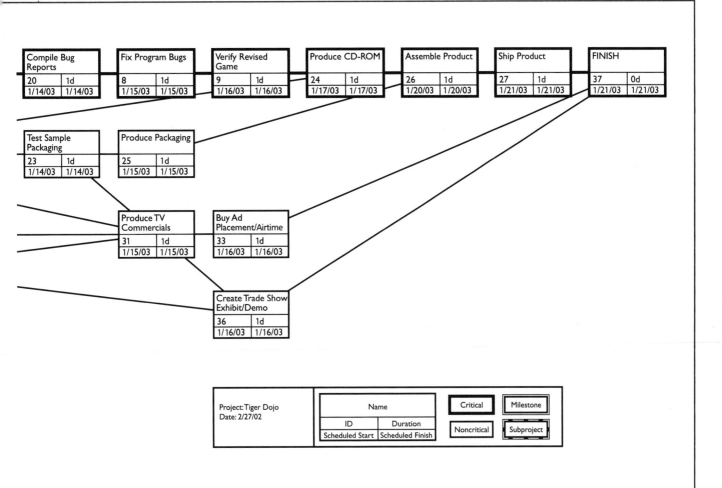

Project: Tiger Dojo
Date: 2/27/02

Name	
ID	Duration
Scheduled Start	Scheduled Finish

Critical   Milestone

Noncritical   Subproject

▲ In this version, there are no durations listed for any activities (a default of one day is used for convenience), nor are there any relationships other than FS dependencies, because those decisions come later.

it "FINISH" and put it at the very end of the board. Now, ask yourself (and your team if you're doing this together) what activities can be started at the beginning of your project. Take those sticky notes from your WBS and put them to the right of the "START" node. Draw arrows from the "START" node to the sticky notes you've placed.

Now, for each sticky note that follows "START," ask yourself (and your team), "What activities can start once this task is complete?" Put those sticky notes after the activity you've chosen, and draw arrows from that task to the new tasks. Work left to right until all the tasks from your WBS have been placed into a network. Draw arrows from the last tasks to the "FINISH" node (see Figure 16-7).

If you're doing this as a team-building activity—which we recommend—you'll find it's an enormous timesaver to get one Network Diagram done start to finish *before* you let the team start discussing options. If you don't, you'll get seriously bogged down.

Rules for Network Diagramming

A network must have a single starting node. We did that by creating a sticky note with "START" written on it. That's necessary when more than one task can begin at the kickoff of the project. It's optional (though still a good practice) when only one task starts a project.

A network must have a single finish node. That's the sticky note marked "FINISH." That's necessary when more than one task live at the end of the project, optional (but good practice) if not.

Every activity in the network must have a predecessor. For every activity (except START, of course), there must be at least one line coming into it from a previous task. The predecessor/dependency relationship may be any of the types we've discussed (FS, SS, FF, SF).

Every activity in the network must have a successor. For every activity (except FINISH, of course), there must be at least one line coming out of it and going to a subsequent task. This successor/dependency relationship may be any of the types we've discussed (FS, SS, FF, SF).

All connections move left to right. There are no loops. In regular flow-charting, loops are extremely common. You might find them useful in this kind of charting because some project tasks may have to be done multiple times. The reason you cannot use them is that these relationships also signal forward movement in time—in the absence of a time machine, loops can't exist in project plans because the end date cannot then be defined.

Finding the Critical Path

In the next chapter, we'll look at techniques for estimating how long these activities will take. You need this information before you can determine the critical path, which will also tell you how long your project is expected to last.

Critical path is the longest path through a schedule network. A sequence of activities from project start to finish, all of which have slack or float less than or equal to zero. Total slack/float is the extra time available to finish a task before it results in a delay to the project. Free slack/float is the extra time available to finish a task before it delays its successor task, whether or not the project is delayed as a result.

To illustrate these concepts, let's look at a project (see Figure 16-8). Here, we're planning to buy software and hardware to build a project management workstation. The critical path is the longest path. It must include Task 1, because it begins the project. Comparing the two branches of the path, we notice that Task 2 is longer than Task 3, and both link back in Task 4. Task 2, therefore, is critical. Task 4 must be critical because it's the only task in that time period. Between Task 4 and Task 8, the final task in the project, there are two paths. The path with Tasks 5 and 7 on it totals six days; the path with Task 6 has three days; Tasks 5 and 7 are critical. Task 8 finishes the project and is critical. Adding up the critical path tasks 1-2-4-5-7-8 gives us a project of twelve days duration.

The twelve days on the critical path are duration, not calendar time. Depending on what day of the week the project starts, there might be one or two intervening weekends, and maybe even a holiday. So the calendar time might be fourteen, sixteen, or seventeen days, counting nonworking time.

It's also unlikely that this project would constitute someone's full-time activity for twelve days. More likely, most of the tasks will be performed on a part-time basis by people engaged in other work or projects. So the level of effort will be a lot less than twelve days. For Task 5 "Delivery Lag," there is no effort—the five days is waiting time until the boxes get delivered. Like waiting for the concrete to dry in our swimming pool, our projects often contain nonworking duration.

Definitions

"Duration" is the number of work days (or other periods) necessary to complete a task or project. This does not count nonworking days, such as weekends or holidays. "Calendar time" is the number of calendar days (or other periods) necessary to complete a task or project. This includes weekends, holidays, and other nonworking days. "Effort" is the number of work hours necessary to complete a task or project. If someone is not working full time on a task or project, the level of effort will be less than the duration. If someone is working full time or overtime, or if more than one person is working full time on the task or project, the level of effort can be greater than the duration.

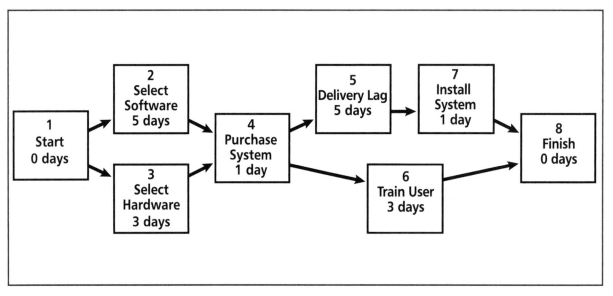

▲ FIGURE 16-8: *Critical path and slack.* The critical path on this project is the task sequence 1-2-4-5-7-8, totaling twelve days of duration. Task 3 is noncritical and has two days of slack. Task 6 is noncritical and has three days of slack.

Performing the Forward and Backward Pass

On this project, you can figure out the critical path just by eyeballing it and using a little bit of logic. If the project involves many tasks, you have to perform a specialized calculation known as the forward and backward pass to determine the critical path and the amount of slack in noncritical activities. Today, most people simply enter the project into project management software and let the software do the calculation for them.

You may never need to perform a forward and backward pass in real life, but it's still a good idea to understand how this technique works. After all, when your project management software tells you that *this* is the critical path, you'd be better off knowing how it came to that conclusion.

First, we need a few more specialized terms. Early Start (ES) is the earliest a task can start, based on the logic and duration of previous activities, as well as any imposed dates. Calculate ES as part of the forward pass. Early Finish (EF) is the earliest a task can finish, determined by adding the Duration to the Early Start. Late Finish (LF) is the latest a task can finish without delaying the project, based on the logic and duration of subsequent activities, plus any imposed dates. Calculate the LF as part of the backward pass. Late Start (LS) is the latest a task can start, determined by subtracting the Duration from the Late Finish. Imposed Date is a mandatory project date that overrides normal calculations of task start/finish. Figure 16-9 illustrates these concepts.

ES		EF
(Early Start)		(Early Finish)
	TASK	
	X	
	(Duration)	
LS		LF
(Late Start)		(Late Finish)

▲ FIGURE 16-9: *Forward and backward pass notation.* **To perform a forward and backward pass, you must develop the Early Start, Early Finish, Late Start, and Late Finish from the duration (X) and the network logic.**

Calculate the LF as part of the backward pass. Late Start is the latest a task can start, determined by subtracting the Duration from the Late Finish.

Forward Pass

Basically, we're going to put a number in each corner of each task in the Network Diagram. Just follow along the process and you'll see how it works (see Figure 16-10).

Let's start. In the upper left corner of the first task in the project, we write "0," because the project begins at its kickoff moment, elapsed time zero. Then you add the duration (X) to the ES—but for a START task with a duration of "0," we get 0 + 0 = 0. "0" is the EF for Task 1. So far so good, but it gets just a little more complex.

For Task 2, its ES = EF of Task 1, which is still zero. Add the five days of duration, and Task 2 has an EF of 5. The parallel Task 3

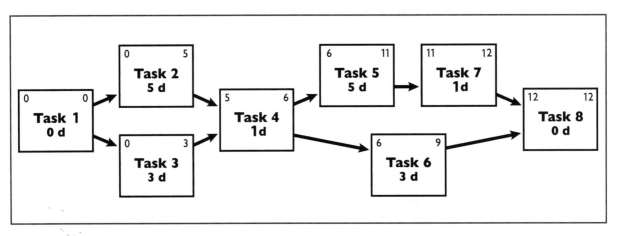

▲ FIGURE 16-10: *Forward pass.* Starting with Task 1 on Day 0, we add the Duration (X) to the Early Start (ES) to get the Early Finish (EF). For the next task, its ES is the same as the EF of the predecessor. If there is more than one predecessor, take the largest EF as the new ES, and keep going until you reach the end of the project.

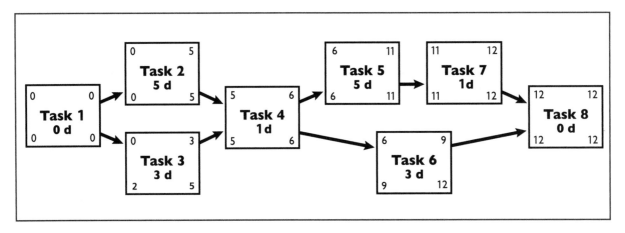

▲ FIGURE 16-11: *Backward pass.* Starting with the final task (Task 8) and its Early Finish (EF) of 12, we work backwards, subtracting our way back to Task 1. First, copy the last task's EF into the Late Finish (LF) spot in the lower right corner. Now, subtract the Duration from the LF to get the Late Start (LS). Move that backward to the tasks on which it is dependent, and keep subtracting. If there is more than one predecessor, take the *smallest* LS and the new LS and keep going. You should end up at 0 on Task 1.

has the same ES because it has the same predecessor, so it starts at zero as well. Add three days of duration to get an EF of 3. Task 4 has two predecessors, finishing on days 3 and 5 respectively. Since Task 4 can't start until *all* its predecessors are complete, it can't start until day 5. So move the largest EF forward (it's the 5) to be the ES of Task 4. Add a day of duration, and Task 4 has an EF of 5.

Tasks 5 and 6 now both have an ES of 5 because of the shared predecessor. Add five days in Task 5 and the EF is 11; add three in Task 6 and the EF is 9. Task 7 starts on day 11 (only Task 5 is its predecessor) and finishes a day later on 12. Task 8 has two predecessors, so again we take the largest EF (Task 7's 12) as the new ES; add zero again and finish with an EF of 12.

We now know this project is expected to take twelve days to complete, based on the Network Diagram. We know the critical path, therefore, has to equal the same 12, but we don't yet know which tasks are on the critical path, and which are not. For that, we need to perform the backward pass.

Backward Pass

Starting with the final task, copy the task's EF into the LF space in the lower right corner. We want the project to finish in no more than twelve days, so we start with that number. Subtract the Duration (0) from the LF to get the LS for Task 8, which is still twelve (see Figure 16-11).

The LS of Task 8 is the LF of Tasks 6 and 7, which we determine by following the arrows backward. For both tasks, subtract the Duration from the LF to get the LS. For Task 7, 12 – 1 = 11; for Task 6, 12 – 3 = 9. Task 7 is dependent on Task 5, so its LS of 11 becomes the LF of Task 5. Subtract 5 to get 6 for the LS of Task 5.

Now, it gets a little tricky. Notice two arrows leave Task 4, going into Tasks 5 and 6. So, thinking backwards, for the project to finish on time, Task 4 can't finish on day 9 (in time for the LF of Task 6), can it? If it does, Task 5 won't start on day 6, and you'll end up late.

In the forward pass, when there was a choice, we moved the larger number forward. So it's not too surprising that in the backward pass, we move the smaller number backward. With Task 4, you have a choice of an LF of 6 or 9, so you choose 6. Subtract

> We now know this project is expected to take twelve days to complete, based on the Network Diagram.

Watch Out for Errors

For the last task in the project, the top and bottom numbers on each side should be the same, and for the first task in the project, you should always end up with ES = LS = 0 at the beginning. There should also be at least one clear sequence of tasks from start to finish where ES = LS and EF = LF. Otherwise, you've made an arithmetic slip-up somewhere in the calculations.

Task 4's 1 day of Duration to get an LS of 5, which becomes the LF of Tasks 2 and 3. For Task 2, 5 – 5 = 0; for Task 3, 5 – 3 = 2. Again, you have a choice going backward; you pick the smaller LS, which is Task 2's zero, subtract Task 1's zero Duration and end up with an LS of zero.

Critical Path and Slack

The critical path consists of the tasks where the top and bottom numbers in each pair are the same (see Figure 16-12). In other words, ES = LS and EF = LF.

To calculate slack or float, subtract the top number from the bottom number on either side, either LS – ES or LF – EF; it doesn't matter. But if you get a different answer from the two calculations, you did something wrong.

If you've done this correctly, you'll always have at least one complete path from start to finish of critical tasks, and that's your critical path. (It is possible to have more than one critical path, but it's not necessarily a good thing.)

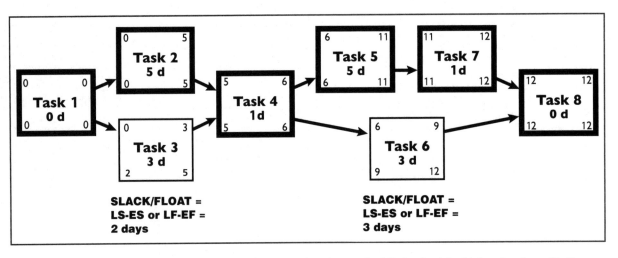

▲ FIGURE 16-12: *Critical path and slack.* The critical tasks are highlighted with thicker borders. Notice that on each, the top and bottom numbers in each pair are the same—ES = LS and EF = LF. The noncritical tasks have a different number in the top/bottom pairs. The difference between them is the slack or float.

It's also possible to have "negative slack," where LS-ES/LF-EF comes out to be less than zero. That's a polite way of saying you're behind schedule.

Using Project Slack as a Resource

Slack is your friend, if you know how to treat it right. There's one automatic and obvious advantage to having slack; it lowers the consequence to the project if that task should slip over schedule. You don't have a deadline problem unless the slippage becomes greater than the amount of slack available. (Of course, it's possible for you to have a budget problem—slack helps the time constraint but does nothing for the cost constraint.)

As a project manager during project execution, you may be able to afford to pay less attention to tasks with plenty of slack. If some of the members of your team are faster (or slower) than others, put the faster ones on critical path activities and the slower ones on tasks with slack.

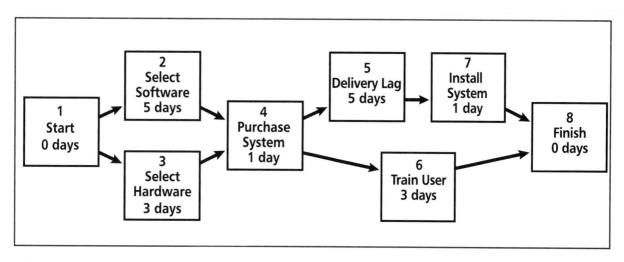

▲ FIGURE 16-13: *Slack as a resource.* The person working on Task 3 "Select Hardware" could be shifted to work on Task 2 "Select Software," either to keep it on schedule in case of slippage, or possibly to speed it up.

Slack as a Project Resource

Most importantly, slack can in some circumstances turn into an extra project resource. Let's go back to our software project (see Figure 16-13).

We know there are two days of slack available in Task 3 "Select Hardware." But if you've assigned a full-time project team member to that job, you have two extra days to play with. You can do a variety of things. You can assign the person to another project for those two days. You can increase the performance standard for the task. You can keep the two days in reserve in case of emergencies. Notice you can only do one of these things—once the two days are spent, they're gone.

Imagine that something goes wrong in Task 2 "Select Software." That's on the critical path, and so if it goes late, the "bumper car effect" is going to push out the deadline. Where can you get help? Slack to the rescue!

There are three possibilities (assuming that the Task 3 resource has the technical skills to be of use on Task 2 and that Task 2 is the kind of job where extra hands can speed it up—neither are always the case): You can wait until Task 3 is done and shift the resource into Task 2 for the remaining two days; you can delay the start of Task 3 (move it from its ES to its LS date) and invest the two days in Task 2 up front (while this might increase risk in Task 3, it could be worth it); or you can interrupt Task 3 in the middle and shift the person up to Task 2.

While in some circumstances you can compress your project so there is no slack left, you may not want to do that, especially if there is a significant degree of risk or uncertainty about the project. Keep a little something up your sleeve in case of emergencies.

> Keep a little something under your sleeve in case of emergencies.

Crashing

Our project schedule says this job should take twelve days, but the boss tells us that's too long. We need to speed it up. Let's take a look at the later part of the project, in particular, Task 5 "Delivery Lag." That's waiting until the boxes get here. You can indicate lag as a simple delay or gap on your timeline, but it's safer to treat it like a task that just happens to contain no effort requirement.

We have a five-day duration for this task, which is the cheap delivery. But if time is the driver, we might want to look at some

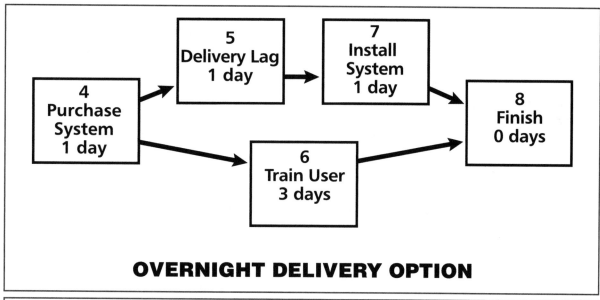

OVERNIGHT DELIVERY OPTION

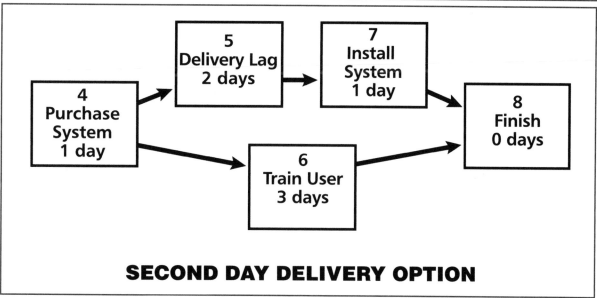

SECOND DAY DELIVERY OPTION

▲ FIGURE 16-14: *Crashing the schedule.* If we go with overnight delivery, Task 5 drops from five days to only one day; if we go with second-day, Task 5 drops from 5 days to two days. But notice Task 6's three-day duration. Overnight delivery doesn't speed up the project any more than second-day.

faster delivery options (see Figure 6-14). There are two listed in the catalog—overnight delivery for a premium price, and second-day delivery for a somewhat smaller premium. If the issue is time, not cost, which is faster?

It may surprise you that in this example, both take the identical amount of time. The reason is that there are two paths: Tasks 5–7 and Task 6, in parallel. Task 6, we know, has three days of available slack. Therefore, if you take one, two, or three days out of the Task 5-7 pair, the deadline moves up. But if you take any more than three days out of the Task 5-7 pair, Task 6 becomes the new critical path. The rest of the Task 5-7 savings is just more slack. Crashing is speeding up a task or project by spending money or resources to shorten activity durations.

Now, if you thought Task 7 was risky, you might go with overnight delivery anyway, just in case. And that's a legitimate decision, as long as you remember that's buying insurance, not speed.

> Crashing is speeding up a task or project by spending money or resources to shorten activity durations.

For more information on this topic, visit our Web site at www.businesstown.com

Chapter 17

Estimating Time and Resources

Process of Estimating

An estimate, by definition, is not a certainty. It's perfectly legitimate that your organization and your customer want good information about how long the project will take, how much money the project will cost, and what human and other resources the project will consume. Yet, certainly at the beginning of the project and possibly well into the project execution, there may be a lot about the project that is unknown. If this work hasn't been done before, you may not have comparables on which to base an estimate.

Estimating involves risk. It's seldom true that you have full control over all the outside events that are capable of having an impact on your project, and depending on those outside events, your costs and time may change, and sometimes change drastically.

The process of estimating involves three areas: data, scope, and tools. Data provides a foundation for the numbers you finally submit, and includes historical data, expert judgment, your own expertise, and comparable projects. Scope is the statement of the project to be done. The more detail and specification you have about what the customer wants, the more accurate your estimate can be. If scope is vague and yet to be defined, then the estimate will be quite general. But if scope is detailed, your estimate can improve its accuracy drastically.

There are numerous tools for estimating, depending on whether you're looking for a general order of magnitude estimate or a detailed cost breakdown. Both general and detailed estimates have use in the project management process, so let's find out how to develop them.

> Estimating involves risk.

How to Build Useful Estimates

If someone asks how much it will cost to build an office building, you don't normally answer, "Exactly $132,428,197.32." Nor is that really the answer the person wants. If we're just thinking about whether we need a new office building, we're looking for a ballpark figure on which we can base further decision-making. It's a number used for the purpose of discussion. If the number is, say, under $100 million, we may forge ahead, but if it's much over $100 million, we'll probably pass for now.

While different estimates have different purposes, they all have one thing in common: We develop estimates because they are useful.

As a result, the first thing you want to figure out is what kind of estimate is required.

In the project process, it's normal to start with a very general figure and slowly refine it into an estimate of increasing accuracy and stability. Figure 17-1 gives you some different types of estimates and their purpose. Please note two important qualifiers. First, the expected accuracy ranges given here are from multiple sources. Individual organizations often have their own nomenclature and their own expectation of what the terms mean and how accurate they are expected to be. There are standards available; the Project Management Institute and the Association for the Advancement of Cost Engineering, among others, publish standard guides and ranges.

Make sure you find out what level of information people expect you to have and how accurate or definitive the estimate must be, normally expressed as a range. If they don't tell you, make sure you qualify any estimate you supply as to how accurate or definitive you intend it to be. It's very frustrating to have a general WAG turned into a cast-iron straightjacket. (WAG–"Wild Assed Guess" or "Wildly Aimed Guess." Some more formal WAGs are called SWAG, or "Scientific Wild Assed Guess." This is a fairly common business expression, and can refer to a conceptual/order of magnitude or feasibility level estimate.)

> Make sure you qualify any estimate you supply as to how accurate or definitive you intend it to be.

Type of Estimate	Information Available	Accuracy Range	Typical Purpose
Conceptual/Order of Magnitude	General category of project	-33%/+233%	General Discussion
Feasibility	General description of project	-25%/+100%	Determination of interest
Preliminary	Project charter	-25%/+75%	Internal budgeting
Budget	WBS/3rd level	-15%/+50%	Job costing/bid preparation
Final	WBS/All levels	-5%/+15%	Cost accounting and reporting
Definitive	Significant work completed	-3%/+5%	Weekly reporting

▲ FIGURE 17-1: *Types of estimates.* **Although names and ranges vary, you need to prepare different types of estimates for different purposes, and have different amounts of information available.**

Two Advanced Estimating Rules

The Three-Quarters Rule:

When you are performing an estimate by analogy, and you've figured out the capacities and sizes of what you want compared to the analogy you have, a good rule of thumb is that the ratio of the cost is equal to the ratio of the sizes or capacities raised to the power of three-quarters. We're building a warehouse with 100,000 square feet and we have the cost of a recently built warehouse with 50,000 square feet: $1 million. The estimating formula is therefore (cost of new warehouse) /$1 million = $(100,000/50,000)^{3/4} = 2^{3/4} = 1.68$ x $1 million = $1.68 million.

The Square Root Rule:

You can estimate how long it will take to manage a project by the Square Root Rule. The idea is that the square root of the ratio of the costs of the new and existing projects equals the ratio of the duration of the two projects. If our 50,000 square foot warehouse took twenty-four weeks to build, we estimate how long it will take to build a 100,000 square foot warehouse by this formula. (New duration)/24 weeks = square root of ($1.68 million/$1 million) = 1.3 x 24 weeks = 31.1 weeks.

Top-Down Estimating/Estimating by Analogy

The first two levels of estimating, conceptual/order of magnitude and feasibility, are often estimated using analogous models. The feasibility estimate, where there's enough information to write a Project Charter or even a general draft of the Scope Statement, may be based on expert judgment models or parametric models. All of these are "top-down" estimating techniques because they generate an overall big picture number without detailed knowledge of the project we are to do. That's why in all cases their accuracy swings significantly.

Analogous models focus on a similar project (or several similar projects), adjust based on our general current understanding of the proposed project, and generate an estimate accordingly.

If we're talking about how much a new office building would cost, it isn't too difficult to find some recent office structures in the same vicinity and find out their cost. We don't decide how many floors we need or what kind of air conditioning we're going to buy—we're just not ready to make those decisions. So, we look at four or five office buildings, figure out where in that range we're likely to be, take the appropriate figure, and we're done. An estimate of this sort can be quickly prepared and has enough accuracy to enable further discussion, and maybe even a decision that, yes, we're going to build a new office building.

The important qualification on estimates by analogy is to make sure the analogous projects are in fact similar. If you use an office building as a comparable but you're planning a shopping center, even if the square footage is identical, you're likely not to get a useful estimate.

Expert Judgment

If someone has done a certain kind of project at a very sophisticated level for a long period of time, it's likely that he or she has developed a pretty good sense of how much certain projects are likely to cost. If you're not personally an expert, you can find one—or more than one. Expert judgment estimates can even include decisions that haven't been made. "I know they're saying right now they don't want a large conference room, but in my experience, before the project is done they're going to ask for one, so I'll estimate accordingly."

There are two qualifications in getting experts to make estimates—first, you want to make sure the person really is an expert, and second, you want to be sure the expert doesn't have a personal stake in the number. The contractor who is going to build your office building is probably (hopefully) an expert; but as an estimator, the contractor isn't exactly a disinterested and objective third party.

Parametrics

You may be shopping for office space and not necessarily committed to a new building. If you call a commercial real estate agent in your area and say, "We're looking at leasing 10,000 square feet of downtown office space. About how much will that cost?" You'll usually get an answer along the lines of, "Downtown office space is running about $35 a square foot."

That means that the annual rent on a 10,000-square-foot space will be about $350,000 a year. Of course, you won't get exactly 10,000 square feet, but rather 9,982 square feet, and the particular building you like is $34.48 a square foot if you go with the five-year lease. Still, it's useful to start with the ballpark number. If one office building wants $50 a square foot for its space, or another is willing to lease to you at $20 a square foot, you'll want to know why their office space is that much out of line with averages. There may be a good reason, but you want to know what it is.

This is an example of a simple parametric model. Parametric models calculate cost and duration on the basis of variables. Here, the variable is number of square feet, and the parametric produces a cost figure. The model probably needs a scale. The price for leasing 10,000 square feet all at once probably has a bit of a discount compared to someone who only wants to lease 200 square feet.

A more sophisticated parametric has a number of variables to use as input. If we go back to building our office building, we may decide that we want an exterior of glass rather than marble, that we want the special high-speed elevators, that we want the parking area covered, and that we want a fountain and a sculpture out front. We make the

The Delphi Method

A variation on the expert judgment method is known as the Delphi method, first developed by the Rand Corporation in 1948. The special problem the Delphi method solves is when the situation is highly complex and the experts are often at odds, for example, in the academic world.

In a Delphi estimate, the estimator experts are each provided with a form to fill out anonymously. The estimates are compared with one another to determine whether they are basically in agreement or diametrically opposed. The parts that are controversial then get sent out as a second form, this including the information and justification the experts supplied in their first answers. Those parts are re-estimated, and the cycle repeats until a consensus estimate is reached.

This method is more time-consuming and laborious than some others, but the accuracy value is quite high, especially when you're estimating something at the leading edges of science.

appropriate check marks, and out comes a cost figure. If we don't like the cost figure, we can go back and change some of our choices.

Parametrics can determine price as well as cost. Make sure you know which you're looking at, and from whose point of view. Both costs and prices are subject to estimates.

If it's a firm fixed price deal you're looking at, the price is fixed, but the cost—to the builder—is still a matter for estimating. The price includes a risk adjustment based on the uncertainty involved, and the fine print of the agreement excludes from the firm fixed price things that are unknown or unknowable before the job actually starts. Your price may end up varying.

Bottom-Up Estimating

Bottom-up estimates can be developed only when the job is defined. In the project management world, that means we have an approved Scope Statement and a Work Breakdown Structure (WBS) for the job. Now, a WBS can be done only to two or three levels of breakdown, or be comprehensive and broken down as far as the job will go. On the level of detail and accuracy of the WBS, we can base a variety of bottom-up estimates.

The method of bottom-up estimating is to look at each job package in the WBS and prepare a cost and time estimate for that package (see Figure 17-2). The packages get "rolled up" in their WBS parents for cost accounting purposes. For example, in "Tiger Dojo," all the systems engineering tasks can be individually priced, and then combined into a total cost for that area of the project. This is usually important in management planning and overall decision-making. Your decision-makers may not always want to see the lower level details, but will want to know that you have done it.

Watch out for the tendency to pad. It's not irrational to decide to put in a little safety margin on your job, say, 10 percent or so. Then the cost account level person rolls up the tasks and tacks on another 10 percent "just in case," and the job ends up with what is presumed to be a safety margin, but really isn't.

In spite of the temptations, we urge you not to pad estimates or let people on your team pad theirs. Why? First, we get into a game of

STREETWISE PM TECHNICAL BASELINE   Total $ 76,000

	SUMMARY	Person-Hours	Cost per Hour	Total Labor	Cash Outlays	Other Resources
A. Writing	**$16,750**					
1 Prepare Outline	$400	8	$50	$400		
2 Write Sample Chapter	$800	16	$50	$800		
3 Perform Research	$2,000	40	$50	$2,000		
4 Write First Draft	$10,000	200	$50	$10,000		
5 Prepare Back Matter	$1,000	20	$50	$1,000		
6 Make Revisions	$1,250	25	$50	$1,250		
7 Proof Galleys	$1,300	16	$50	$800		$ 500
B. Editorial	**$10,150**					
1 Find Author	$600	12	$50	$600		
2 Review Samples	$1,000	20	$50	$1,000		
3 Negotiate Contract	$1,500	15	$50	$750		$ 750
4 Review First Draft	$2,000	40	$50	$2,000		
5 Copyedit Manuscript	$4,000	80	$50	$4,000		
6 Prepare Cover Copy	$150	3	$50	$150		
7 Prepare Turnover Package	$900	8	$50	$400		$ 500
C. Production	**$32,850**					
1 Prepare Mockups	$1,000	8	$50	$400	$ 200	$ 400
2 Design Cover	$1,050	16	$50	$800		$ 250
3 Design Book	$2,500	40	$50	$2,000		$ 500
4 Produce Art/Graphs	$3,500	40	$50	$2,000	$ 1,000	$ 500
5 Prepare Art	$4,300	20	$50	$1,000	$ 2,500	$ 800
6 Coordinate Printing	$20,500	10	$50	$500	$ 20,000	
D. Marketing	**$16,250**					
1 Develop Promo Plan	$3,000	40	$50	$2,000		$ 1,000
2 Prepare Catalog	$3,000	10	$50	$500	$ 2,000	$ 500
3 Prepare Sales Materials	$1,750	15	$50	$750	$ 500	$ 500
4 Develop Mailing List	$950	4	$50	$200	$ 250	$ 500
5 Send Review Copies	$850	2	$50	$100	$ 250	$ 250
6 Implement PR Campaign	$6,700	12	$50	$600	$ 5,000	$ 1,100

▲ FIGURE 17-2: *Bottom-up estimate.* This spreadsheet was based on the WBS for the *Streetwise Project Management Book* Project (see Fig. 7-3 for the WBS data used). This allows detailed item-by-item budgeting to be rolled up into summaries.

"liar's poker" with our managers, because the managers know perfectly well that the temptation is there, and some get a bad case of "ten-percentitis" and slice 10 percent off the top. So after a while the pad grows to 20 percent—so there'll be 10 percent safety left after the expected 10 percent cut, and therein lies madness.

If the project has high risk, account for the risk and if that involves a cost adjustment, make it clear and obvious, not secret. You can legitimately argue for safety margins on projects, or contingency money for potential risks, and you'll be a lot stronger throughout if you are honest and up front about it.

Five Steps to Exceptional Estimating

Here are some good rules to follow in improving your own ability to estimate:

1. Use actual information when possible. To estimate how long a task will take in a current project, start with actual time estimates for the same work in similar projects.
2. Develop a network of experts. Look for people who can give you good information. Watch out for the natural tendency to be an optimist or a pessimist—but if you know how somebody leans, you know how to adjust his or her numbers.
3. Research history of vendors, subcontractors, and team members. Always early? Always late? Over budget? Under budget? You may have to use imperfect people, but know what to expect.
4. Look for standard references and tools. A lot of people have had this problem, and that normally implies there's a lot of material to help you. Check it out.
5. Build your own skills. You can train yourself to overcome your own natural tendencies. Make a WAG-type estimate before you estimate or run the project. Write it down and then look at it when the project is over. You'll learn your own biases and that helps you correct them.

> Develop a
> network of experts.

For more information on this topic, visit our Web site at www.businesstown.com

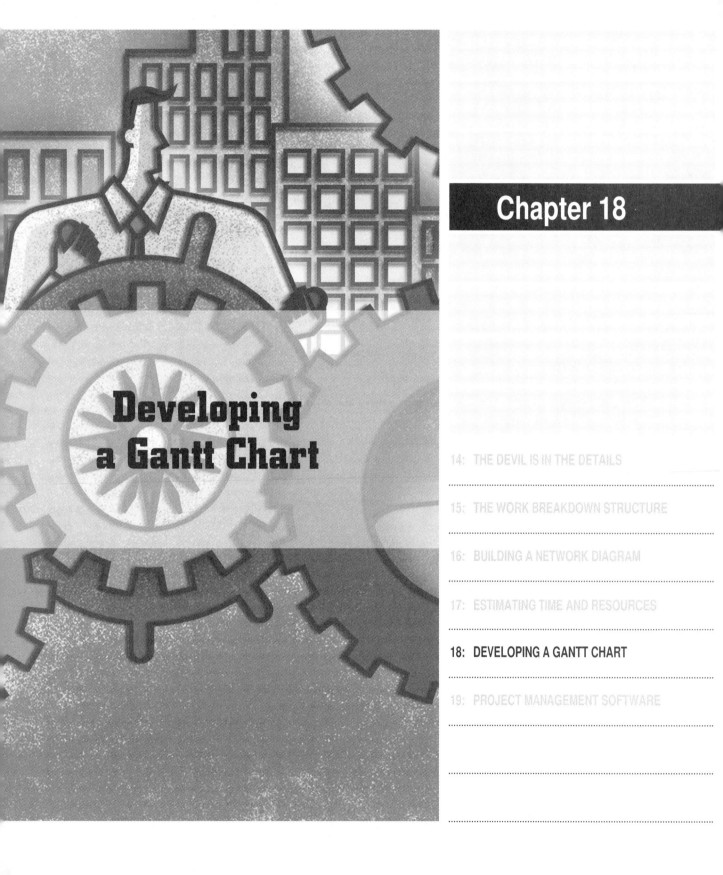

Chapter 18

Developing a Gantt Chart

The Swiss Army Knife of Project Management

For the majority of small to medium-size projects, the Gantt Chart is the most frequently used planning tool. Although it has some limitations, it's still a very practical tool, useful in scheduling, resource management, milestone planning, and tracking. In its various special forms it can serve as an aid to delegation, a briefing and summarizing chart for senior management and customers who don't necessarily have an understanding of project management mechanics, and much more. The Gantt Chart, in many ways, is the "Swiss Army knife" of project management.

> The Gantt Chart, in many ways, is the "Swiss Army knife" of project management.

Advantages and Limitations of the Gantt Chart

Advantages	Limitations
Easy to design and build	Doesn't show how the project works as a system
Simple to understand, especially for people with little PM experience	Doesn't show dependency relationships without extra symbols
Can show ahead/behind schedule	Can't show early start/late start
Can link progress to calendar	Not always clear how a particular late activity affects deadline

Turning Your Network Diagram into a Gantt Chart

To build a Gantt Chart, either manually or by computer, you need the following information:

- A list of all the tasks in your project
- The duration of each task
- Dependency relationships of each task

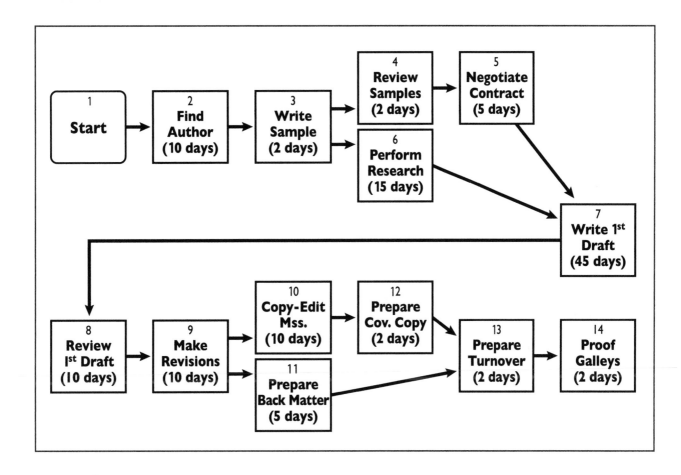

You develop the list of tasks in building your WBS, and then you develop dependency relationships in constructing your Network Diagram. After you estimate duration of each task, you enter that information into your Network Diagram. As a result, you should be able to organize all the Gantt Chart information by referring to your Network Diagram.

Let's start with the Network Diagram for our *Streetwise®* *Project Management* book project, which we developed back in Chapter 5 (see Figure 5-4).

▲ FIGURE 18-1: *From Network Diagram to task table.* All the information needed to develop your Gantt Chart is contained in your completed Network Diagram.

Defining Milestone

A milestone is a task with a duration of zero. Milestones serve as markers for significant project events, such as starting, finishing, or completing a major phase, or for mandatory reviews or interim completions. In project management software, normally entering "0" in the "Duration" field turns a task into a milestone automatically.

How to Build a Task Table

You set up the task table in four columns: Task Number, Task Name, Duration, and Predecessors. The first task in our project, obviously enough, is Task No. 1, and it's "Start." Because it's just a milestone, or a marker, it doesn't actually have duration, so under "Duration," we write "0." And since nothing comes before the project start, we write nothing in the "Predecessor" column.

The second task in the project (Task 2, obviously) is "Find Author," and it has a duration of ten days. When can it start? Only after the starting gun has been fired, so in the "Predecessor" column you write "1," which indicates that "Find Author" is dependent upon "Start."

For Task 3, we have "Write Sample Chapter." It has a duration of two days and is dependent upon Task 2 "Find Author," so write "2" under "Duration" and "2" under "Predecessor." But wait a minute! Isn't "Write Sample Chapter" also dependent upon "Start"? After all, the project must start before we can write the sample chapter.

Technically, the answer is no. You only look at the previous arrow connection on the Network Diagram, which connects to "Find Author" because "Find Author" in turn connects to "Start."

Now, we encounter something new. You'll notice on the Network Diagram that following Task 3, there are two parallel tasks, Task 4 "Review Samples" and Task 6 "Perform Research." Task 5 "Negotiate Contract" follows Task 4 "Review Samples." By inspecting the arrows, we see that Tasks 4 and 6 have the same predecessor—they are both dependent on Task 3 "Write Sample Chapter." In other words, neither task can start until the sample has been written. For Task 5, notice that the arrow only goes back to Task 4, and doesn't involve Task 6 at all. So for Task 5, the predecessor is simply Task 4.

But what about Task 7 "Write First Draft"? Two arrows come into that box, meaning that Task 7 is dependent on Task 5 "Negotiate Contract" and on Task 6 "Perform Research"! All that means is that you must write both task numbers in the "Predecessor" column. The convention is to separate them with commas. (You'll actually enter them in exactly that way when you use project management software to do this.)

The Critical Path

But wait! It's clear that Task 6 (fifteen days) is the critical path—it's longer than adding Tasks 4 (two days) and 5 (five days) together. Do you still have to write down both predecessors? Yes, absolutely. Why? Because sometimes tasks get delayed. If the contract negotiation gets bogged down, it could stretch out fourteen days, or even more, which would change the critical path on the project and delay the start of Task 7.

Write down all dependency relationships in your task table, not only those on the critical path. When surprises and delays happen, your critical path can change—and you'll need the information to adjust your schedule appropriately. Figure 18-2 is the completed task table for the *Streetwise Project Management* book project.

Now let's look at how to build a Gantt Chart by hand, and then we'll do it again using project management software.

Drawing a Gantt Chart by Hand

To draw a Gantt Chart, all you need is graph paper and a straightedge ruler. You can also make a Gantt Chart using a drawing program or even a spreadsheet/graphing program like Excel or Lotus 1-2-3. Remember, all the information you need to develop your Gantt Chart is contained in the task table. We're going to use the task table in Figure 18-2 and build the Gantt Chart from it.

Start the Gantt Chart by listing the tasks in order down the left side. Put a time scale across the top, because a Gantt Chart displays work over time. Because we're only considering duration (work days), not calendar time (including weekends and holidays), we're using a scale of one block equals five days.

The first task is "Start," and as you remember, that's a milestone because it has zero duration. Now, it's tough to draw a line of zero width and have it easily seen. So, the Gantt Chart convention is to represent a milestone with a diamond (◆). This particular milestone starts the project, so it goes in the very first block at the left edge (start-of-business of project Day 1).

The second task is "Find Author." It's dependent on "Start," which means that its bar starts exactly where "Start" ends. In this case, since "Start" is a milestone, "Find Author" also starts at the

> To draw a Gantt Chart, all you need is graph paper and a straightedge ruler.

Task No.	Task Name	Duration	Predecessors
1	Start	0 days	None
2	Find Author	10 days	1
3	Write Sample Chapter	2 days	2
4	Review Samples	2 days	3
5	Negotiate Contract	5 days	4
6	Perform Research	15 days	3
7	Write 1st Draft	45 days	5,6
8	Review 1st Draft	10 days	7
9	Make Revisions	10 days	8
10	Copyedit Mss.	10 days	9
11	Prepare Back Matter	5 days	9
12	Prepare Cover Copy	2 days	10
13	Prepare Turnover Package	2 days	11,12
14	Proof Galleys	2 days	13

▲ FIGURE 18-2: *A completed task table.* **This task table now contains in an organized form all the information you need to prepare a Gantt Chart. If you are using project management software, all you will have to do is type this information directly into the appropriate fields of the program.**

Watch Calendar Space

When starting out with Gantt charts, make sure your lines cover all the calendar space, rather than just float in the middle. If you don't pay attention to start-of-business and close-of-business with the bars, your chart can easily slip a day or two off schedule without you noticing it.

beginning of the project. It has a duration of ten days, so draw a line from the left edge of the first block to the right edge of the second block. Voila! You've now shown graphically the task's duration and start and finish times.

Task 3 is "Write Sample Chapter." It is dependent on "Find Author." That means it cannot begin until "Find Author" is complete. (That's only true if it's an "FS" dependency, as you recall, but unless

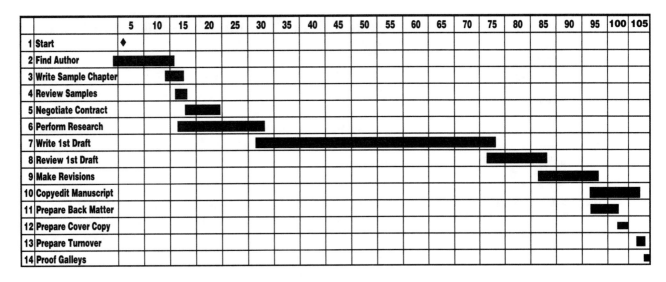

		5	10	15	20	25	30	35	40	45	50	55	60	65	70	75	80	85	90	95	100	105
1	Start	♦																				
2	Find Author	■																				
3	Write Sample Chapter			■																		
4	Review Samples			■																		
5	Negotiate Contract				■																	
6	Perform Research			■																		
7	Write 1st Draft							■														
8	Review 1st Draft																■					
9	Make Revisions																		■			
10	Copyedit Manuscript																				■	
11	Prepare Back Matter																		■			
12	Prepare Cover Copy																				■	
13	Prepare Turnover																					■
14	Proof Galleys																					■

specified otherwise, "FS" is the default.) To find the start of Task 3, you locate the finish of its predecessor, Task 2. Drop down a line and start your next bar. The duration of this task is two days, so your bar is two days long.

On the task table, you'll note that both Tasks 4 and 6 are dependent upon Task 3. If two tasks have the same predecessor, they start at the same place on the chart. Find the end of Task 3 and go down to the Task 4 and 6 lines, respectively. Task 4 has a duration of two days, and Task 6 has a duration of fifteen days.

Now, back to Task 5. It's dependent on Task 4, so you place the start at the end of Task 4 and draw a line to cover five days of duration.

Here's the potentially tricky part. Task 7 "Write First Draft" is dependent on two predecessors, Tasks 5 and 6. Worse, those two predecessors end at different times (Task 5 ends on Day 19 and Task 6 ends on Day 27). Logically, if Task 7 can't begin until both are done, finishing Task 5 on Day 19 doesn't mean you can start Task 7. It has to wait until Day 27, when the other predecessor is done, so it can start.

If a task has multiple predecessors, it can't begin until the latest finish of all its predecessors. Now you're ready to finish the Gantt Chart on your own. Complete the remaining lines on the task table, then check your work by looking at Figure 18-3.

▲ **FIGURE 18-3:** *A completed Gantt Chart.* **This chart provides a graphic display of all tasks in the project in a calendar format, showing when each job is to be performed.**

What If Your Plan Requires More Time Than You Have?

Now that you have a Gantt Chart, what good is it? How does it help you manage your project? In a first-draft Gantt Chart, you may discover that your finish comes later than your deadline.

Do we have a problem? Not yet. This is a first draft Gantt Chart, not a final. Now that we know we have to save time, we can look for ways to shorten this schedule.

Techniques for Shortening a Project's Duration

There are numerous ways to shorten a project schedule. Not every technique will work for your personal project situation, so plan on looking at all the tools to find out which ones will.

If you've got a firm deadline, plan your project to end early, giving you a safety margin for things that go wrong.

Shorten Individual Critical Path Task Times

The most obvious way to compress your schedule is to alter the estimates for individual tasks. It's only helpful to do this on the critical path, because if you shorten a noncritical task, all you get is more slack/float. Of course, you can't change an estimate unless you have a legitimate reason to justify it. Consider these possibilities:

1. *Add resources to tasks.* If you add resources (people, equipment, money) to a task, it can shorten the expected duration. First, make sure you have the resources available when you need them. Second, you usually need a plan for how you will use the extra resources—if you don't plan, extra resources don't necessarily speed things up. They can even make things worse! Third, not every task can be sped up even with extra resources, so you can't do this anywhere you like.
2. *Change task scope.* Another way to make a task take less time is to do less work. Are there luxuries or nonessentials that can be cut or scaled back if time is tight? Are there elements that can be added to the final product at a later stage, when more resources and time may be available?

3. *Finish late.* Time is not always the driver of your project. Resources and performance may be more important. If that's the case, perhaps you can simply plan on a later finish.

Alter Dependency Relationships

When dependency relationships change, always check to see if the critical path has changed. If we make the change, will we simply make a new critical path? If so, we may not necessarily end up any better off than before.

Realize that changing dependency relationships may alter the way tasks are done, forcing you to alter your estimates. Again, until we do the arithmetic, we can't be sure if that cancels out the advantages.

Realize that not all dependency relationships can be changed. We know we can't pour the concrete for our swimming pool until the hole has been dug, no matter how convenient that might be. Make sure you can develop a strategy for getting the work done within the proposed change.

> When dependency relationships change, always check to see if the critical path has changed.

Use Dependency Types Other Than Finish-to-Start (FS)

So far, we've used FS dependencies throughout the project, but that's not necessarily the best way to go. Maybe a Start-to-Start (SS) dependency with a lag of, say, 50 percent would work.

To create this dependency in Microsoft Project, we changed the predecessor to read "3SS+50%." The first number is the Task ID of the predecessor. The letters SS give the dependency type (Start-to-Start). If you want lead time (move right on the chart), type a plus sign; if you want lag time (move left on the chart), type a minus sign. You can specify the amount of lead or lag either as a percentage (50 percent), or as duration (17w). The difference is that if the predecessor task is early or late, the start of the successor will move to remain at 50 percent, but if you use "17w" instead, the task will always start seventeen weeks into the predecessor, regardless of its length. Use whichever one fits your situation best. While this is specifically for Microsoft Project, you'll find that other project management software packages operate in a similar manner.

Assigning Resources to Tasks

Another aspect of project planning we haven't looked at yet is assignment of resources. How many team members do we need to get the work done? How do we assign them? The Gantt Chart is a good tool for this purpose. The team for project "Tiger Dojo" is probably pretty large, so let's take a look at another project to see how you do this important work (see Figure 18-4).

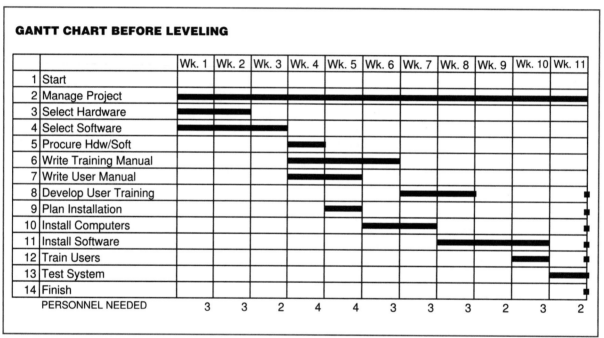

GANTT CHART BEFORE LEVELING

		Wk. 1	Wk. 2	Wk. 3	Wk. 4	Wk. 5	Wk. 6	Wk. 7	Wk. 8	Wk. 9	Wk. 10	Wk. 11
1	Start											
2	Manage Project											
3	Select Hardware											
4	Select Software											
5	Procure Hdw/Soft											
6	Write Training Manual											
7	Write User Manual											
8	Develop User Training											
9	Plan Installation											
10	Install Computers											
11	Install Software											
12	Train Users											
13	Test System											
14	Finish											
	PERSONNEL NEEDED	3	3	2	4	4	3	3	3	2	3	2

▲ Figure 18-4: Note that staff needed ranges from two to four people, with three most commonly needed. By leveling the project, we reduce the need for peak staff by shifting work into periods where there are more resources.

Here, a marketing company is trying to automate its call center. (There's a hint in the project plan that suggests we're on a tight schedule. Can you figure out what it is? Task 12 "Train Users" starts one week before the end of Task 11 "Install Software." In other words, instead of waiting for all the computers to be fully operational, we're getting one or two workstations up to speed and doing training while the remaining software installation is taking place. If we weren't under time pressure, we'd probably wait until all the software is installed.) The boss asks us how many people we need to do the project. If you assume (for convenience's sake only)

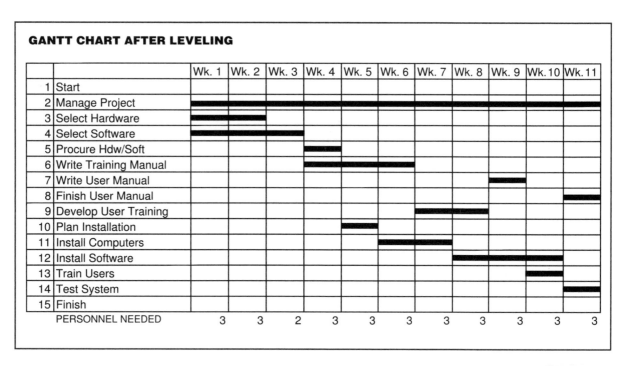

GANTT CHART AFTER LEVELING

		Wk. 1	Wk. 2	Wk. 3	Wk. 4	Wk. 5	Wk. 6	Wk. 7	Wk. 8	Wk. 9	Wk. 10	Wk. 11
1	Start											
2	Manage Project	████	████	████	████	████	████	████	████	████	████	████
3	Select Hardware	████	████									
4	Select Software	████	████	████								
5	Procure Hdw/Soft				████							
6	Write Training Manual				████	████	████					
7	Write User Manual									████		
8	Finish User Manual											████
9	Develop User Training							████	████			
10	Plan Installation					████						
11	Install Computers						████	████				
12	Install Software								████	████		
13	Train Users										████	
14	Test System											████
15	Finish											
	PERSONNEL NEEDED	3	3	2	3	3	3	3	3	3	3	3

that each task takes one person working full time, how many people would you need?

Determining Team Size

Look at the first week of the project. You'll see three tasks going on in that week (Tasks 2, 3, and 4). If each task takes a full-time person (our assumption), then we need three team members for that week. The same is true for Week 2. Week 3, on the other hand, only needs two team members. Weeks 4 and 5 need four team members, and so forth. So the team size needed to run the project fluctuates between two and four people. How many do you need?

You could ask for four, but you're unlikely to get them. After all, you only need the fourth person for a single two-week period (Weeks 4 and 5). The person would be unnecessary the rest of the time. While having a little extra margin is good for project managers, that's excessive. A team size of three people sounds about right (see Figure 18-5).

▲ FIGURE 18-5: In this leveled Gantt chart, we have taken "Write User Manual" and moved it to the end of "Develop User Training." We split it into two segments (Tasks 7 and 8) to avoid creating a 4-person problem in week 10 of the project. The new schedule needs no more than three staff at any time.

Unfortunately, that leaves us with two problems: What about the weeks when we have three people but need two? And what about the weeks when we have three people but need four? We'll take the easier problem first.

Managing Excess Resources

We only need two people in Weeks 3, 9, and 11 of our project. As a project manager, you may decide to keep these excess resource weeks unscheduled. If you have a problem or delay, you've got three person-weeks of staff to throw at them. If you don't have a problem, then you'll have to find something else useful for them to do, but that's usually fairly easy. Don't feel you have to preschedule every resource for every minute of your project.

In a multiple project environment, technical specialists often do the same work for first one project, then the next. Sometimes, it may appear as if you have excess resources in your schedule, but if that excess resource time is already scheduled on another project, it's already gone. You can't spend it twice.

> Resource leveling is a process of adjusting a schedule based on resource constraints.

How to Level a Project Gantt Chart

In the two weeks where you need four people but you only have three, there are two basic categories of solutions. The first is to get some temporary resources to cover the overload. These can include overtime, borrowing a specialist for a brief period, contracting out, or any one of a number of techniques.

The second technique is to shift the schedule around to eliminate the overload. This is called "leveling" your project. Resource leveling is a process of adjusting a schedule based on resource constraints, such as maximum number of people who can be working at any one time.

To the extent that it's possible to move your overload into periods where you have excess resources, you can "level within slack," which has the effect of eliminating the excess resource loading without extending your deadline. If you can't accommodate all the overload into your slack, then you either have to accept a later project deadline or get temporary resources. Let's see how we could level this project.

Week 4 is the first time in our project we encounter a problem. There are four tasks in that period: Task 2 "Manage Project," Task 5 "Procure Equipment," Task 6 "Write Training Manual," and Task 8 "Develop User Training." For now, let's assume there are no other resources available, and the project manager can't take on another task.

You can't shift out either Task 2 or Task 5 because they are critical. Moving them immediately pushes out the deadline. Instead, look at the two noncritical tasks, Task 6 and Task 8. Instead of doing them in parallel, we could choose to make Task 8 dependent on Task 6. That would shift the overload out of both our problem weeks. Unfortunately, it moves the overload into Weeks 7 and 8 instead. The problem is not solved.

It's not unusual for a leveling problem to take more than one step. Looking at Weeks 7 and 8, we decide this time that we'll make Task 7 "Write User Manual" dependent on Task 8 "Develop User Training." This moves Task 7 into Weeks 9 and 10, and actually helps us. Week 9 only had two tasks in it, so we have a person available. Alas, in Week 10 we're back to the overload problem.

To get around this, let's try something new. Instead of planning to write the user manual as a single start-to-finish activity, we're going to split it into two segments, each a week long. The first week remains in Week 9, where it's safe. We make "Finish User Manual" dependent on "Train Users," and now we've moved the second half of the work into Week 11 in our project, where we had only two tasks! We've solved the resource overload problem and the deadline remains the same.

Resolving Resource Conflicts

Now, we've got a three-person project team, consisting of Larry, Moe, and Curly. Moe, of course, is the project manager, so we assign him to Task 2. Larry and Curly have to divide up the remaining tasks.

Let's put Larry on Task 2 and Curly on Task 3. When Larry finishes Task 2, notice that we have a problem. There is no new task starting at that time. This makes Larry a slack resource for the third

Working Project Manager

On small to mid-size projects, you're often expected to be a "working project manager," doing task work on the project you also manage. Even if you're a full-time project manager (not expected to do other work), you still have to account for the cost of project management—your time—on the project.

In this example, we're listing "Manage Project" as a task, which is one of the ways to provide this accounting. Notice that the only thing dependent on "Manage Project" is the finish milestone. That is, no task is waiting for the project manager to finish managing the project. The duration of "Manage Project" will always exactly equal the duration of the project.

week in our project. This isn't necessarily a bad thing. If anything goes wrong with Task 4, Larry is available to help. Larry can also work on nonproject work, or do a task for another project, if the timing works out right. In some cases, Larry can even work on later activities in the project to get a head start.

Curly finishes Task 3. There are two tasks beginning at the end of Task 3: Task 5 "Procure Equipment" and Task 8 "Write Training Manual." And there are three possibilities for Curly:

1. Curly can do either task. If Curly can do either task, assign team members with more specific skills first and assign Curly to what is left.
2. Curly can do one task but not the other. If Curly can only do one of the tasks, then assign Curly the appropriate task and hope you have someone else with the skill set and availability to do the other.
3. Curly can't do either task. If the tasks are highly specialized, an otherwise-useful employee might experience a situation in which he or she is unable to do anything starting in that week. In this case, you've got an extra week of excess resources and a new resource overload problem, which you'll have to resolve by either getting a replacement resource or by leveling the project once again.

Let's go ahead and assign Curly to Task 5 and Larry to Task 6. That makes Curly the technical person and Larry the training expert, so we divide the rest of the tasks accordingly, resulting in the following Gantt Chart.

Preparing a Resource Gantt Chart

It can be very useful in delegating work to team members to provide them with an activity timeline for their own work. Once you've assigned work to team members using your project management software, you can sort all the tasks by who will be performing them, and display the information in the form of a Resource Gantt Chart.

> It can be very useful in delegating work to team members to provide them with an activity timeline for their own work.

Using project management software, you can identify the number of hours each team member has been assigned work, cases in which a team member has been double-booked for the same period, or even the cost of using the resource! All of this information can be extremely useful to you as a project manager and to members of your team. Unfortunately, there is a price: Even though the theory behind some of the functions is pretty straightforward, the practice gets quite complicated when you have multiple staff with multiple skills on multiple projects.

Using project management software, you can identify the number of hours each team member has been assigned work.

For more information on this topic, visit our Web site at www.businesstown.com

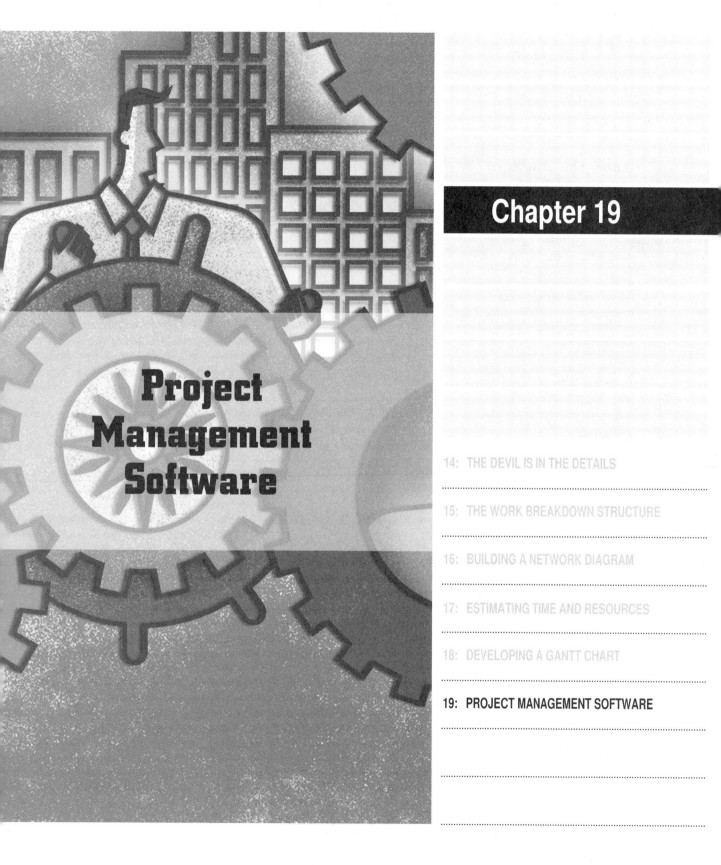

Project Management Software

Chapter 19

The Popularity of Project Management Software

In many ways, the development and wide distribution of project management software has been the triggering event that moved the discipline of project management from an esoteric engineering and construction world into its current wide acceptance. The problem with project management was never particularly the concepts, but rather the implementation, which can become complicated and time-consuming quite rapidly.

The popularity of project management software has not been an unmixed blessing, however. First, confusion of project management software with project management has led in some cases to a blizzard of paper accompanied by little or no actual understanding. People thrown into project management with only a software tool and no training tended to find themselves in over their heads quite rapidly. And a "one-size-fits-all" approach to projects within an organization has led to the imposition of hugely complex and overpowering formal structures to manage projects we could organize on the back of envelopes.

A Tool, Not a Solution

In some ways, it's a misnomer to describe these software tools as "project management" software because they don't perform project management. You do. Software automates certain tools of project management. That's definitely a convenience, but make sure you keep the software in proper perspective. It's a tool, not a solution.

First, you need to decide if you have a situation that requires use of project management software at all. Second, you need to determine what you want the software to do for you. And third, you must make sure you understand enough about project management for the tool to be of use for you.

The more you know about project management and its tools, the more software can do for you. But always remember to buy a clue first . . . and software afterward.

Benefits of Project Management Software

In spite of these cautions, project management software can be highly useful and a great timesaver. As the quality and power of the software tools have improved, the number of project managers who can benefit from them has greatly expanded.

Depending on your project and your needs, here are some of the advantages and benefits you can gain from use of the right software tools:

- Quick and accurate production of Gantt Charts and Network Diagrams
- Automatic calculation of the critical path
- Ability to track resource assignments and report on resource utilization
- Easy maintenance of multiple iterations of the plan
- Ability to track actual performance against plan and forecast the likely course of the remaining project based on actuals
- Performance of Earned Value Method calculations
- Project budgeting and cost baselining for time-dependent variable costs
- Ability to create and build templates for common project types
- Ability to distribute information electronically, including Web-based Internet/Intranet shared access
- Ability to integrate timesheet information into project status
- Organize project financial data for cost accounting
- Tracking and management of resources across multiple projects (For the facts on this extremely important area of project management, see my book *The Juggler's Guide to Managing Multiple Projects*, Newtown Square, Pennsylvania: Project Management Institute, 1999.)
- . . . and much more.

Just because a function is available in the software, it doesn't mean that it's a function you should use in your project. Remember that it takes time and effort to input project data. Focus on the value you can get as a project manager to determine what parts are right for you.

Buy the Least Powerful Software

Theoretically, there's no reason you can't drive carpet tacks with a sledgehammer. But when the tool is selected out of proportion to the problem, it becomes harder to use and may make things worse. Because of the learning curve and the costs of complexity, you're likely better off buying the least powerful project management software that will meet your current needs, and upgrading to more powerful software when—and if—your needs mature.

Don't Drive Carpet Tacks with a Sledgehammer

In the case of the man who wanted to swap Microsoft Project for Primavera to manage projects more suitable to graph paper, we find an important caution about proper scale. Because projects come in a wide range of sizes, from building the International Space Station to organizing a company picnic, tools come in a variety of grades of complexity and power. There's a right audience for each tool, but you need to focus on the tool that's right for you.

People often buy more computer than they need at any given moment because they realize there's a good chance their needs will increase, and the extra power isn't all that expensive. However, what may be arguably appropriate for computer hardware doesn't necessarily apply to computer software.

Buy at the bottom edge of what you need, not the top. With project management software, extra power requires extra complexity and a greater array of options. Often, handling a simple project in software designed for complex ones becomes far more difficult.

Limits and Dangers in Project Management Software

The limitation in project management software is that it doesn't do project management. The danger in project management software isn't in the software, but in the mindset of the user.

When you understand what project management software is capable of doing, and partner that with a strong understanding of the tools, techniques, knowledge, and skills of project management, there is no danger. The appropriate use of project management software is clearly positive.

A general difficulty that even experienced users sometimes find is that the ease with which you can understand how to do something isn't necessarily matched by the ease with which you can actually do it. An example is resource leveling across multiple projects. You learned the theory in the previous chapter, and it's not that difficult.

In practice, however, trying to allocate fifteen or twenty people across fifty or sixty projects can eat up an unbelievable amount of time!

Information costs money. While in a perfect world, you'd manage your projects with perfect information, you can't always afford it. The bigger the project, the easier it becomes to justify the costs of putting the resources into formal project management methodology. In small projects (especially multiple small projects, which is disproportionately difficult), you must make tradeoffs, and if you can't afford the information, then you have to live without it. Software won't solve all those problems.

The Three Levels of Project Management Software

In rough terms, there are three major power grades of project management software. These aren't quality grades—there's good software in each category—but rather measurements of the size and complexity of the projects they can handle, and the number of reports, functions, and charting options they provide to you. There are numerous choices in each category, and there are people who are right for each niche as well.

For management of mammoth projects, programs such as Primavera give the project manager the fullest range of expert tools for the job. For smaller projects, a complete Primavera installation is disproportionately large (though a PC version is available as well as the traditional mainframe/network version).

Microsoft Project is currently the most popular tool, and it's a representative of the middle power grade. Running on a personal computer, programs in this category offer both Gantt Chart and Network Diagram options, schedule and track resources, and offer a variety of reports.

At the low power end, there are programs that provide basic Gantt Chart functions and not much more, but there are a number of people who don't need to use or plan to use anything more than a Gantt Chart. There's no particular value in spending money for a bunch of functions you have no intention to use. You can always change your mind if you change your needs.

Factors to Consider in Project Management Software

Before shopping for software, analyze your situation and your expected needs first. You want to consider the following factors:

- How large are the projects you manage (numbers of team members, dollars, tasks, etc.)?
- What gaps and problems in project management do you currently face (resource juggling, keeping on schedule, communicating project status to team members and stakeholders, etc.)?
- What types of reports, charts, or data do you believe would help you better manage your projects (Gantt Charts, WBS, Network Diagrams, Resource Utilization)?
- What types of reports, charts, or data do your managers, customers, and stakeholders expect or want you to provide them (make sure your software can deliver)?
- How good are your technical skills in project management? (The more you know how to work the tools you need, the easier you'll find the software to learn and use.)

When project management software first became commercially common, the first users, obviously enough, were people who had been doing it by hand for a long time. Because they knew what the software was supposed to do, they found the initial learning curve to be fairly easy to master. Now, more and more people are encountering project management software before they have gained an understanding of project management itself.

Project management software, in the right hands, can speed up a lot of the mechanics of project management. It's still the case that the software works best for people who best understand project management. Work on those skills first, and the rest will follow.

How to Choose the Package That's Right for You

Project management software, like most commercial software categories, changes so quickly that any recommendations made here would likely become obsolete in short order. In addition, individual situations are so varied that you need to do your own research to find the best personal choice.

Most major computer magazines run periodic reviews of available project management software with checklists to help you select what is most likely to meet your needs. Check your local library.

The most thorough and comprehensive information source comes from the Project Management Institute. *The PMI Project Management Software Survey* offers an efficient way to compare and contrast the capabilities of a wide variety of project management tools. The reference has comprehensive information on system features, what they do, and how they handle multiple projects, project tracking, charting, and much more. The survey is a valuable tool to help narrow the field when selecting the best project management tools. It's available in printed form and on CD-ROM.

PART V

Risk, Quality, and Other Planning Concerns

- **What the nine knowledge areas of project management are and what they mean for your project**

- **How to develop and apply a comprehensive risk management plan**

- **How to develop a systematic plan to ensure your project achieves your quality objectives**

- **How to develop a comprehensive budget for your project using activity-based costing methods**

- **How to manage uncertainty on your project using the PERT tools and techniques**

- **How to perform schedule analysis using the CPM tools and techniques**

The Nine Knowledge Areas of Project Management

Organization Structure

So far, we've looked at project management from the perspective of the project life cycle, from initiation through to closeout of the project. There is another vision of project management, described in this chapter, that slices through the work sideways. It's a good tool to expand your understanding and insight into project management.

Project management as a discipline can be broken down into component processes, or knowledge areas. This particular organization structure comes from one of the fundamental standards in the project management business, the Project Management Institute's *A Guide to the Project Management Body of Knowledge.* (In the profession, it's generally referred to as the PMBOK, pronounced "Pimm-bock." Say it that way, and people will think you're really in the know.)

Later, when we talk more about project management as a profession, we'll learn about a certification available for project managers, the "PMP," or "Project Management Professional." To earn a PMP, you must (among other requirements) pass a test on the PMBOK.

Aside from potential certification issues, there are other reasons to be familiar with the PMBOK and its role in project management. For one thing, you'll find many project managers and many organizations use the PMBOK as a common language and a common framework to help us work together more effectively. For another, the PMBOK provides a comprehensive picture of project management in all its variations—you may not need it all, but it's nice to know it's there in an organized form.

The nine knowledge areas that describe the project management body of knowledge are:

- Project integration management
- Project scope management
- Project time management
- Project cost management
- Project quality management
- Project human resource management
- Project communications management
- Project risk management
- Project procurement management

> Project management as a discipline can be broken down into component processes, or knowledge areas.

Project Integration Management

As we've learned, the way to manage a project is first to break it into tasks. Often, different people take their tasks and go off in a corner to complete them. Different stakeholders focus on the aspects of the project that most concern them. At some point, however, all these disparate pieces have to be assembled into a whole. How can we be sure the work is done in a compatible manner?

In this sense, being a project manager is at least a little like conducting a symphony orchestra. The pieces of your project won't automatically blend together, and it's therefore one of your responsibilities to make sure that they do.

The process of project integration management is about making sure that the various elements of the project are properly coordinated. You do this through developing the plan, through your role in executing the plan, and through the process of making sure that changes to the project during execution get coordinated across the entire project.

In addition to making sure that the pieces of the project fit together, the project manager is often responsible for making sure that the project work is integrated with the ongoing operations of the company. Finally, project integration management involves making sure that the process of doing the project work coordinates with the actual product to be delivered.

Integration Management in Plan Development

We've focused our discussion of planning so far on the mechanical processes. The goal of planning, of course, is to develop a document that will govern the process of achieving the project goal. In evaluating the quality of your plan, look at how the steps flow together. Where will people on one task need to coordinate with people on another task, or even people outside the formal project structure, in order to get the information or input necessary to complete their task in a way that supports the overall goal? Where does the task definition have to be carefully monitored so that people do their work in a way that will fit together in the final product? Where does the project's goal put additional constraints on the way some tasks will be managed?

> The project manager is often responsible for making sure that the project work is integrated with the ongoing operations of the company.

Integration Management During Project Execution

Considering integration management during the planning phase is important, but managing this process during the project execution phase is also a key to ensuring a satisfactory project outcome. Here, the project manager exercises the range of more general management skills, including organization, supervision, negotiation, and the like, in support of achieving project goals.

Two additional tools in this phase are work authorization and status review. Work authorization is a formal process of approving project work to make sure the work is done at the right time, in the right way, and in the proper sequence. Later, we'll show you a control system to aid you in this process. Status reviews, either through meetings or reports, are how you obtain and verify more detailed information about project status.

Integration Management of Project Changes

As we've observed (and as you've no doubt noticed if you've managed very many projects), change is a fact of life with most projects. An old project management joke has it that your project is in trouble when the rate of change begins to exceed the rate of progress. Frequently, you don't have the power to avoid project changes. Instead, focus on developing your ability to manage project changes.

The first thing you can do is see which project changes can be predicted in advance. If you're working for a customer who always changes his or her mind about the layout of the book, you can wait until the review stage and then modify your project plan, or you can design the plan to provide a rework task following the customer review milestone. If it happens all the time, put it in your plan instead of letting it become a project change.

The second vital part of change management is to establish a process for project changes. The minimum ingredients in a change control process include a provision that all changes be in writing, that the impact of the change is assessed before the change is approved or rejected, and that the authority to make changes in the project is clearly set forth. As the project manager, you don't necessarily need to be the one approving each change, but you definitely

> Two additional tools in this phase are work authorization and status review.

want to see a proposed change early enough to analyze its impact, and you want it clear who can order a change and who cannot.

The third vital part of change management is ensuring that a change is fully integrated into the project and the product. Often a change in this area will force modification of other areas of the project. Someone–this means *you*–has to take responsibility for tracing the change throughout the project and ensuring all necessary adjustments get made.

Project Scope Management

You know how important scope management is for the project from our previous work. Does the project include all the work necessary to complete it? Have we excluded the work that is properly *not* part of the project? Are the major stakeholders aware what's in the project and what is not? Is there agreement on this issue? How will we handle proposed or necessary changes to scope during the project life cycle? These are important questions for the project manager, and make up the knowledge area known as project scope management.

Take Control During Initiation

Your first and most important opportunity to get control of scope management issues is during the project Initiating phase, where the initial decisions and authorizations take place. As you remember, it's good practice to develop a written Scope Statement to establish a clear and correct understanding of scope at the outset. Through the WBS, you define scope in detail as a set of project deliverables. In the Executing phase of your project, you verify that the project scope is completed and accepted, and manage and control changes to project scope.

Project Scope and Product Scope

There is a difference between project scope and product scope, even though they coexist in achieving the project goal. Product scope consists of features and functions that define a product or

Overlapping

You can probably see how scope management tends to overlap integration management, and that's no accident. The project management processes don't work independently of one another; they merge with each other to form a coherent overall strategy for project management. By separating them, we can see more deeply what each involves, but operationally, you'll find it less clear exactly which knowledge area you're working in.

Projects Within a Product

Besides writing, editing, and design, there are other projects needed to complete the product of this finished book. Usually, a production manager or print buyer is a type of "customer" of our project, because our output (manuscript, files on disk, illustrations, etc.) is the input for the next part of the project. To the printer, the project starts with the completed package and ends with books in boxes being loaded on trucks. To the trucking company, the project begins with boxes on one loading dock and ends with boxes on another loading dock. Then the distributor has a project and the retailer has a project . . . and then you have a project of learning what you need to know about project management! There can be many projects in producing a single product.

service. Project scope, on the other hand, consists of the work that must be done to deliver that product.

In the project *Streetwise Project Management*, the product is what you're holding in your hands. The product scope consists of such elements as a certain number of words and pages, diagrams and illustrations, case studies and examples, and format-specific elements such as boxed text, a glossary of terms, and a bibliography. Some of these were specified in the contract, others in documents such as writer's guidelines. These documents serve the purpose of a Project Charter and Scope Statement.

The project scope consists of the work necessary to complete the product. The project scope was defined in the WBS (Figures 5-1 and 5-2) and Network Diagram (Figure 5-4). While everyone is working together to get the product out, the work of the project is assigned to different people. The writing tends to take place independently of the editing and the graphic design, for example.

Sometimes, important ingredients of product scope are completely independent of project scope. The printing of the book is clearly part of product scope—otherwise, you're holding nothing at all in your hands! Yet as far as the project team is concerned, the book is out of our hands when it goes to the printer, except for such review functions as proofing page galleys.

Project Time Management

There is a sense in which project management can be considered an "upscaled" version of time management. Although time is only one of the Triple Constraints and is not necessarily the driver of your project, it's frequently the case that time does matter.

When time is the driver, remember the traditional definition of a deadline: a line across which something—or someone—dies. When you hear that definition, you usually know they're talking about you.

When time isn't the driver—even if it's the weak constraint—it's never safe to ignore time issues on a project. The passage of time normally affects the expenditure of money, because people get paid. Many people are surprised when they read about a project that was not only ahead of schedule, but also under budget, or about a project that was not only late, but also over budget. Neither should be a surprise. Because people get paid, a late project normally results in increased expenditures. On an early project, people are released early to get on with other work, and fewer staff dollars get consumed.

Time and the Schedule

You manage time on the project in the process of developing the schedule. The first step in the process is defining the activities that have to be performed. Each activity requires a certain amount of time and must obey any requirements of sequence. If one task must follow another, the total duration of your project will be greater than if the two tasks can proceed at the same time. You often have choices to make as you do this, and although time is not and should not be the only factor on which your choice is based, you will normally at least consider the impact of decisions on deadlines.

Problems and Issues in Estimating Duration

How long will each activity take? This important estimating question makes you look at a variety of time-related issues, since there's normally a range of potential outcomes. Will you have one person working on this task, or several? Are people experienced in doing this work (learning curve advantage) or brand-new? Is doing it fast and "good enough" the preferred method, or will the customer be more satisfied with the product if we take more time to do it thoroughly? These are value-driven decisions with significant impact on your project results.

What could go wrong in these activities that might make the project take longer to complete? Should you consider allowing extra time in a task definition to deal with something that might go wrong, or are you better off putting extra resources on the task?

Are you dependent on outside forces for time control? If you're ordering parts, the supplier isn't normally part of your project, but if the supplier is late, then all activities that depend on the parts arriving are at risk.

Aside from the main project deadline, are there interim deadlines you must meet? These are normally indicated on the project as milestones. At each milestone, you may have to have some activities

> Will you have one person working on this task, or several?

complete. Even if the overall project looks like it will meet its deadline, missing a milestone often has consequences of its own.

How solid are your time estimates? If you say an activity will take two weeks, do you mean that it will take ten days of duration (two work-weeks), that it will be done on the fourteenth calendar day from today, or do you mean two weeks plus-or-minus a few days either way? (When other people give you time estimates, be aware they may be looking at the estimate through any of these perspectives.) You may not be able to make a firm estimate for activities that are experimental or new—how long will it take you to come up with a new concept, for example? Often, a range or even a WAG is the best you can do. (There are various project management techniques for this kind of uncertainty, which we'll address in Part VI of this book.)

Controlling Schedule Performance in Project Execution

Of course, no matter how good your scheduling and estimating skills, you must still manage and control schedule and time during project execution in order to achieve the deadline.

Measure project performance by tracking the baseline schedule. How are your actual results comparing to what you originally planned? Is there slippage? Is the slippage on the critical path, or is it on activities that have slack or float? If it's the latter, the slippage doesn't actually threaten the final deadline (at least until the slippage exceeds the amount of slack or float that was available), although it may affect resources, budgets, or achievement of milestones.

Perhaps the slippage isn't currently significant but suggests a trend. If, say, the first tasks are showing a consistent variance of 10 percent over schedule, you might check to see if there is an underlying reason for all the slippage. If the trend is likely to continue, then you might want to take the opportunity to act early.

If you have significant slippage, what can you do? Your risk management plan and other work done in the planning phase may point the way to a solution. Otherwise, look at later tasks on the critical path that might be shortened, look at work that might not need to be done, or look for additional resources you might use to get the work done faster.

> Measure project performance by tracking the baseline schedule.

Change Control in Project Execution

Change control on projects is a scheduling issue, too. If there is a change to project scope, there may now be more work to be done, but the original deadline may still be vital. How will you achieve more work in the same amount of time? Will you spend money or resources or modify some of the other work on the project?

On the other hand, is there flexibility in the deadline? Are the consequences of going over budget or failing to get the work done to a certain performance level worse than the penalty for exceeding the deadline? Is negotiation an option?

Project Cost Management

How much will it cost to complete this project, considering money, resources, materials, and tools and equipment? Is the amount within the approved budget for the project, or are you starting with funds and resources insufficient to do the job the way you would like to do it? How and where will funds be allocated to do the work? How is our actual performance comparing with the planned budget, and what will we do if it is not? How will proposed changes to the project affect the costs associated with it? These issues are part of the area of project cost management.

Financial Issues Outside of Cost Management

Not all financial issues surrounding the project are part of the project's cost management. In the *Streetwise® Project Management* and "Tiger Dojo" projects, there are income considerations as well as cost considerations. For both projects, the project manager is accountable for how much is spent in developing the products.

We've already noted that the printing, warehousing, and shipping costs get allocated to other budgets. However, the amount of money available to do these projects is obviously affected by the revenue projections. How many copies can be sold? What retail price will be charged? These decisions are normally not made within the project, but influence the cost picture of the project. Therefore, even if making them is not your job, knowing about them most certainly is.

> How and where will funds be allocated to do the work?

While it might seem logical that costs and price are related, that's not necessarily the case. The price is what someone is willing to pay you, which is related to the value they perceive. Some products and services get sold for many times their cost, because they are extremely valuable to the people who buy them. Other products and services don't get offered in the marketplace at all because the price someone is willing to pay is less than the cost of providing the product or service.

Cost Competition among Project Phases

Printing, warehousing, and shipping are costs associated with the product that aren't part of the project we're managing. However, they are part of many other projects. Money for these costs comes from the same source as your money: the projected revenue for the book or game. More money for your part of the project means less money for these other necessary activities. The expected result is a certain degree of competition for available funds, which is resolved normally at a higher level of management. The reason you don't get some extra money when you ask is that the rest of the money pool has already been allocated. If management decides to give you extra money, then something else gets less.

It doesn't always have to be a zero-sum game, however. If the desired change for which you want some more money means that more copies will be sold, you may be increasing the money pool, making it easier to justify why you should get more of it. That's why even if you're not at the executive level, you need to hone your skills at seeing the Big Picture. It makes you stronger.

Project Quality Management

The difference between the performance criteria and quality is simple: Performance is what you do; quality is what the customer wants or needs. Quality on a project is not an accident, it must be planned and managed in order to be achieved.

The processes for project quality management involve three areas: (1) planning, to determine what the quality objectives need to be and how they will be achieved; (2) quality assurance, to measure

> More money for your part of the project means less money for these other necessary activities.

what the project is producing against a standard; and (3) quality control, to ensure that quality standards are met and fix the situation (with emphasis on underlying causes) when they are not.

As with scope, quality applies both to the project and to the product. The product portion is fairly clear—the customer has certain needs and objectives that need to be met. If in meeting the customer's needs we damage our ability to do the work—burning out staff, using up capital resources, or overspending—then our ability to do future projects is harmed.

While a discussion of quality has been an ongoing subject in this book, Chapter 22 is completely devoted to this process.

Project Human Resource Management

Unless your project is quite large and takes place over a long period of time, you might not think of human resource management as an area specific to project management. But think for a moment of all the people who are connected in some way with your project. Here are some potential categories.

Organizational Planning

Even if a formal organizational chart is inappropriate for your project, it may be worth thinking through the question of who does what. In addition to people who do the project work, there are often people who review and approve the project output, or who must be consulted in its development. They are every bit as much a part of the project team as the official members, because without them, you can't get the project done.

As one example, let's say that the legal department has to review and sign off on the material you develop. Although they are normally outside your official range of control as a project manager, their performance affects yours. How long will it take them to complete the review? What is the likelihood of change requests? How serious will it be if they do ask for changes or reject the work? Who specifically in the legal department will do the review? What else is on that person's plate, and is there anything you can do to ensure that your needs take priority? If they can't (or won't) do the review

---

Who's on the Project Team?

- The project manager
- Members of the project team
- The customer and the customer's team members
- The project sponsor
- Managers and team members of other projects related to the same product
- Consultants, vendor team members, and other non-core contributors to the project
- Project managers and team members of other projects with whom you share resources
- The project sponsor and other senior managers of your organization with an interest in your project
- Functional managers from whom you borrow resources or who do work in support of your project

in the time you need, what kind of influence can you exert (from asking nicely to calling in senior management's help)? Will early notification help speed your work through the system? How about pre-reviews to identify potential sticking points while there's still a chance to change them? All these questions need to be considered in your planning process.

Staff Acquisition

Although a common lament among project managers is that they don't get to choose their own teams, you may be able to influence the process somewhat. Who do you want, and will asking early help? Who else will be competing for the staff you want and need? If you get people on your team who aren't your first choice, how can you ensure they get the work done?

In the absence of perfect people, you know that when you hire according to someone's strengths, you get their weaknesses as well. If you can't prevent all problems (and you can't), awareness may be the second-best strategy.

In acquiring and assigning staff, it's good to realize that negotiation is a perfectly legitimate tool, especially given the common reality that the project manager is often not the supervisor of significant numbers of team members. Ask for whom you want; negotiate assignments and conditions to get the best people.

Team Development

A project's core staff forms a team. In order to work effectively, teams normally need some team development. Consider involving project members in the planning process to get better buy-in and understanding. Establish ground rules and set clear expectations for team participation—it's surprising how much influence you have when you are clear about what you want even when you don't have supervisory powers over people.

How can you reward people who work effectively and participate actively on your project team? Even when you don't have certain traditional rewards (bonuses, good performance appraisals), you can always make sure you write thank-you notes, praise people to their regular supervisors, make sure credit is fully distributed, and more.

> In the absence of perfect people, you know that when you hire according to someone's strengths, you get their weaknesses as well.

Project Communications Management

Everyday communication is often the lifeblood of projects, and much communication takes place without the necessity of formal process. But there is a lot of project communication that does require a formal process, and that part fits into project communications management.

First, consider the need people have for the project, both members of the team and those whom the project serves—customers, sponsors, and others inside and outside the project organization. Who needs information? What do they need? How often do they need it? What form is best for the information (meetings, memos, or graphics)? What tools will you use (software, e-mail, graph paper, sticky notes)?

The performance measurement part of project management is a communications environment. Progress reports, status meetings, updates of project charts, all are part of communication. And in the wrap-up of your project, measurement and lessons learned on the project just completed are vital tools for long-range improvement.

It's sobering to realize that 90 percent of a project manager's time can quickly be taken up by all these forms of communication. While cutting back on communication can add short-term advantage while creating long-term problems, consider ways to improve the efficiency and reduce the burden on you to keep up with project communication. Distribution lists for standard materials such as project updates, and even a good old-fashioned bulletin board to serve as an unofficial project "war room" are ways that preplanning can reduce the work of communication.

> It's sobering to realize that 90 percent of a project manager's time can quickly be taken up by all these forms of communication.

Project Risk Management

Getting formal about risk management is extremely valuable, and is one of the most powerful and immediate benefits you can get from adopting a project management methodology. Although risks involve uncertainty, there are certain fundamental risk characteristics that allow risks to be analyzed and managed in a logical fashion.

A risk is not a problem—yet. Risks are uncertainties that may or may not occur. If they occur, they will have a positive or negative effect on the project, in the process becoming either a problem or an

Understanding Your Role

Understanding how your role as a project manager involves managing each of these areas throughout the project's lifespan is a good way to keep yourself focused on how elements work together, what ongoing concerns require your attention, and why it's important to have a good plan and a good process.

opportunity. Risks have causes and risks have consequences. You can describe a risk with three components: the event, the probability of the event's occurring, and the impact of the event if it occurs.

The overall study of risks is risk management planning. The steps involved are the identification of risks, the assessment of impact and likelihood, the numerical quantification of impact and likelihood, establishment of appropriate strategies, and then the implementation of those strategies in the execution of the project, all of which are covered in Chapter 21.

Project Procurement Management

In many projects, you must acquire goods and services from outside your own organization. This can be as simple as making a petty cash purchase and as complex as arranging a multibillion-dollar, multiyear contract involving thousands of people in numerous locations. The process of planning for the acquisition of goods and services is therefore an important knowledge area for project managers.

Buying Decisions

"Make or buy" decisions start with the initial planning process. While sometimes it will be very clear even in the earliest project stages whether key items will be procured, other times there is significant project work to analyze in detail where procurement is appropriate. As you identify the areas of your project where acquisition from outside is appropriate, you are starting the process of procurement planning.

From whom will you acquire the goods and services you need? Are there multiple sources? What are the specific requirements and characteristics of the goods and services we need to acquire? This is solicitation planning—getting ready to contract or purchase.

For more information on this topic, visit our Web site at www.businesstown.com

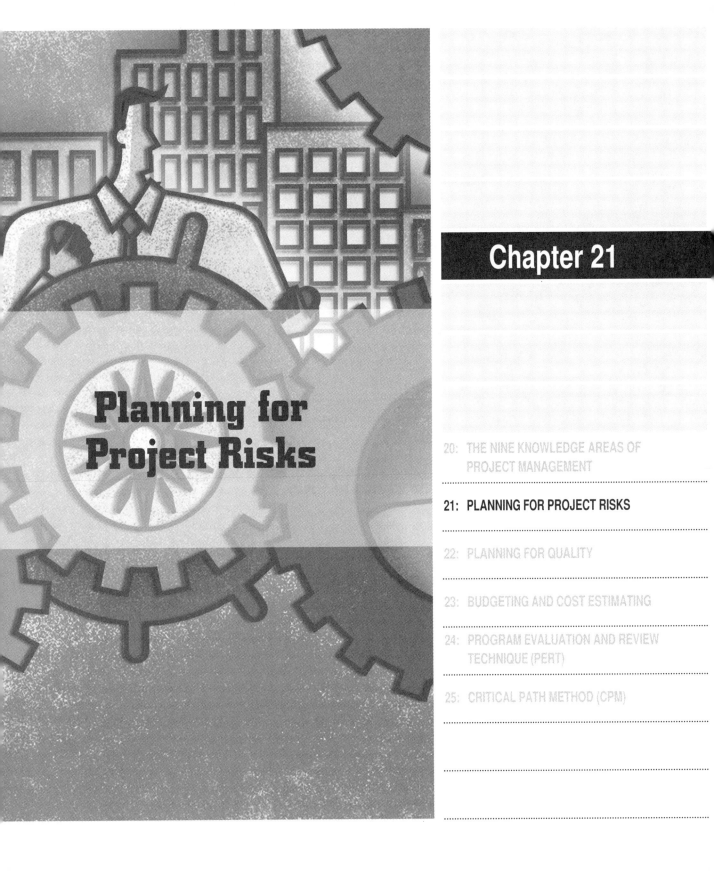

Planning for Project Risks

Chapter 21

Risk Management

Because not everything is ever under your complete control, risk is an unavoidable aspect of project management. Murphy's Law—"Everything that can go wrong, will!"—and its corollary—"Murphy was an optimist."—is cited by many project managers as a fundamental reality of the project world. It's not hard to find reasons to sympathize with that perspective. If you've managed very many projects, you've likely had more than one occasion to feel that way yourself.

The discipline of risk management, which we will cover in this chapter, doesn't pretend that it can provide you with an absolute security blanket. Uncertainty and probability can be tamed to some extent, but almost never completely caged. Still, with our project manager's motto of "Better is better," even a partial solution to the dilemma of risk is better than none.

Risk management is one of those skills that makes the truly excellent project manager stand out. It's worth your while to master this topic.

> The discipline of risk management doesn't pretend that it can provide you with an absolute security blanket.

Categories of Risk

A risk is not a problem. The distinction is at the heart of the Godzilla Principle, which we discussed in Part I. "Risk" is future tense; "problem" is present tense. If you have developed a list of potential risk events for your project, some may occur, others may not. (And a few items not on your risk list may show up like an unexpected dinner guest!)

The basic methodology for risk management is advance preparation. Some potential solutions are possible only if thought of well in advance. You might think of them when the risk turns into a problem, but it's too late. You're O-B-E, "Overtaken By Events." In addition, surprise disasters tend to create stress, if not downright panic, and for most of us, panic doesn't increase our intelligence or judgment. (There are a few people who truly do work best under pressure, but even with them, there's a limit to how much pressure they can handle.)

The Triple Constraints and Risk Management

A risk is not merely an uncertain event. It has a specific type of impact on your project, particularly on the Triple Constraints. The three kinds of risks are those that threaten to delay your project (time risk), threaten to increase your use of money and other resources (cost risk), or threaten to degrade the quality or functionality of the deliverables (performance risk). It can, of course, hit more than one of the three simultaneously. If the risk you're considering won't do any of those things, it's not a risk—it's merely an event.

The potential seriousness of a risk, then, is influenced based on which Triple Constraint(s) it affects. If a risk threatens your driver, it's far more serious than if the risk threatens your weak constraint. If it only threatens the weak constraint, you may decide you have enough flexibility there to soak up the damage, and accordingly choose not to worry about it any further.

The Triple Constraints also suggest a risk response strategy: exploit the weak constraint. If cost is the weak constraint, your first thought for many risks should be, "Can spending money fix this?" If it's time, "Can letting the project finish slip fix this?" And if it's performance, "What can I drop or modify to fix this?"

Business Risk versus Insurance Risk

Another way to divide risks is between business risks and insurance (or "pure") risks. A business risk has the opportunity for gain as well as for loss. A stock market investment is an example of business risk—you can make money or you can lose money. You might think of risks as generally something to avoid, but business risks are sometimes actively chosen for their upside potential.

A pure, or insurance, risk is one that only has the opportunity for loss. If you're running a construction project, there's the chance that a worker will be injured, or that a wall will collapse. Because the outcome is only negative, you want to avoid the risk if feasible. One obvious strategy for managing a pure risk is to buy insurance, which is why it's also known as "insurance risk." You'll need to distinguish between these two types of risk in developing your strategy.

> A business risk has the opportunity for gain as well as loss.

Difference Between Good Luck and Bad Luck

Risk management includes maximizing positive outcomes as well as minimizing negative ones. If you're managing a project that has business risk, you know there are opportunities for gain and for loss. If you can minimize either the chance of loss or the amount of loss, that's good for the project. Similarly, it's worth thinking how you could maximize the chance for gain or the amount of gain.

While pure risk is always negative, there also exists the possibility of good luck and positive opportunity on your project. We frequently don't take the time to walk through our project plan and ask ourselves, "Could we get some good luck on this task, and if so, how?" You might be surprised.

Murphy's Law notwithstanding, we would expect random events to distribute themselves more or less evenly between good luck and bad luck, but that's not our operational experience. We seem to experience negative random events on projects much more commonly than positive ones. What's the reason?

There is a structural difference in the way the two types of luck operate. Bad luck is automatic. If you lose, say, $100, it requires no additional effort on your part to suffer all the consequences of the loss. Good luck, on the other hand, normally requires a deliberate effort on your part to gain its value. If there's $100 lying on the street, you might not notice it's there. If you do notice, you're under no actual obligation to pick it up. You might be suspicious that it's a trick of some sort. It might be raining. You might be in a hurry. And if you do pick up the $100, you might not spend it wisely. You only get the benefit of the $100 as a result of deliberate, conscious action.

That has implications for project management as well. Ignoring the opportunities good luck may provide is wasteful. When analyzing risks, take a little time to consider the upside, too.

Upside and Downside Risk

Imagine that you're offered a stock market investment. Invest $5,000, and within six months, you will either receive $50,000 (70 percent chance) or lose the $5,000 (30 percent chance). Interested? Assuming the facts check out (and we'll assume they do for the purpose of this example), it looks like a pretty good deal.

> While pure risk is always negative, there also exists the possibility of good luck and positive opportunity on your project.

The expected value of this transaction is (.7 x $50,000) + (.3 x =$5,000) = $35,000 + (-$1,500) = $33,500. In other words, if you made this investment over and over again, winning and losing according to the percentages, you would earn an average of $33,500 per transaction.

Does this sound like a "no-brainer"? In surveys, most people will turn this offer down. It could be because they don't know how to do the math. It could be because any deal that looks that good deserves deep suspicion. It could also be because of an essentially emotional reaction to any sort of financial risk. But there's a deeper reason to consider as well.

If you're an experienced investor and you've got at least $5,000 in your portfolio looking for a higher-risk/higher-gain investment, then you'd probably jump at this offer (after, of course, due diligence to make sure it is what it's represented to be). But imagine instead that the $5,000 you'd have to put up is the mortgage and family food budget for next month. Even though that $50,000 looks very attractive, you can't take the risk.

Upside risk and downside risk aren't necessarily proportional even if they're both expressed in units of currency. It's perfectly rational to consider both the consequence of loss as well as the benefits of gain.

Tolerance for Risk

Tolerance for risk is a complicated issue. Personal tolerance for risk is partly a matter of style and emotional preference and partly determined by your circumstances and the effect of gains and losses. While there's nothing inappropriate about emotions, personal circumstances, and style preference playing a role, examine your own biases and tendencies to ensure that your final risk decisions really are those that are best for you.

In your role as project manager, you'll also have to take into account your organization's tolerance for risk, which may be greater or less than your own. Discovering organizational tolerance for risk isn't always easy. Some managers talk a good game of taking risks and seizing opportunities. Unfortunately, when failure happens as a result of risk-taking, they look for the easiest victim to shoot for it.

> Upside risk and downside risk aren't necessarily proportional even if they're both expressed in units of currency.

Other managers urge more caution, but are actually willing to accept intelligent risk-taking in a more positive spirit. Ask about risk tolerance, but also observe actual response to risk events and consequences.

How to Determine Your Project Risks

In Chapter 7, we learned that the steps in an overall risk management strategy consist of:

- *Risk identification.* This is the process of identifying potential risks on the project.
- *Risk quantification.* For the identified risks, assess the probability and the impact to determine which risks are worth action.
- *Risk response planning.* For those risks you decide are worth action, develop potential responses, either with preventive or corrective actions or contingency plans.
- *Risk response control.* In the execution phase of your project, implement the plans that you have developed.

All these steps must be performed throughout the project life cycle because some risks drop in significance and others rear their ugly heads for the first time within the project.

Risk Identification

Not all the risks—even the really big risks—are necessarily obvious from a first glance at the project. It's good practice to make the process of risk identification methodical. Follow the processes described below to help identify risks. It's important to remember that each of these methods has biases and limitations. The more varied techniques you use, the better the result will be.

Document Analysis

Even in fairly early stages of the planning work, you are already amassing a number of documents that will facilitate your risk planning. These include any contractual documents, the Project Charter,

---

Bad Ideas for Managing Risk

- Pad your schedule and budget.
- Pick a scapegoat to blame when things go wrong.
- Learn to grovel and beg for forgiveness.
- Renegotiate the project goals whenever anything goes wrong.
- Don't check for problems so you won't find any.
- Cut training, documentation, and quality assurance.
- Shrug your shoulders and say "Hey, it happens."
- Get transferred to another project before anybody finds out.

Scope Statement/Statement of Work, and any correspondence with the customer. Review them for areas of possible risk.

If you have a formal project management methodology already in place, you should have "lessons learned" files on any similar projects the organization has previously performed. They are a powerful source of realistic risk information.

Depending on the technical area of your project, you might also have systems engineering documentation, life-cycle cost analysis, and industry-specific risk management information from which to draw. It's worth it to do a little digging to discover these resources.

Interviews

Interview your stakeholders on risk issues. Customers, project sponsors, team members, and other affected parties can address the risk identification process from their own points of view. While all risks affect the underlying project, different stakeholders may be more or less affected by the same risk, and as a result can focus on the ones most important to them.

Discussing the risk process with stakeholders not only gives you good information, but also helps prepare stakeholders for the reality that things go wrong on projects. This can benefit you later in the project, since many stakeholders find unpleasant surprises worse than expected potential problems.

In addition, interview project managers who have done similar projects as well as technical experts on the disciplines that are part of your project (especially those that may be outside your own areas of expertise). Also interview sponsors and other senior managers in your own organization to determine issues of risk tolerance and policy implications.

Assumptions Analysis and Brainstorming

In the preparation of your Project Charter, you identified a list of constraints and assumptions. The assumptions—those that you weren't able to resolve into facts—also become risks for your consideration. If the charter assumes you will have people with the necessary technical skills when you need them, there's a risk that maybe they'll all be busy on other work. If the charter assumes that building the

Schedule Meetings

To get your team fully engaged in the risk management process, schedule specific meetings during the Planning and Executing phases to specifically discuss risks and risk management. During the closeout phase, when you're developing your "lessons learned" file, make one of your agenda items a discussion of risks and problems.

game engine involves no new technology, it's possible that you might find that you need new technology to make your vision work.

Part of your risk meeting work should be brainstorming about possible risks. This is a good way to identify global project risks, such as the risk that a key staff member will leave the project. Like with all brainstorming, accept any suggestions uncritically at first and analyze them only after the brainstorming period has passed.

Plan Analysis

The stages of your planning process also have risk implications. Some risks are global—they affect the entire project, or can happen at any time. Others are specific—they appear within a specific task or activity. Analyze your WBS for risk. In each task, what could go wrong? How would it affect the project?

Creating Network Diagrams and managing the scheduling process have risk implications as well. When you make strategic choices about how to set up your Network Diagram, you will find that the different options have different consequences. There are four different values that you consider in laying out your project. Three of them are the Triple Constraints—how this proposed schedule affects time, cost, and performance. The fourth is risk. Different layouts create different amounts and types of risks.

Risks involving tasks along the critical path are made more serious because any delay in one of those tasks immediately delays your project completion. Risks on tasks involving slack may be at least partially mitigated because a certain amount of delay has no discernable project deadline consequences.

Risk Quantification

The process of risk quantification is concerned with measuring the seriousness of the risks you have identified. Not all risks rise to the threshold where a response is necessary. It's just not realistic to mitigate every conceivable risk on a project.

The fundamental formula for risk quantification is: $R = P \times I$.

The quantified value of a risk is equal to the probability (P) of it occurring times the impact (I) if it does occur. This gives you a risk

> Creating Network Diagrams and managing the scheduling process have risk implications as well.

score or risk category so that you can develop an appropriate and proportional response.

If there's a 50 percent chance (based on previous history) that a vendor will be late in shipping a key part, and the resultant delay will cost us $3,000 in extra overtime costs to meet the deadline, the risk score is 50% x $3,000, or $1,500. If paying for "rush" delivery would cost us an extra $500, it's probably a good idea to get the rush delivery.

If there's a machining error of greater than $1/1000$" in our manufacturing process, the final product will fail its quality control test. If there's a 10 percent chance (again, based on our history machining that kind of part) of this occurring, and the cost of a product failure is $15,000, then the risk score is 10% x $15,000, or $1,500. If buying a new lathe that has better reliability costs $5,000, and we don't need it for other work, then it's probably better to accept the risk of product failure.

Of course, that's not an absolute. There could be other consequences of product failure that we can't easily quantify, and if so, we might choose to make the investment in a new lathe anyway. For example, we might feel that our reputation for no-fail quality is important enough to justify the extra expense.

It's valuable to run the numbers in risk quantification, but the numbers aren't an absolute way to determine the risk response decision. It's appropriate to consider other factors in deciding what to do.

Decision Trees

Sometimes, you have a choice between decisions that each contain risk. If we're considering purchasing a new lathe, maybe we have two to choose from. One lathe costs $50,000 and has an error rate of 4 percent. The other lathe costs $60,000 and has an error rate of 3 percent. We make 10,000 widgets a year. Each error costs us $200. Which machine should we buy?

In the decision tree in Figure 21-1, the total cost of the first option is the $50,000 for the lathe plus $80,000 for the cost of errors (4% x 10,000 = 400, at $200 apiece). For the second option, it's $60,000 for the lathe, plus $60,000 for the cost of errors (3% x 10,000 = 300, at $200). The first year total cost for the cheaper lathe

> There could be other consequences of product failure that we can't easily quantify.

is therefore $130,000, and for the more expensive lathe is $120,000. Paying for the more expensive lathe saves us $10,000 in the first year. It's fairly obvious which is the right decision.

$$(\$50{,}000 + ((.04 \times 10{,}000) \times \$200)) = \$130{,}000$$

$$(\$60{,}000 + ((.03 \times 10{,}000) \times \$200)) = \$120{,}000$$

▲ FIGURE 21-1: *Decision tree.* **A decision tree compares alternatives, in this case, a purchase decision between two machines. Here, the machine with the higher initial purchase price is actually less expensive based on its lower defect rate.**

You can consider any number of options in a decision tree, not merely two. Often, however, if the numbers are close, it's not appropriate to make the decision based on numbers alone. For example, how accurate is the percentage failure rate in the above case? If the accuracy is ±1 percent, then the first branch of the decision tree is actually a range between $110,000 and $150,000 (3%–5% failure rate), and the second branch is actually between $100,000 and $140,000 (2%–4% failure rate). They overlap by $30,000. Now, your decision to purchase the more expensive machine isn't necessarily justified on economic grounds alone. Don't give your numbers more credence than they deserve.

Risk Buckets

It's often the case that you have a general idea about probability, but there's no legitimate way for you to assign a firm number. You can rank risks into categories by using a risk impact assessment chart such as the following (see Figure 21-2).

It's often the case that you have a general idea about probability, but there's no legitimate way for you to assign a firm number.

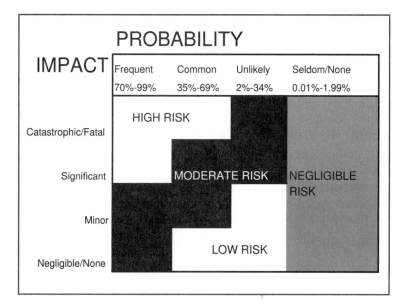

PROBABILITY

IMPACT

	Frequent 70%-99%	Common 35%-69%	Unlikely 2%-34%	Seldom/None 0.01%-1.99%
Catastrophic/Fatal	HIGH RISK			NEGLIGIBLE RISK
Significant		MODERATE RISK		
Minor				
Negligible/None		LOW RISK		

▲ FIGURE 21-2: *Risk categories.* **A sorting technique is a valuable way to quantify risks when precise probability information is unavailable.**

Filtering

Another technique for risk quantification is filtering, in which you use screening questions to sort risks requiring immediate action from those that can wait or safely be ignored. Some sample filtering questions include:

- *Filter 1.* Will the impact of this risk affect the driver or otherwise significantly affect customer perception of the result?
- *Filter 2.* Has this risk happened before? Are there conditions and circumstances that make this risk more likely?
- *Filter 3.* Does this risk require immediate action or can action be taken later?
- *Filter 4.* Does this risk lie inside project scope, or is there someone else who is responsible for it?

> Has the risk happened before?

Comparative Risk Ranking (CRR)

In CRR, the risks are listed, and then each pair of risks is rated by team vote as to which is most significant. In the following example, each risk is compared to every other risk. The team votes which one is the most significant. In the first pair, Risk B is more serious than Risk A. Risk A is more serious than Risk C, and Risk D is more serious than Risk A. Risks A, B, and D each get one point, and Risk C gets none.

In the second round, Risk B gets two points and Risks C and D get none. Risk A is not in this round because all of the risks have already been compared to Risk A. In the third round, we make the remaining comparison, and Risk D wins another point. Summing up the results and ranking them in order, we conclude that Risk B is most serious, followed in order by Risks D, A, and C (see Figure 21-3).

> In CRR, the risks are listed, and then each pair of risks is rated by team vote as to which is most significant.

▶ **FIGURE 21-3: *Comparative risk ranking.* This technique assigns values to risks based on their seriousness compared to other risks.**

Comparative Risk Ranking

A.	Delivery is late	B.	Wrong item shipped
A.	Delivery is late	C.	Color doesn't match
A.	Delivery is late	D.	Hole too big
B.	Wrong item shipped	C.	Color doesn't match
B.	Wrong item shipped	D.	Hole too big
C.	Color doesn't match	D.	Hole too big

Scoring:

A — 1 vote

B — 3 votes

C — 0 votes

D — 2 votes

Comparative Risk Ranking:

Risk #1— B

Risk #2— D

Risk #3— A

Risk #4— C

Finalizing the Process

After applying the appropriate techniques, you should end up with a list of risks that have been quantified and prioritized. You will have to set some sort of threshold that distinguishes risks that you plan to deal with and risks you will not. You might set a dollar or score threshold, or you might look ahead to your risk response planning work and decide to drop every risk where the cost of cure is greater than the cost of the risk.

Whatever method you use, show your risk management plan to sponsors and stakeholders to get their approval. You need your stakeholders to be aware of which risks you can effectively manage, and which ones you simply must accept.

Risk Response Planning

Taking your prioritized list of risks, you now must come up with a potential strategy or solution for each. Depending on available resources and options, there may be a finite limit as to how much of the list you'll be able to treat.

> Whatever method you use, show your risk management plan to sponsors and stakeholders to get their approval.

Strategies for Risk Response

As we learned earlier, there are four strategies for risk response planning. These are:

1. *Avoidance.* Modify the project plan or strategy to remove the root cause of a risk. You can eliminate either the probability or the impact in avoiding the risk.
2. *Mitigation.* Reducing either the probability or the impact of the risk. There is still a risk and still project consequences of the risk, but the score is reduced.
3. *Transfer.* Making someone else responsible for the risk event, or at least some portions of it. Insurance is a common method of risk transfer. Contract forms also transfer risk. In a fixed-price type contract, the seller owns the financial risk of something going wrong. In a cost-plus type contract, the buyer takes on that risk.

4. *Acceptance.* Deciding not to act in response to a risk. This could be because the probability, impact, or risk score fall below a threshold, or because the cost of mitigating, avoiding, or transferring the risk is greater than the risk itself. In passive acceptance, you plan to take no action even if the risk occurs; in active acceptance you may implement a contingency plan if the risk occurs (such as a rain date for a picnic).

Modifying the Plan for Risk

For each risk on your action list, consider if you can modify the plan to deal with the risk. If there's a chance that a vendor delivery will be late, you might alter the schedule for that task so that a certain amount of lateness does not pose a problem. (If the task is non-critical, this may be easy; if it's critical, this may not be an option.) You can add money or resources to a task, modify its position in the Network Diagram, or change some aspect of its performance criteria. You can use the techniques of avoidance, mitigation, and transfer in this way. Acceptance, of course, doesn't modify the plan.

Contingency Planning for Risk

Sometimes, you would prefer not to incur the cost of dealing with a risk unless it's almost certain that the risk is going to occur. Instead of renting a tent as part of the original picnic plan, you might decide to check a few days before the picnic to see what the long-range weather forecast looks like, and rent the tent then if it looks like rain. Contingency planning falls under the category of active acceptance. Initially, you plan to do nothing—acceptance—unless you reach a triggering event or pass a threshold.

Risk Response Control

As with other elements of the planning process, you should end up with a written document, in the form of a table or narrative as you choose, that describes your risk management plan for the project. If you do similar projects, you can use previous risk management plans to build a template. Over time, as your understanding of risk improves, the document will become increasingly valuable to you and the organization. Identify major risk action points in your project schedule. You can use a milestone (a task with a duration of zero to serve as a marker) to do so.

Schedule risk management meetings periodically throughout your project, probably not as often as project status meetings, but regularly nonetheless. Set a standard agenda for these meetings that involves reviewing the current plan, determining whether circumstances or improved knowledge changes any of your risk response strategies, identifying risks that have decreased and increased as project results have come in, and identifying new risks that only now have become apparent.

Updating and Maintaining the Plan

Either you as the project manager or a team member who has been designated "risk manager" for the project should be operationally responsible for the plan. Use version numbers for document control and identify the list of those who need current risk information—these likely include team members, the customer, and the project sponsor, and may include other important stakeholders.

Keep a record of decisions and alterations made as a result of your periodic risk review meetings. Prepare an archival report on risks and surprises for the project "lessons learned" file at the end.

Managing Residual Risks

Residual risks are risks you decided to accept and the remaining part of risks you have mitigated. By definition, these should be fairly minor—unless, of course, you've made a mistake or some risks have turned out to be far more serious than you expected.

Serious or not, the risks on your project require attention. Are you seeing slippage on the critical path, budget creep, or tasks with lower quality outputs than expected? Day-to-day project adjustment is not unusual, and that becomes one more of your responsibilities.

In your "lessons learned" at the project's end, review the residual risk issue. Were the risks indeed residual, or were some more serious than you expected? Were there triggering factors or special circumstances that you would expect again? What would you do differently given the experience you just had?

> Keep a record of decisions and alterations made as a result of your periodic risk review meetings.

Chapter 22

Planning for Quality

What Is Quality?

Although project management as a discipline grew up parallel to quality management, and not as a part of it, quality tools are now considered one of the core disciplines of the project manager. And that's as it should be. Customer satisfaction is the final measurement of project success, and quality is, above all, about pleasing the customer.

The subject of quality goes far beyond our focus on relating it to project management. Discussion of the various quality philosophies is necessarily limited, and we recommend continuing your study on this vital topic through some of the books listed in the Bibliography.

Definitions

We've given two definitions of quality earlier in this book. The first definition is from W. Edwards Deming, "exceeding customer

A Brief History of the Quality Movement

Formal thinking about management effectiveness, efficiency, and quality is a product of the last two centuries. The history of formal management thinking goes back to the beginnings of mass production. The drive for efficiency—faster production cycles, and reduced scrap and waste—led to the publication of Frederick Winslow Taylor's classic *Principles of Scientific Management* in 1911.

Statistical Process Control (SPC), the root of quality management, was developed by Walter A. Shewhart, an engineer in quality control at Western Electric, beginning in 1924. Theory X, Y, and Z models of supervision grew from Taylor and expanded as insights from psychology made their way into the domain of management. From Management By Objectives (MBO) and its close partner Management By Exception (MBE) in the 1960s and 1970s, we get such tools as the ubiquitous mission statements and the concept of empowerment. While criticisms exist for all these systems, each has made contributions to our current understanding of the best way to get the job done.

In the 1980s and 1990s, the one central, dominating force in American business was the renewed focus on, even obsession with, quality, a reaction to growing Japanese domination of one market after another. The various philosophies and systems generally known as Total Quality Management (TQM) were implemented in one business after another, with, predictably, a range of outcomes. People like W. Edwards Deming, J. M. Juran, and Philip Crosby led the field with comprehensive philosophies of what quality was and how to achieve it.

While TQM as such is treated by many as a fad whose day has passed, many of the ideas, tools, and systems within the TQM field are now simply assumed as a part of business.

expectations." The second is from Philip Crosby, "conformance to requirements." There are others. Deming also referred to quality as meaning "continuous improvement" (originally "never-ending improvement," but changed at the request of Ford chairman Philip Caldwell because "never-ending" sounded like too long a time).

Homer M. Sarasohn, who was in charge of helping the Japanese start postwar manufacturing and who first asked W. Edwards Deming to lecture to the Japanese on quality control, defined it as "a fitness of a process, a product, or a service relative to its intended purpose." J. M. Juran called quality "fitness for use." Howard D. Wilson, director of Quality Management Systems at IBM, identified "delight factors" as an essential part of the definition of quality. Japanese quality expert Kaoru Ishikawa (developer of the "fishbone diagram") focused on a quality product as "the most economical, most useful, and always satisfactory to the customer." The International Organization for Standardization (the "ISO" in ISO-9000) defines quality as "the totality of characteristics of an entity that bear on its ability to satisfy stated or implied needs."

It's clear that all these definitions are aimed at the same underlying idea, but the reality is that a complete, comprehensive, operational definition of quality doesn't quite exist. We know it when we see it (and so do our customers), and we have some general ideas about how to get there. Focus on quality planning at the beginning of your project, and you'll find it easier to get high-quality results at the end.

Quality as a System

The famous GIGO ("garbage in, garbage out") points to one of the odd truisms by which computers work. It's true in the sense that if you have a badly designed program, it delivers consistently bad results. Similarly, every system works in the sense that it delivers what it's designed to deliver—which, alas, is not always what you want it to deliver.

The breakthrough fundamental idea in quality management is that quality is ultimately what the system produces, or fails to produce. If a product is defective, the question is "why?" Tracing back through the system, we look for the root cause that led to the defective product.

> The reality is that a complete, comprehensive, operational definition of quality doesn't quite exist.

Working Backward

"If you don't know where you're going," Yogi Berra is alleged to have said, "you're likely to end up somewhere else." In a sense, the entire project management process ideally works backward—from the concept of a satisfied customer back to initial goals and standards. A project is a means to an end, rather than an end in itself.

If we can eliminate the root cause, we eliminate the reoccurrence of that defect. Through continuous improvement, we make the system better, which in turn makes results better.

In applying this approach to a project, there is a major hurdle: Projects are temporary activities to produce unique results. If you were only planning to make one product, eliminating future causes of the same defect doesn't accomplish anything. That tells us that project quality management must focus on designing the system to "do it right the first time," a Crosby slogan.

Measuring "Good Enough" and "Perfect"

A project management approach to quality, therefore, has to recognize how the special characteristics of a project both limit and modify standard quality management approaches. Both project management and quality management share the same ultimate aim of customer satisfaction. Because finding out whether the customer likes it after all the work is done is a risky proposition, the first focus in project management must be to identify customer needs and desires, and express them in terms of project requirements and specifications. That's the initiation part of the process.

The process of quality planning involves developing appropriate quality standards and measurements for the project. We recommend the dual approach of determining two control points: What is "good enough" and what is "excellent" or even "perfect." An understanding of one often leads to a better understanding of another.

The understanding of "good enough," because it identifies the core needs of the customer, can help guard against fake quality—features and detailing put into a product because it suits the personal style or artistic whims of the creator, not because it relates to the needs of the customer. In addition, it provides a fallback position if factors beyond your control hamper your ability to deliver.

The understanding of "excellent" or "perfect," on the other hand, also has benefits, even in cases where it's unlikely (usually because of resource or time constraints) that you'll reach it. First, not all elements of excellence necessarily take more work or more time or more money to achieve. Occasionally, dramatic improvements are possible with minimal extra effort. (Remember that value is not always proportional to cost.)

To be useful in planning, both goals must be made specific and measurable. How can you achieve this?

Measuring Quality Objectives

You normally begin with at least a general description of the product that is desired, but the description is normally not developed enough to allow specific definitions of quality objectives. The tools you can use to develop these objectives include:

- Interviews
- Cost/Benefit Analysis
- Benchmarking
- Experiments

Interviews

You don't have to be a subject matter expert to be a customer. You need only two things: a need for a product or service and the wherewithal to pay for it. Customers often start a project largely in ignorance of what they really want and need at the level of detail necessary for a project manager to deliver it. Before you can start your job as a project manager, you often have to perform an additional role as a project consultant—an advisor, an investigator, a confidante—to help the customer properly define his or her own needs. Consider developing a question list in advance to focus your inquiry with the customer. On a project to build an e-commerce site, for example, your questions might include:

> You don't have to be a subject matter expert to be a customer.

1. What kind of customers will use the site?
2. How familiar are they likely to be with your products and services?
3. Is the only positive outcome that a visitor places an order, or are there benefits you can get from a customer who simply browses?
4. What do you think the current best e-commerce Web site is?

5. What do you like best about that site?
6. What other sites have features that you think would work well with your customers?
7. What kind of response do you think is a reasonable expectation?

. . . and so forth.

Cost/Benefit Analysis

Tradeoffs among valuable aspects of the project are common in project management. Because of project constraints, more of "A" often results in less of "B." Through your initial interview and initial project documents, identify potential tradeoffs and do an economic analysis. Even if it's out of the question to get more money, try to find out what features or benefits would be worth more money to the customer. Those features and benefits are often what will delight the customer. Perhaps you can achieve some of them within your budget or other constraints.

Present the customer with cost/benefit tradeoffs to gain a better idea of relative importance or relative merit of different options. As you determine which items are most important, emphasize them in your subsequent planning and execution.

> Present the customer with cost/benefit tradeoffs to gain a better idea of relative importance or relative merit of different options.

Benchmarking

How good do you have to be to be the best? The measurable answer is "better than the competition." Your customer and end user often have options. Identify and measure the quality of the options. Interview the customer about the best characteristics of the competitive option as well as about any perceived weaknesses or limitations in it. This sets a quantifiable and specific excellence target for your project. Respect your benchmarking competition. It's safer to overestimate them than to underestimate them.

Experiments

It's not unusual to find yourself with a project that is not merely unique, but virtually unprecedented. How, then, can you identify quality objectives when you can't necessarily even see your way clear to the goal? Sometimes, an experimental approach is the only reasonable way. You have to try something, measure it, then try again using the first results as input. (Try not to do this on a fixed-price contract basis.)

Tools for Quality Management

Just about everyone in management ought to have a working familiarity with what are generally referred to as the "Seven Basic Tools of Quality." You'll find some variation in lists of what the seven tools include, but the most common list goes as follows:

1. Benchmarks
2. Cause-and-Effect Diagram (Fishbone Diagram)
3. Checklists
4. Control Charts
5. Flow-charts
6. Histogram
7. Pareto Diagram

We've covered benchmarking already. Let's review the other tools.

Cause-and-Effect Diagram

This tool is variously referred to as a Cause-and-Effect Diagram, as a Fishbone Diagram, and as an Ishikawa Diagram, after its originator, Kaoru Ishikawa. It is used to work backward from an effect to the multiplicity of potential contributors (causes) of that effect. With your team, you brainstorm potential contributors in a set of established categories, and end up with something like the following (see Figure 22-1).

Improve Quality Throughout the Organization

It's almost axiomatic that quality is profitable, because there is a cost associated with doing things wrong. The expenses associated with improving quality are almost always paid for by reduction in the cost of poor quality. Project managers have an enormous opportunity not only to improve quality on our own projects, but also to take a leadership role in improving overall quality throughout the organization.

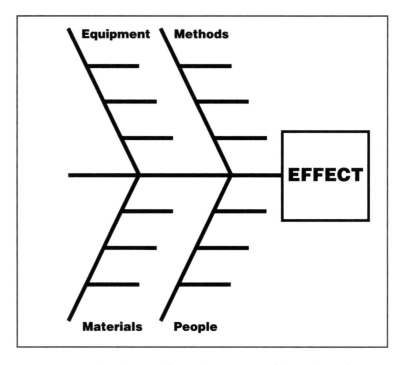

▲ FIGURE 22-1: *Cause-and-Effect Diagram.* **This diagram shows the various potential causes of an effect, used in the study of quality problems.**

In this Cause-and-Effect Diagram, imagine that the effect we are discussing is an unacceptable CD-ROM manufacturing defect rate for our "Tiger Dojo" project. We write that in the "Effect" box at the right side of the diagram (the "head of the fish"). Working backward, we start with "Methods." How could our methods of manufacturing be contributing to these defects? Could it be a problem with our inspection process? Or maybe it is that we are putting on the disk label before burning the disk? The frequency of maintenance checks on our CD burners?

When we've listed everything we can think of, we next do "Equipment." Is the age of our equipment a problem? Is there a problem with the vendor or manufacturer of the equipment? Could there be power surges or climate issues that are damaging the equipment?

> When we've listed everything we can think of, we next do "equipment."

Then comes "Materials." Are we buying a nonstandard brand of blank disks? Have other people reported problems with the materials? Have the materials been properly stored prior to burning?

And finally "People." Are people properly trained? Are they using the training? Are we pushing them too fast?

Notice that the defect rate could be primarily from one item, but others often contribute. And unless all the causes are analyzed and appropriately addressed, we won't ultimately solve the underlying problem and the defects are likely to continue.

Checklists

Developing checklists is a way to make processes more consistent and reliable. Although captains of passenger jets are normally quite experienced, every one uses a checklist to ensure that everything is done before the plane takes off. When a process must be done the same way, or when certain things must be checked and verified before an action takes place, checklists are a valuable tool.

Control Charts

The Control Chart was the very first of the tools, originally developed by Walter Shewhart to help workers measure their own processes. In a Control Chart, you are looking for the difference between common cause variation and special cause variation. Common cause variation is the normal variation inherent in a system. If a bus follows the same route each day, there is some expected variation in arrival times because of ordinary random causes such as red light patterns and other traffic. Special cause variation includes reasons capable of improvement—breakdowns, new or untrained drivers, or special events requiring schedule and equipment modifications. By identifying special cause variations, you can begin to improve your process and bring it under control.

You normally start by measuring actual variation over a period of time to get a median value and distribution for the

> You normally start by measuring actual variation over a period of time to get a median value and distribution for the process.

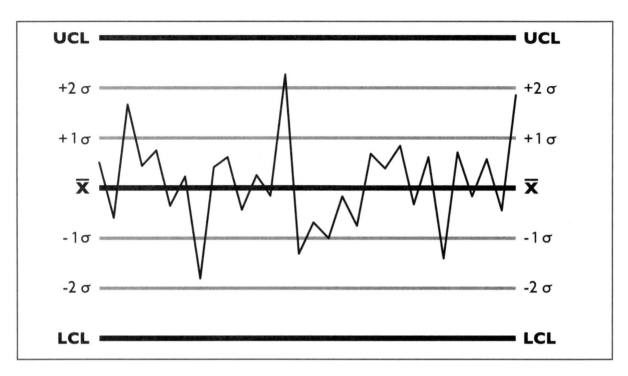

▲ FIGURE 22-2: *Control Chart.*
This diagram shows the various potential causes of an effect used in the study of quality problems.

process. The upper and lower control limits are set at 3 σ (sigmas, or standard deviations from the mean), with dashed lines at 1 σ and 2 σ, as shown in Figure 22-2. Look for special causes for the outlying points and eliminate those causes, which shrinks deviation (and may move the mean as well). Over time, you bring the process under control. Variation will still remain, but it's common cause variation.

Flow-charts

You can't expect to improve the quality of a process you don't understand. Along with Cause-and-Effect Diagramming, flow-charting is a powerful way to get insight into a process. In fact, you've already used process flow-charting in the development of a Network Diagram. In understanding the e-commerce Web site, you might consider a flow-chart of likely buyer actions and company responses (see Figure 22-3).

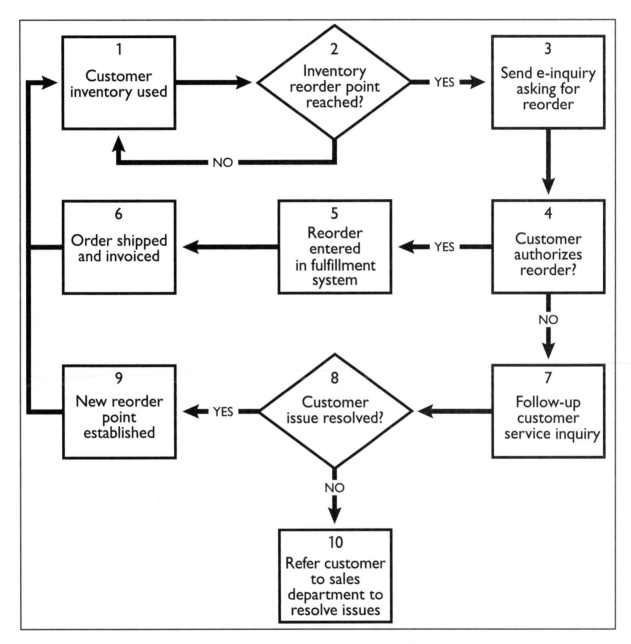

▲ Figure 22-3: *Flow-charting.* A flow-chart describes and makes visible a process.

Histogram

A histogram is a graphic similar to a bar chart, in which data is grouped into a series of bins that can be compared against one another. In our company, the tech support people get numerous problem inquiries. To improve software quality for your next update release, you want to know what problems are most frequent, so you ask tech support to classify each incoming call. The problem bins you define include bug reports, unintuitive processes, incompatibility with other software, and missing features. Over a period of three weeks, tech support tracks this information, resulting in the following histogram (see Figure 22-4).

> A histogram is a graphic similar to a bar chart, in which data is grouped into a series of bins that can be compared against one another.

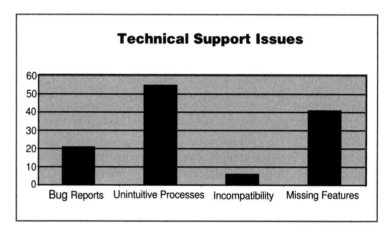

▲ **FIGURE 22-4:** *Histogram.* **A histogram is a bar chart that groups and displays data in bins for further analysis.**

Pareto Chart

If the histogram is a description of why some customers are dissatisfied, what would you have to do to reduce dissatisfied customers by, say, 40 percent or more? To answer this, re-plot the factors in descending order and show the cumulative percentage of the total problem represented by the factors in order. This is known as a Pareto Chart, and it looks like this (see Figure 22-5).

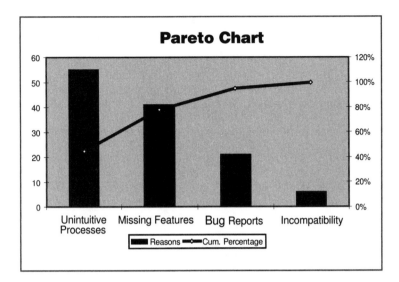

▲ FIGURE 22-5: *Pareto Chart.* The Pareto Chart is a type of histogram that shows rank ordering of causes in order to focus your attention on the actions that will have the greatest total impact on the problem.

How Will You Measure and Control Quality?

The two quality processes that take place during the execution and monitoring phases of your project are quality assurance and quality control. Quality assurance involves the operations within the quality system itself–the overall process of making sure that the project will satisfy the established quality standards that you developed in your planning process. Quality control is the monitoring of specific results of the project, and is more associated with the product, rather than the project's process.

The tool most associated with quality assurance is the quality audit. The audit that enables a company to earn ISO-9000 certification, for example, is a quality audit. Quality audits are also important in the evaluation, or "lessons learned" process that is part of project closeout, because it helps you to do the next project better.

> The tool most associated with quality assurance is the quality audit.

Quality control tools include inspections, statistical sampling, and trend analysis, as well as the seven tools previously described, all to ensure that the project satisfies its quality objectives.

Projects to Improve Quality

There is another very important way in which project management overlaps quality management, and that is in the area of continuous improvement. The process of improving an organization's overall quality normally involves analyzing existing processes and improving them. This is normally done as a series of projects, and here project management directly uses the tools of quality management as its own inherent process.

You not only use the seven tools extensively in this work, you use one other very important element of the quality movement, the PDSA Cycle, also known as the Shewhart Cycle (see Figure 22-6). (You'll also see this referred to sometimes a the PDCA (the C stands

> Project management directly uses the tools of quality management as its own inherent process.

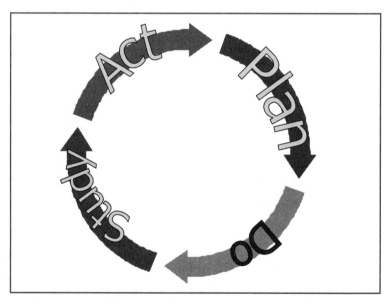

▲ Figure 22-6: *PDSA Cycle.* The four processes of Plan, Do, Study, and Act form a model to improve the quality of projects.

for "Check") Cycle or the Deming Cycle. Deming credited the tool to Shewhart and felt that "PDSA" was a better description of the process than "PDCA.")

The PDSA Cycle is a process for continuous quality improvement. The first step is Plan. Identify an area requiring improvement, using such tools as histogramming and the Pareto Chart to focus on the best targets. Second is Do. Determine a corrective or improving action to take and implement it. Then comes Study. Analyze what you've done. Has quality been improved? Is the change sustainable? Do the benefits outweigh any costs? Finally, Act. Depending on the results of the study, make a decision: Implement the change and make it permanent, decide the particular experiment has not been productive and start over, or decide that while some benefit has been achieved, there is more to achieve as well. Modify and start over.

By following the PDSA cycle, you and your team can manage any number of continuous improvement projects, leading to higher and higher levels of sustainable quality.

Does Quality Pay?

DaimlerChrysler—Reduced development cycle for new vehicles from as long as sixty months to thirty-three months.

Ford Motor Company—Cut person-hours per vehicle in half, and cut number of parts in a bumper from over 100 to only ten in the Ford Taurus.

IBM—Achieved "six sigma" (no more than 3.4 defects per million) on some products, and cut defect per million rate by 32 times.

John Deere & Co.—Reduced cycle time of products by as much as 60 percent, and saved 30 percent of traditional development costs.

For more information on this topic, visit our Web site at www.businesstown.com

Budgeting and Cost Estimating

Chapter 23

Learn the Organization's Procedures

The financial management of your project is usually important not only to you as a project manager, but also to others in your organization. It's not unusual to spend more time justifying the budget than presenting almost any other aspect of your project.

Your individual organization drives a significant portion of this project according to its own rules and procedures, and project managers do well when they take the time to learn those rules and work within them.

In business, it may surprise you to know that it's actually unusual for the cost constraint to be the driver of the project. Most projects are undertaken because the perceived benefit significantly outweighs the cost. If that's the case, then going over budget is usually a better choice than failing to complete the project in a manner that delivers the benefit. However, expenditures in the present are

How Much Is 2 + 2?

There is a joke about the CEO who wanted to know how much was 2 + 2. She began by calling the head of the information technology group. "How much is 2 + 2?" she asked.

The head of IT shook his head. "Well, I'll need to order a new Cray and hire six additional programmers. With luck, I'll have an answer for you in six to nine months. The good news is that I can guarantee accuracy to 40 decimal places!"

The CEO sent him away and called in the head of marketing. "How much is 2 + 2," she demanded.

"Fortunately," said the head of marketing, "we've been doing focus groups on just that topic lately. Our consensus is that it's around 3.6 right now, but we're forecasting that it will be 4.8 by the end of next fiscal year."

She dismissed the head of marketing and called in the head of finance. "How much is 2 + 2?" she asked.

The head of finance shrugged. "I don't know. How much do you want it to be?"

In some ways, that's only a slight exaggeration. Real money—the kind most of us don't have personally—operates by more complex rules, and what seem to be straightforward and simple questions don't always have straightforward and simple answers. That can put you at a serious operational disadvantage if you don't have at least a basic grasp of key concepts. Finance is the language of senior management and executives, and if you don't speak that language, regardless of your other virtues, you won't ever be considered eligible for the top jobs.

easier to see than potential benefits in the future, so the emphasis on cost control is normally greater in practice than the underlying project dynamics would suggest.

While nothing will take the place of you learning your own organization's procedures and issues, there are some common elements of budgeting and cost management that project managers need to know.

Escalating the Cost Constraint

Because of the central nature of finance in business processes, it's normal that the problems in getting a budget and expending money on your project are numerous. From fiscal limits to political tensions, from operational issues to the overall economic environment, financial pressures and issues can be enormous.

Why are money matters so difficult?

People Issues

First, people have a stake in money decisions because every dollar on your project comes from somebody and goes to somebody. This naturally influences money matters, from the price a vendor charges to the size of the budget your manager allows. What's good for the project is only a single variable among many.

Risk Issues

Second, projects have risks. It may be true that your project, if completed successfully, will earn us a million dollars. It would seem, therefore, that as long as you spend less than a million dollars in accomplishing the project, there's a profit. But that assumes that you successfully complete the project and that it performs to expectations and forecasts. How likely is that? If there's a 50-50 chance the market will embrace the project, then the expected value is only 50% x $1 million, or $500,000. Expect the organization to want to keep your budget more in line with the expected value, or even less.

Career Advancement

Even in cases where cost is not the driver, paying attention to the financial performance of your project is good project management practice. It will not only pay in terms of the fiscal health of your organization, but it will also show that you take your management obligations seriously—a help in your own career advancement.

Visibility Issues

Third, lost money shows up more clearly on the bookkeeper's sheet than the cash value of a missed opportunity. If we pass up the opportunity to go for the million-dollar project, that doesn't show up on the books as a loss. But if we spend $100,000 and have nothing to show for it, that's extremely visible, and could be damaging to our career prospects. There's a saying that "what gets measured gets performed." Sometimes the measurement issue militates against even worthwhile risks.

Control/Hierarchy Issues

Fourth, control of money is one of the central defining characteristics of management. Surrendering control of money is surrendering control, period. And not everyone is happy about surrendering control. Keeping rein on the purse strings is a way to keep control of the project.

Empty Pockets

Finally, sometimes the money just isn't there or is committed to other worthwhile projects. It's not that someone doesn't want to give you the resources you need, it's that they can't. Money is also a symbol, and it means different things to different people. If you know the "why" behind the money issue, you'll be stronger in dealing with it.

> Money is also a symbol, and it means different things to different people.

Strategies for Managing Budget Politics

Now that we see the problem, what about a solution? Here are some ideas.

Remember, no matter how effective you become, there's no guarantee that the project budget will come out the way you want. However, there are ways to increase the odds in your favor.

Learn the System and the Context

Who controls the purse strings? What policies, procedures, and histories influence their decisions? Who else is competing for the money you need? Understanding the dynamics that surround you is an important tool.

Be Honest about Your Own Weaknesses

When we're trying to sell our project and our budget, we often emphasize the strong parts and de-emphasize any areas of perceived weakness or vulnerability. That isn't necessarily the best strategy, because the managers reviewing your project can tell they're being "sold." Instead, go through the project as they see it, addressing weaknesses and vulnerabilities in your own approach. Oddly, you'll find in most cases you're perceived better—not overoptimistic, not intending to pull the wool over management's eyes.

Avoid Padding

Of course, padding is the traditional answer to perceived arbitrary management budget cutting. If they always chop your budget by 20 percent, it seems obvious that if you pad your budget by 20 percent, you'll end up okay. And it does work, for a while—until management figures out the game and starts cutting 40 percent. This way lies madness.

Although padding is a bad strategy, there are legitimate ways to achieve much the same goal. Develop a risk contingency plan that shows the extra costs of coping with specific events. If you use PERT or CPM (Chapter 24), you'll automatically be providing budgetary options based on risk and reward. Why aren't these the same as padding? Because you don't have to keep them secret. The costs show up clearly in your planning documents.

Develop Allies

If you're up against someone in senior management who chooses to take an irrational view about your budget, the only response is to find another manager of equivalent (or higher) rank to work on your behalf. Start with your project sponsor and work from there. Provide good staff support to your champion; make sure he or she has the figures and the facts.

Adjust the Rest of the Project

If cost becomes the driver, then it follows that another constraint must be weak. To manage the project within acceptable costs, you may have to make adjustments in the other constraints. Make sure you show clearly and objectively that you've tried to accommodate the cost pressures into your project with minimum compromise, but show the compromises you have to make.

Activity-Based Costing in Project Management

Each direct cost on a project occurs within an activity, or task. If there is a charge for labor, it's labor on a task. If you purchase equipment and supplies, it's part of a task. By assigning costs based on the activities in your project, you end up with a budget that reflects the course of the work of the project, making it easier to track and measure variance.

Your organization may look for other types of cost groupings, based on how it organizes and tracks its own expenditures. This is one reason why the second level of your WBS is sometimes known as the "cost account" level. In developing a WBS, you can establish the cost accounts as headers, and then classify each task under the cost account most suitable for it. Of course, tasks by their nature often cut across any set of categories you might set up. Therefore, expect that forcing tasks into cost accounts will lead to some borderline fits.

You might be expected to group costs by categories such as labor, materials, and services. In this sort of costing, each task is likely to have elements in each category. This may fit the organization's accounting needs better, but makes it much more difficult for you as a project manager to track costs and identify variances. Although you must, of course, do what the organization wants, you may find it useful to create your own activity-based costing linked to your own WBS for the purposes of internal tracking and monitoring.

Types of Project Costs

There are a number of different types of costs, each with special characteristics, that can affect the management and internal operations of your projects.

Direct Costs

Direct costs to manage your project include the actual cost of labor, materials, supplies, and outside services. It's usually possible to assign direct costs to tasks, which is useful for project tracking.

Always find out what costs are charged against your project, and what costs are not. This can often affect your planning and the methods you use to attain your goal.

You aren't always charged directly for what could easily be considered direct costs. One example is the cost of using employee labor on your project. In many organizations, your direct project budget isn't charged for employee labor costs. You must only account for costs that involve the actual payment of funds to someone outside the organization. That isn't a good project management practice from the organization's point of view, because it pushes you to make decisions that aren't in the financial best interest of the organization. Notice that in this case, it's always cheaper for your project budget to do it in-house, even if it really isn't. Now, if you didn't make the rules, then all you're obligated to do is to follow them. It's still appropriate to inform your project sponsor of what's going on.

Fixed Costs

A fixed cost doesn't vary with quantity. If you are making a new product, there are huge costs associated with getting the first one manufactured. Tooling, art costs, preproduction, setup—these costs can mount up quickly. Let's imagine that there is $1 million in up-front fixed costs. If you make only one item, all these costs will have to be counted against that one item, meaning it will cost $1 million plus the variable cost of manufacturing for one copy. But if you make a million, then only one dollar would have to be charged against each product. That's why it's often substantially cheaper on a per-unit basis to order larger quantities.

> A fixed cost doesn't vary with quantity.

Variable Costs

Even though we don't have to pay for tooling for each additional item coming off the production line, there are still some costs involved. We need the material for each item, the press or production time for each item, the cost of assembling the parts, and the cost of packaging and shipping. These are variable costs because they vary with the number of units produced. Let's imagine there are $5 in variable costs in manufacturing each item. The cost for one item is $1,000,000. The cost-per-piece for 100,000 is now ($1,000,000 + (100,000 x $5)) / 100,000, or $1,500,000 / 100,000, or $15 apiece. But the cost-per-piece of one million is only $1 + $5, or $6 apiece.

Indirect Costs/Overhead

What percentage of the office electric bill is properly charged to your project? Obviously, you consume lighting and power for your computer. But maybe the light shines on more than one cubicle, and the network is shared among many machines. It would be silly to try to figure out these costs in detail, yet they are real. We classify these as indirect costs, because they can't easily be apportioned among multiple projects. In many situations, indirect costs won't be charged against your project at all, because you don't control them. Management will work in general to keep overhead under control.

When overhead is billed against your project, it's often billed as a percentage. If you spend $1 million in actual costs and there is a 20 percent overhead, then the project charge is $1.2 million.

If your project is a grant or government contract, an allowable overhead rate is part of the contract, and your organization will

Dangers in Cost Estimating and Budgeting

There are some very common dangers in the process of estimating and budgeting project costs. Here are some to look out for:

1. *Scope problems.* Was the scope properly defined? Are there omissions in scope that you'll later have to handle? Have people misinterpreted what they have been asked to do?
2. *Optimism.* In designing the project, is there a hidden assumption that there will be no surprises and no problems? Is the schedule realistic only if we assume everything goes perfectly?
3. *WBS.* Have we accurately broken the project into all the tasks? Have we left out anything?
4. *Individuals.* Have we figured out what skill levels we're attaching to what tasks, and how the different salary levels and skills will affect how much it finally costs and how long it will take?
5. *Risk.* Have we accounted for likely risk issues? Have likely contingencies been estimated and budgeted?
6. *Geography and time.* Does the project cut across national borders with currency exchange rates? Has rate fluctuation been taken into account? Does the project extend over years? If so, have inflation and general economic conditions been taken into account?
7. *Overhead.* Have we used the proper rates for overhead, G&A, and indirect costs?

probably pocket that money at the beginning, leaving you the remainder. If the total price of the contract (remember that price is not cost) is $1 million, and there is a 20 percent overhead, then you have only $800,000 to spend.

Creating the Cost Baseline

The cost estimate on a project represents your idea of what it will cost to do the project. The budget, on the other hand, is a request for actual funds or the statement of actual funds available. Ideally, the numbers are related, but not in all cases.

Cost estimate is an estimate of the costs that will be incurred on a project. Budget is the proposed and/or accepted costs for a project organized by categories. Cost baseline is a comparison of actual costs to planned costs for the purpose of monitoring.

Operational Project Budget

Your operational project budget is the sum of the task budgets plus any general overhead burdens placed on the project. That ends up being true no matter which way you go. Sometimes, you develop the project budget by developing activity budgets for each task and summing them by cost account category. Of course, it's not unheard of to hear back from management that your budget has been cut by 35 percent. Operationally, this means that the 35 percent cut has to be taken out of individual tasks, and an across-the-board meat axe approach is likely to spell disaster. Try to resolve conflicts like this before you get started.

Tracking Performance and Variances

In the actual management of your project, known as the Executing phase, you will want to track actuals against the plan. To do this, you need a cost baseline. By breaking down the project in terms of tasks and showing the associated costs for each task, you can track your cumulative performance and thus identify any variances. Significant variances will demand action on your part.

> Sometimes, you develop the project budget by developing activity budgets for each task and summing them by cost account category.

There are several ways to build a cost baseline. Figure 7-1, on page 68, is a fairly simple one. Figure 23-1 shows another example.

This project is in a little bit of trouble, at least in its opening phases. It looks as if just about all the programming tasks took longer than expected. On the good side, the art and design seemed to go better than the plan suggested. Nevertheless, we're looking at a variance thus far, and need to make sure at a minimum that the rest of the project holds the line.

On the other hand, we're looking at a variance on the order of $20,000 in a $1.5 million project, which is a variance of a little over 1 percent. If we stay in the range of 2–3 percent total variance, we're probably okay, unless we have other issues.

▼ FIGURE 23-1: *Cost baseline.* **Use a model such as this to ensure current information on project performance against plan.**

WBS	Activity	Fixed Cost	Hours	Rate	Total Labor	Supplies	Total Cost	Cum. Plan	Actual	Cum. Actual	Variance
1.1	Software Engineering										
1.1.1	Construct Game Engine		1440	$ 40	$ 57,600	$ 360	$ 57,960	$ 57,960	$ 60,250	$ 60,250	$ (2,290)
1.1.2	Build Level Editor		960	$ 40	$ 38,400	$ 240	$ 38,640	$ 96,600	$ 40,100	$ 100,350	$ (3,750)
1.1.3	Write AI Character Routines		960	$ 40	$ 38,400	$ 240	$ 38,640	$ 135,240	$ 48,178	$ 148,528	$ (13,288)
1.1.4	Compile Art Files		240	$ 35	$ 8,400	$ 60	$ 8,460	$ 143,700	$ 7,120	$ 155,648	$ (11,948)
1.1.5	Turnover Game to Playtest		1	$ 40	$ 40	$ 0	$ 40	$ 143,740	$ 40	$ 155,688	$ (11,948)
1.1.6	Fix Program Bugs		960	$ 35	$ 33,600	$ 240	$ 33,840	$ 177,580	$ 53,500	$ 209,188	$ (31,608)
1.1.7	Verify Revised Game		320	$ 35	$ 11,200	$ 80	$ 11,280	$ 188,860	$ 14,120	$ 223,308	$ (34,448)
1.2	Art & Design										
1.2.1	Script Game		480	$ 30	$ 14,400	$ 120	$ 14,520	$ 203,380	$ 12,150	$ 235,458	$ (32,078)
1.2.2	Design Characters		240	$ 30	$ 7,200	$ 60	$ 7,260	$ 210,640	$ 6,100	$ 241,558	$ (30,918)
1.2.3	Build Character Animations		1440	$ 45	$ 64,800	$ 360	$ 65,160	$ 275,800	$ 55,000	$ 296,558	$ (20,758)
1.2.4	Design Levels and Backgrounds		2880	$ 35	$ 100,800	$ 720	$ 101,520	$ 377,320	$ 100,950	$ 397,508	$ (20,188)
1.2.5	Develop Licensing Packages	$ 2,500	400	$ 30	$ 12,000	$ 100	$ 14,600	$ 391,920	$ 14,600	$ 412,108	$ (20,188)
1.2.6	Design Package Art		120	$ 45	$ 5,400	$ 30	$ 5,430				$ -
1.3	Production Department										
1.3.1	Design Playtest Plan		160	$ 30	$ 4,800	$ 40	$ 4,840				$ -
1.3.2	Manage Playtests		320	$ 25	$ 8,000	$ 80	$ 8,080				$ -
1.3.3	Compile Bug Reports		80	$ 25	$ 2,000	$ 20	$ 2,020				$ -
1.3.4	Design Product Packaging		120	$ 30	$ 3,600	$ 30	$ 3,630				$ -
1.3.5	Subcontract Packaging Work		20	$ 25	$ 500	$ 5	$ 505				$ -
1.3.6	Test Sample Packaging		20	$ 25	$ 500	$ 5	$ 505				$ -
1.3.7	Produce CD-ROM Disks	$ 75,000	10	$ 25	$ 250	$ 3	$ 75,253				$ -
1.3.8	Produce Packaging	$ 110,000	30	$ 25	$ 750	$ 8	$ 110,758				$ -
1.3.9	Assemble Product		1200	$ 10	$ 12,000	$ 300	$ 12,300				$ -
1.3.10	Ship Product	$ 9,000	160	$ 10	$ 1,600	$ 40	$ 10,640				$ -
1.4	Marketing Department										
1.4.1	Write Marketing Plan		240	$ 20	$ 4,800	$ 60	$ 4,860				$ -
1.4.2	Produce Print Materials		120	$ 20	$ 2,400	$ 30	$ 2,430				$ -
1.4.3	Produce TV Commercial	$ 75,000	640	$ 20	$ 12,800	$ 160	$ 87,960				$ -
1.4.4	Produce Catalogs/Sellsheets	$ 20,000	160	$ 20	$ 3,200	$ 40	$ 23,240				$ -
1.4.5	Buy Ad Placement/Air Time	$ 500,000	40	$ 20	$ 800	$ 10	$ 500,810				$ -
1.4.6	Hire Publicist	$ 50,000	20	$ 20	$ 400	$ 5	$ 50,405				$ -
1.4.7	Execute Publicity Campaign	$ 100,000	120	$ 20	$ 2,400	$ 30	$ 102,430				$ -
1.4.8	Create Trade Show Exhibit/Dem	$ 100,000	200	$ 20	$ 4,000	$ 50	$ 104,050				$ -
TOTALS		$ 1,041,500	14,101		$ 457,040	$ 3,525	$ 1,502,065				

Displaying the cost baseline graphically makes all the relationships easier to see, and also puts the variance into perspective (see Figure 23-2).

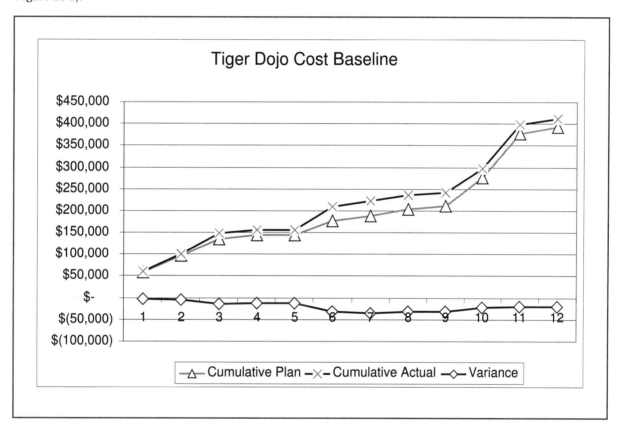

▲ FIGURE 23-2: *Cost baseline chart.* This shows our financial performance on the project to date.

For more information on this topic, visit our Web site at www.businesstown.com

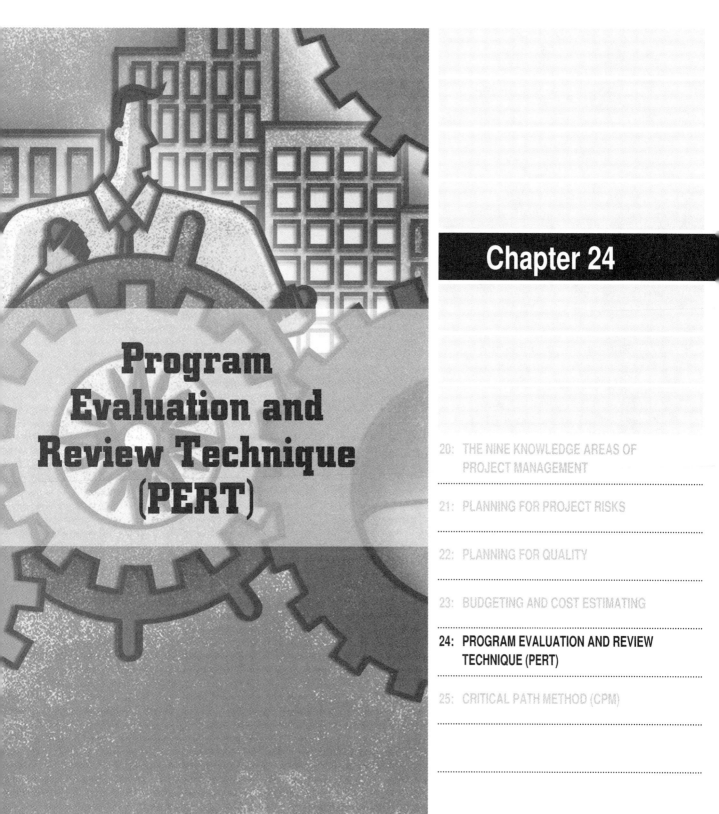

Program Evaluation and Review Technique (PERT)

A Brief History

While some project management techniques are as old as projects themselves, and others (such as the Gantt Chart) date back to the beginning of the twentieth century, most authorities date the development of "modern" project management to the 1960s, when use of mathematical models for large project control began to become widely used.

The two most famous mathematical approaches are known as PERT (Program Evaluation and Review Technique) and CPM (Critical Path Method). (We'll cover CPM in the next chapter.) PERT was developed in the late 1950s by the U. S. Navy's Special Projects Office working with the consulting firm of Booz, Allen, and Hamilton, and was first used on the Polaris Weapons System project.

The basic problem that PERT was trying to solve had to do with uncertainty. While we explored methods of developing time and cost estimates in Chapter 17, we learned that it's not always possible to develop a firm, crisp, reliable estimate. This is particularly true in R&D-type work, where if we really knew in detail how long something would take, it wouldn't really be R&D! For many projects, the inherent uncertainty in estimating is a critical problem. Let's see how PERT can help you bring this problem under control.

PERT isn't for everybody or every project. Use this chapter to get an idea what it's all about, and then decide when—or if—it applies to you.

> The two most famous mathematical approaches are known as PERT (Program Evaluation and Review Technique) and CPM (Critical Path Method).

What Is PERT, and How Can You Use It?

The whole area of new product development projects is rife with uncertainty. How long will market research take? How fast can our programmers design a new system? How long will it take to debug the not-yet-developed system? If you're working with a deadline, these are crucial questions that go to the heart of whether you'll succeed on your project. At the same time, these questions have so many unknowns in them that it's hard to see how any answer can be meaningful.

We do have some useful information, however. Even if we don't know the details of a task such as "Market Research" or "Design System," we do know that these tasks have to be done. We can also establish predecessor/dependency relationships. "Debug Program," for example, will clearly be placed after "Design System" in our schedule. This means we will be able to lay out a Network Diagram for the project. (PERT was one of the first systems to use a Network Diagram for project management.)

And even though you don't know exactly how long many of the tasks will take, that doesn't mean you are completely in the dark. Often, you have a sense of the range of possible times—best-case and worst-case scenarios. Even if you haven't done this particular project before, you may well have done something similar enough to get a general sense how long things might take. Armed with this information, you actually have enough data to develop a useful plan. Let's see how you do it.

The Importance of Managing Uncertainty

To manage uncertainty, we'll follow the PERT process. First, we'll identify the tasks; next, we'll put them in a Network Diagram; and then, we'll come up with some time estimates. This is pretty much what we've done before, but there are a few differences in the PERT method.

We've started by identifying what we do know. Our project generally will have the following characteristics:

> These tasks may be started and stopped independently of one another, within the sequence that you establish.

1. It consists of a well-defined collection of tasks or activities. When those activities are completed, the project will have been accomplished.
2. These tasks may be started and stopped independently of one another, within the sequence that you establish.
3. The tasks are to be performed in some type of sequence, required by logic or chosen by the project manager.
4. Each task will take some amount of time, normally with both a minimum and maximum value.

There are some arguments about whether these assumptions are valid in all cases, which we'll cover a little later. In the meantime, let's act as if these are completely true.

Arrow Diagramming Method

Once the tasks have been identified for your project (by development of a WBS or other means), you need to put them into a Network Diagram. So far in this book we've only considered the Precedence Diagramming Method (PDM), because it's the overwhelmingly popular choice in today's software.

That wasn't always the case. Before modern PC project management programs became available, another layout technique, known as the Arrow Diagramming Method (ADM) or the Activity-On-Arrow (AOA) technique was often used. (PDM is sometimes referred to as AON, or Activity-On-Node.) Although you'll see it used less and less frequently, it's possible that you'll still run into it. If you understand PDM, learning ADM will be little trouble.

Comparing Systems

The major difference between the two systems is that in PDM, the task is the box, or "node," and the arrow simply shows precedence relationships. In ADM, the task is the arrow, and the node connects the arrows in precedence order. Figures 24-1 and 24-2 compare the two:

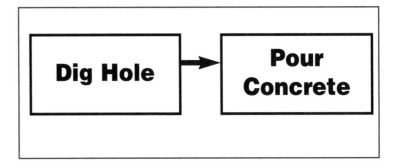

▲ FIGURE 24-1: *PDM/AON.* This Network Diagram lists the activities in the nodes; the arrow only shows the dependency relationship.

> Once the tasks have been identified for your project, you need to put them into a Network Diagram.

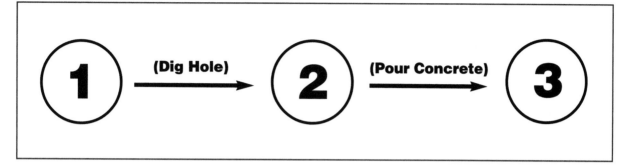

You might feel at this point that a difference that makes no difference is no difference, but back when computer-processing power was extremely limited, ADM allowed linear programming to be done with less memory than PDM. You can get by with only PDM charting for the most part, but it's valuable to know about ADM anyway. It sets you apart from most project managers.

▲ FIGURE 24-2: *ADM/AOA.* This Network Diagram lists the activities on the arrows; the node only shows the dependency relationship.

The Dummy Task

The ADM method for laying out a project introduces a special complication that doesn't appear in PDM. Let's look at the first part of our project *Streetwise Project Management.* In Figure 5-4, we did a PDM-style Network Diagram. Here's the first part of the same project, now done in ADM/AON style. To illustrate the complication (see Figure 24-3), we've added a task "Get Permissions," which is dependent upon "Perform Research," but not dependent on "Write First Draft."

Notice that we can express a task relationship in terms of its nodes. "Find Author" is Activity 1,2; "Write Sample" is Activity 2,3. By naming the activity, we also name its predecessor and successor tasks. That's an advantage.

The corresponding disadvantage shows up in Activity 7,9 "Write First Draft." Its predecessors are Activity 5,7 "Negotiate Contract" and Activity 3,6 "Perform Research." Activity 6,8 "Get Permissions," though, is also dependent on Activity 3,6 "Perform Research." That means that the arrow for Activity 3,6 must be in two places at once! Because we're an arrow short, we add a

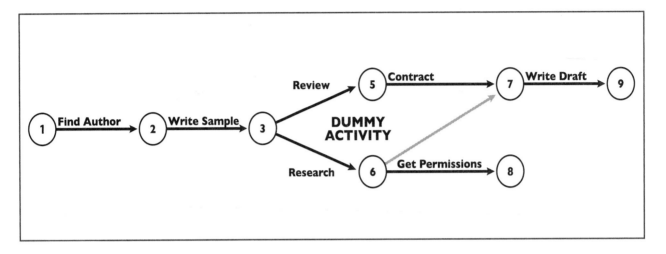

▲ FIGURE 24-3: *ADM Network Diagram showing dummy activity.* **The task "Write First Draft" is dependent on both "Negotiate Contract" and "Perform Research." "Get Permissions" is dependent only on "Perform Research." We need a "dummy activity" to show the extra dependency link between "Perform Research" and "Write First Draft."**

"dummy activity," an arrow to show the precedence relationship of Activity 6,7. The dummy activity doesn't represent work, or resources, or time; it only shows a relationship that you can't show any other way.

Because in PDM, the task is the node and not the arrow, you can draw any number of arrows to show any precedence relationships you choose, and there's no need for the dummy.

PERT Time Estimating

Now that we've got our Network Diagram built, we next develop time estimates. Of course, this is a big problem because this is a project with inherent uncertainty. "How long will it take you to create something brand new?"

As we suggested, you may not be able to determine the actual time required, but it's often possible to come up with a range. In PERT, you develop three time estimates for each task: an Optimistic estimate (O), a Pessimistic estimate (P), and a Most Likely estimate (M).

The Optimistic estimate assumes everything goes right and is the shortest possible time it will take to complete the task. The Pessimistic estimate, on the other hand, assumes bad luck dogs you at every turn. Don't take those excessively literally. While it's (barely) possible that you'll solve your design problem when aliens show up to give you their already developed technology, that's excessively optimistic. Similarly, coping with the effects of nuclear holocaust is a little too pessimistic. Don't consider any event with less than a 1 percent probability in determining either extreme.

Developing the Three Estimates

Given that PERT is about uncertainty, how do you develop the three estimates, O, M, and P? There are a number of ways:

1. *Previous experience.* You may have high uncertainty even in a type of project you do all the time. This means that over time you accumulate a range of data. Activity A has never taken less time than X, or more time than Y. It usually takes about Z, more or less. Therefore, O = X, P = Y, and M = Z (more or less).

2. *Specific contingencies.* You may have a specific scenario in mind for each outcome. If A happens (good), the task will take only X. If B happens (bad), then it will take Y time. If C happens, it'll be in the middle, more or less, at Z. Again we have O = X, P = Y, and M = Z (more or less).

3. *WAGs/SWAGs.* If it's really new, we may have to go on gut feeling (which is an unquantifiable estimating technique). If we're lucky, it might only take X time; if it's really bad, then Y; but probably Z (more or less).

Even if you can't justify the precision of your estimates, the process of statistical averaging will make some degree of error less harmful to your schedule than would otherwise be the case.

Determining the most likely time is based either on what you think is the most likely scenario, or on any comparable experience you've had on another project. It may well be the case that you can't determine the precise point of maximum probability, but PERT is robust enough to handle a reasonable guess.

The PERT Formula

For each task, you now calculate an "expected time," (E), using the following formula: $E = (0 + 4M + P) / 6$. This is a *weighted average*, or how long we would expect the activity to take on average if we did it numerous times. Of course, we may only plan to do the activity once. Still, we have numerous tasks in our project, and each of them may have some degree of uncertainty.

Overall, then, we would argue that there's a high likelihood that some of the tasks in our project will come out around their Optimistic times, some will come out around Pessimistic, and the majority should trend pretty close to Most Likely. In other words, we're creating a *probability distribution*. Given a random distribution of good luck and bad luck, we should expect that a schedule of all "E" values should come out fairly close to that target in reality.

> If we have a standard probability distribution, then we're in the realm of statistics and probability.

The Standard Deviation

If we have a standard probability distribution, then we're in the realm of statistics and probability. This means that a number of tools become available to us. (By the way, if you're knowledgeable about statistics, you may notice some shortcuts and holes in the PERT theory. Because we have to define an entire probability distribution with only three points, PERT does take some liberties with statistical theory.)

How close will our reality get to the PERT time estimate we've prepared? The answer is related to the standard distribution (represented by the small Greek letter sigma, or σ, which in PERT is calculated by the formula: $\sigma = (P - O) / 6$.

One measure of the uncertainty of our project is the amount of distance between the Optimistic and Pessimistic estimates. If we are completely certain of our time estimate, then O, P, and M are all the same number, and P – O = 0. If P – O is a small number, then there's little uncertainty in our project. If P – O is very large, then there is a large amount of uncertainty in our project. The standard deviation, therefore, is a measure of the uncertainty of our project.

Standard Deviation for a Path or Project

The formula we just listed gave the standard deviation for each task. When we insert all these values into our Network Diagram, we want to know how long it will take to do the entire project, and what the standard deviation is for the entire project. When we calculate the critical path using our forward and backward pass techniques (Chapter 16), we find it easy to determine a value E for the entire project. Unfortunately, calculating the standard deviation for the whole path isn't just addition. For each task on the critical path, you square the standard deviations, add them up, then take the square root of the sum to get the standard deviation for the path (this is called the "root sum square").

Likelihood of Finishing on Time

You can use the standard deviation to determine the likelihood of finishing on a particular date. The "E" time is considered the probability median. Half the time you expect the project to take E or less time; the other half E or more. But because there's more likelihood of finishing near the Most Likely time than at the extremes, roughly 68 percent of the time your actual end should be within one standard deviation of E. You'll end up within two standard deviations around 95 percent of the time, and within three standard deviations almost always a whopping 99.7 percent probability.

To figure out your chances, first determine how far the desired finish date (D) is from E in terms of the standard deviation, using the following formula: $Z = (D - E) / \sigma$ (we'll call the answer "Z"). Then use the table in Figure 24-4 to determine the probability of meeting the deadline.

Using Portions of PERT

In spite of the large-project concerns with PERT, a number of people use portions of PERT, such as the three time estimates, and integrate them into a normal project, achieving a tradeoff that works for them. If you do this, please be aware that you may not get the same quality of answer as you would if it were done properly, but you may find some useful insights into your own project situation.

Standard Deviations from E	Probability of Meeting Date
+3.0	99.9%
+2.4	99.2%
+2.0	97.7%
+1.4	91.9%
+1.0	84.1%
+0.4	65.5%
+0.0	50.0%
-0.6	27.4%
-1.0	15.9%
-1.6	05.5%
-2.0	02.3%
-2.6	00.3%
-3.0	00.1%

▲ FIGURE 24-4: *Probability of achieving due dates.* A standard normal distribution table will provide percentage probabilities for a wide range of times.

> PERT is a well-documented, well-developed methodology that has been used in a variety of projects and industries for many years.

Problems and Issues with PERT

PERT is a well-documented, well-developed methodology that has been used in a variety of projects and industries for many years. However, there are some problems and issues both in PERT theory and PERT practice you should consider in making your decision whether to implement this technique on your projects.

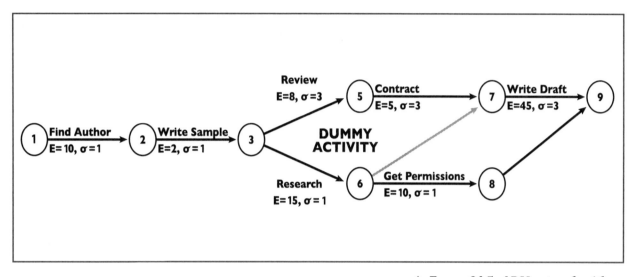

Critical Path May Not Be Critical

If you calculate E for the project, you may actually be using an overly optimistic completion time. Here's why. Imagine that you have the critical path and another path that's close in total time but has a larger standard deviation (see Figure 24-5). In practice, it may turn out that the other path turns critical!

Let's continue with our previous example. This time, we've added times (E) and standard deviations (σ) for each task. (We also adjusted the time for task "Review Samples" so it would illustrate this problem better.) Now, using the table below (see Figure 24-6), we've listed each task, its time, its standard deviation, and the square of the standard deviation (the variance). Remember, the value of the standard deviation for a path is the square root of the sum of the variances for the tasks on that path.

According to everything we've done so far, it's easy to see that the second path is critical at seventy-two days. But not so fast! Notice that path has a standard deviation of 3.46 days. That means we think there's roughly a 68 percent chance that the actual time will be somewhere between 68½ days and 75½ days. (When dealing with these calculations, round your answers to sensible time units.)

▲ FIGURE 24-5: *ADM network with standard deviations.* We've modified the previous chart by adding times (E) and standard deviations (σ) for each task.

Task	Time (E)	Std. Dev	SD sqd.
Find Author	10	1	1
Write Sample	2	1	1
Review Samples	8	3	9
Perform Research	15	1	1
Contract	5	3	9
Get Permissions	10	1	1
Write Draft	45	3	9
Path 1,2,3,5,7,9	70	5.39	
Path 1,2,3,6,7,9	72	3.46	CRITICAL
Path 1,2,3,6,8	30	2.00	

▲ FIGURE 24-6: *Critical path and variance.* **This table organizes the information from the Network Diagram in Figure 24-5. There are three paths through the network, and the second of these is the critical path because it's the highest number.**

Now look at the first path. It takes seventy days officially, but with a standard deviation of 5.39 days, it could take anywhere from 64½ days to 75½ days. In practice, either path could turn out critical, and in some cases the shorter path could actually turn out to be statistically the longest in practice! Make sure you consider this possibility in your projects. (You can use a Monte Carlo simulation to get around this problem, which we'll discuss shortly.)

Is it accurate to assume that the activity times vary in a standard distribution?

Problems in the PERT Assumptions

Is it accurate to assume that the activity times vary in a standard distribution? Perhaps there are only a few specific cases that are possible. For example, it takes three days to do Step A, but it doesn't always work the first time. Therefore, A might take three, six, nine, or twelve days, but no values in between them. Or what if the times are not in a series? Task A could take three days, but if it fails it will take five, if it fails again nine, and if it fails again seventeen.

Are the tasks really independent, in that the time it takes to do one job doesn't have an influence on how long it takes to do another job? If a critical task goes late, it's likely that you'll be looking to shorten future critical path tasks. The time it takes to do the first task would then influence how long it took to do the others. If there's a limited resource availability, and Task A takes extra time, then the resource may not be available in time to start Task B, making it take longer automatically.

Or, is it always possible for you to define all the tasks before the project begins? Perhaps the research nature of your project is such that you don't know all the tasks that will turn out to be necessary. Similarly, there may be other dependencies than the ones you initially planned.

In practice, you will likely find that these assumptions hold true in most instances. But if your project is an exception to the general rules, you may find that you don't get particularly useful information from PERT.

Level of Effort

With computing power much cheaper today than in the late 1950s and 1960s, it's plausible to attempt this method on smaller projects, but PERT can still be a handful. PERT is expensive to maintain just in terms of feeding it all the data. It's labor intensive, and if you are the only manager on your project, you may not have time available to keep up with it. PERT provides extensive detail, perhaps more than you may need to manage your project effectively.

When organizations use PERT, it's often at the demand of a client or customer. The Department of Defense, for example, used to require PERT for relating costs and schedules on major contracts. This turned into a major cost accounting headache for even large companies, resulting in two sets of books—one for their use, and another to satisfy their performance requirements with the customer.

When to Use PERT, and When Not To

Give serious consideration to using PERT if any of the following apply to you and your situation.

> When organizations use PERT, it's often at the demand of a client or customer.

The Monte Carlo Simulation

One of the newer tools available for project managers is software to perform a Monte Carlo simulation of a project network. In project management, a Monte Carlo simulation of your project involves running it thousands of times to determine the range of possible outcomes.

For each task, the simulation generates a random time within the frequency distribution that has been set for the task. If O = 1, P = 11, M = 3, and E = 4, on one run the program might choose 5 as the value, on another 3, and on another 8. Times within a standard deviation of E are selected more often than those outside, just as you would expect in reality.

At the end of the run, the program determines the project completion date, then does it over and over. The final graph shows actual completion times and the probability of each one. This method overcomes the PERT difficulty with more than one potential critical path.

1. Your project is very large (hundreds of millions of dollars at a minimum).
2. Uncertainty is high, and time is a factor in project success.
3. You have enough knowledge, experience, and understanding to develop the PERT information.
4. You have the money and staff to keep the system running (a comprehensive PERT implementation can run into hundreds of thousands of dollars).
5. Your customer requires it.

It is probably not a good idea to try PERT if you believe your project does not have the theoretical conditions listed above, and especially if you are starting a project in which very little of its future can be seen clearly. You may find yourself planning as you go along, with the data from early steps necessary to continue to stretch your schedule into the future.

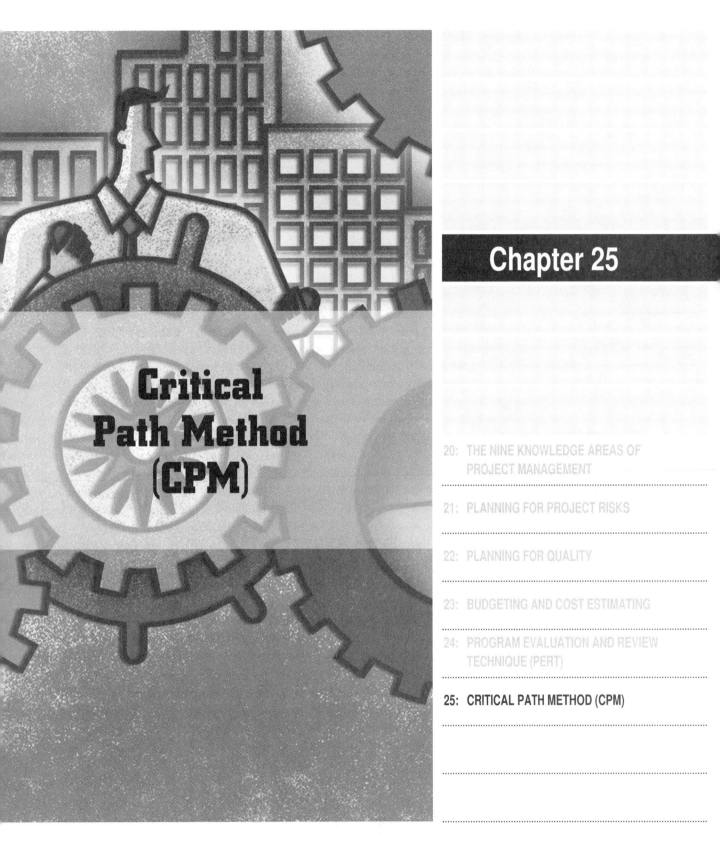

Critical Path Method (CPM)

Chapter 25

Looking for Tradeoffs

Managing a project with uncertainty is a challenge, and PERT evolved to meet that challenge. There are other challenges in project management, of course, and tools have evolved to meet those challenges as well.

Construction, in general, is a well-understood business. If we know how many bricks a skilled bricklayer can lay per hour, we can estimate with a good deal of precision how long it will take one bricklayer to build a ten-foot high wall. If we put two bricklayers on the job, we estimate that the wall will be completed in half the time. The hourly cost of building the wall goes up when we use two bricklayers, even though the task time goes down. What, then, is the best tradeoff between resources and time? Would it be profitable to put on two bricklayers to get the job done quickly? How about three? Four? Twenty?

Questions about time and cost tradeoffs can be very important in how you plan and schedule the tasks in your project. How you analyze these questions and determine your answers is the goal of the Critical Path Method, or CPM. CPM was developed in the mid-1950s at DuPont, working with Remington Rand, and was first tested in the construction of a major chemical plant in 1958.

Like PERT, major ideas in CPM are still widely used in project management, but often not in their purest academic form. You may find that certain practices in your organization are referred to as either PERT or CPM, but are quite different from what you see in this book. If that's the case, don't worry about it. Still, there's real value in understanding the fundamentals of this powerful tool.

CPM analysis is a valuable way to look at your project plan, even if you decide the full system is not for you. Look for the tradeoffs that save time and money, and when you find them, use them!

> CPM analysis is a valuable way to look at your project plan, even if you decide the full system is not for you.

Project Costs

The time estimate you establish for many of the jobs in your project is a function of the level of resources—people, equipment, money, and materials—you plan to devote to them. More resources are often a recipe for less time, and conversely, fewer resources means more time. Depending on the driver of your project, you can see the possibilities from both sides.

There are exceptions, of course. As the traditional project management joke has it, the fact that it takes one woman nine months to have a baby doesn't mean nine women can get the job done in one. Some task time estimates are independent of level of resources assigned.

Direct and Indirect Project Costs

Whether you're forced to account for them in your project budget or not, certain indirect costs are incurred on your project based on the time it takes. If a project takes longer, the costs of employee benefits and general management services rise, equipment rentals continue to be billed, and staff salaries continue to be paid. If you shorten the time to complete the project, the indirect project costs decrease.

The cost of the actual resources to get the job done are direct costs. If we add resources to complete the project earlier, the direct costs of the job tend to increase. That sets up the first tradeoff question for CPM: Do the savings in indirect costs from early completion outweigh the additional direct costs to achieve the savings?

Penalties and Incentives

In addition to the direct versus indirect cost tradeoff, there are other financial considerations. If you're managing a contract, sometimes there are incentives for early completion and penalties for late completion. Therefore, in considering whether to increase direct costs to speed up time, you not only consider the savings in indirect costs, but also the value of any incentives or penalties on the job. If your indirect cost rate is $500 per day and there's a $1,000 bonus for every day early you complete the project, then it's worth spending up to $1,500 on extra resources for every day they shorten the job.

Notice that penalties and incentives work differently. If you're dealing with a late completion penalty, that money only counts if your schedule shows you are going to be late. If the penalty is $1,000 a day and indirect costs are $500, then it's worth spending up to $1,500 to avoid being a day late. It's only worth $500 a day to beat the deadline, because you do save the indirect cost.

If there's an incentive, it's the other way around. You get $1,500 a day for beating the deadline ($1,000 + $500), but if you were going to be late anyway, it's only worth $500 a day to reduce the lateness.

Too Many Cooks Spoil the Broth

You can put too many people on a job, and when you do, the time it takes goes up! There's actually a proof in the computer world that demonstrates adding more programmers to a late project invariably makes it later. New people need to be brought up to speed on the project by existing staff, which takes time. People given tasks to complete code written by others have to do a lot of analysis merely to understand what's already there. In addition, programmers often have their own style preferences, which results in workable code being rewritten. So, extra resources aren't a panacea for all project problems.

Extra Revenue

People offer incentives and penalties because they have opportunities and costs associated with your project performance. If you're building a new factory, and the factory will start generating $5,000 a day in profit as soon as it's up and running, then it's worth up to $5,000 a day to get it up and running earlier. If it's a contract job, you want to offer an incentive to your contractor because you can realize a profit from it. If it's an in-house job, the same logic applies. It's worth it to spend extra money (the amount of the potential revenue or avoided cost plus any savings in indirect cost) to achieve earlier performance.

Crashing

You've heard of a "crash" priority, right? This term comes from CPM, and suggests that you want to throw all your resources at the job to get it done ASAP! Remember back in Chapter 16, when we considered spending money on express delivery to get our computer here quicker? Now we'll look at this approach in greater detail.

Crashing is speeding up a task or project by spending money or resources to shorten activity durations. CPM is a technique for analyzing your crashing options on a project and determining which ones are desirable. In using CPM, we have to make some assumptions (shown in the sidebar).

CPM can be dangerous on a project with high inherent uncertainty, because you don't always receive the reward the system says you should.

As in our discussion of PERT, these assumptions may not hold true in all cases. Sometimes, this means that CPM can't be used effectively on a particular project. Other times, it may mean that it's a lot more difficult and time-consuming to do so, or that you must be aware that your results are fuzzy. (With all project management techniques, remember that the numbers that come out of a model are never any better than the numbers that went in.) Let's plan a sample project using CPM to see how it's done.

Optimizing Your Project Schedule in CPM

While CPM, like PERT, originally employed the ADM/AOA method of network diagramming, you'll find that you can also do it in PDM. We'll show you both. First, the ADM method (see Figure 25-1).

In the sample project shown here, the critical path is 1, 2, 3, 5, 7, 8 (the top route), and totals forty-seven working days. Task 2,4, Task 4,6, and Task 6,7 have a total slack of four days among them (twenty-eight days compared to thirty-two days on their critical path counterparts). That means, you'll remember, that all three tasks together can be a total of four days late before the project is delayed.

For each task, we've listed the normal time (no extra resources) and the potential crash time. The crash time is the fastest possible time for the job assuming unlimited resources. That means regardless of your willingness to spend extra money, the task cannot take less than its crash time. For the purposes of this exercise, you can make the task take any amount of time between its normal and

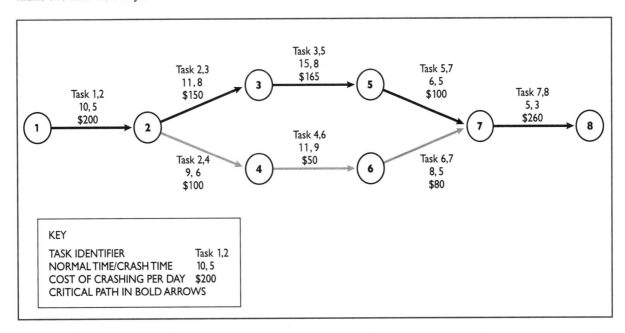

▲ FIGURE 25-1: *CPM Network Diagram.* This ADM-type network shows the information necessary to calculate the cost of crashing activities, and the potential time to be saved.

Base Cost Not Included

Please note that the cost of crashing doesn't include the base cost of doing the work. It could be hundreds of dollars or thousands of dollars, but for the purpose of this analysis it doesn't matter. You'll spend that money (called "sunk costs") whether you crash a task or not. Right now, you only have to worry about the extra cost to shorten its time from the normal value.

crash times. You will have to spend the cost of crashing per day for each day you want to shorten a task.

The remaining piece of information you need is the overhead cost, the sum of all the indirect time-related costs on this project. Let's make that equal to $250 per day. Follow along as we do this exercise, and see if you get the same answers before we do!

First Crash

The obvious place to look for savings is in parts of the project where only one activity is taking place. Here, Task 1,2 and Task 7,8 fit that condition. Crashing Task 1,2 is easy. We spend $200 per day to reduce the task by five days, and gain back $250 per day in saved overhead! The project time has now dropped from forty-seven days to forty-two days, we've saved $250 (5 x $50), and the critical path is unchanged (see Figure 25-2). Task 7,8, on the other hand, costs $260 per day to crash, but that's more than the $250 per day we gain. We leave that task alone.

Second Crash

It doesn't make any sense to try to shorten Tasks 2,4, 4,6, or 6,7; at least for now. That's because they aren't on the critical path. Shortening them leaves the total project length unchanged, and so we would save nothing in overhead costs.

Instead, we look at the critical tasks 2,3, 3,5, and 5,7. Remember that the critical path is only four days longer than the noncritical path below it. Therefore, it's only worth our while to crash these three critical path tasks by a total of four days. Any more simply switches the critical path to the bottom, and again we don't save any additional overhead cost.

Of the three tasks, the cheapest one to crash is Task 5,7. Unfortunately, we can only shorten it by one day, but we save another $150 ($250 – $100). The second-cheapest task to crash is Task 2,3. We can cut it by three days, saving $100 per day, or $300.

Now, we've shortened the project by four more days to thirty-eight days, and our total savings are $700 (see Figure 25-3). All tasks in the project are now critical.

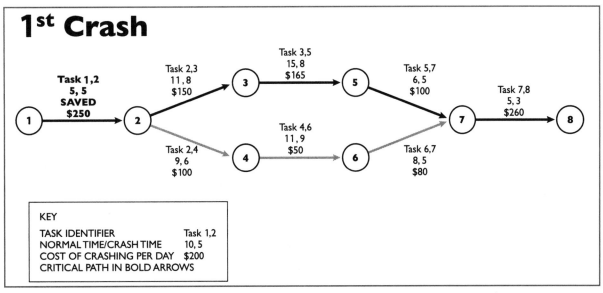

▲ FIGURE 25-2: *CPM after first crash.* We've shortened Task 1,2 by five days and saved $250.

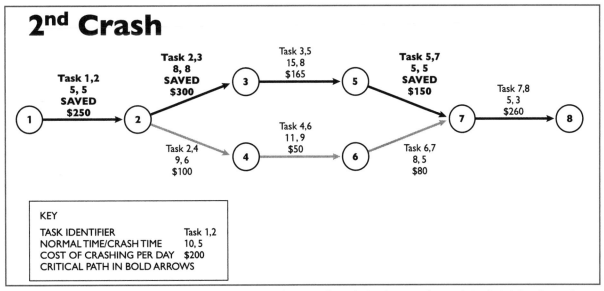

▲ FIGURE 25-3: *CPM after second crash.* We've shortened Task 5,7 by one day and Task 2,3 by three days, and saved another $450. All tasks are now critical.

During the CPM process, you can suddenly find that you have a new critical path. Activities that earlier weren't worth considering for crashing now are; other activities that looked promising before now aren't.

Third Crash

To reduce time any further, we will have to cut a day from the path 2-4-6-7 for every day we reduce 2-3-5-7, because we now have two critical paths. Neither Tasks 2,3 nor 5,7 can be crashed any further, because they are both at their minimum already. To find any further crash opportunities, we have to look at Task 3,5. It can be cut a total of seven days before it reaches its minimum of eight.

To cut Task 3,5 by one day, we will have to cut one of the three tasks below it by one day. If we don't, the critical path simply shifts to the path 2-4-6-7, and we don't save any overhead costs.

Start with the cheapest combination, which is Task 3,5 with Task 4,6. The combined crash cost is $165 + $50, or $215 per day, giving us a savings of $35 per day, and we can cut a total of two days before Task 4,6 reaches its minimum of nine. The critical path is now thirty-six days and total savings are $770 (see Figure 25-4).

Fourth Crash

Now we look at the pair of Task 3,5 and Task 6,7. The total crash cost for the pair is $245, which is just barely below our $250 threshold. Nevertheless, we can save three more days before Task 6,7 reaches its lower limit. The critical path is now thirty-three days and total savings are $785 (see Figure 25-5).

Fifth Crash

We still have two available crashing days in Task 3,5, so we look at our final pairing with Task 2,4. Unfortunately, the total cost to crash this pair is $265, which is more than we save. We're now finished with crashing this project. The critical path remains at thirty-three days, with the total savings at $785.

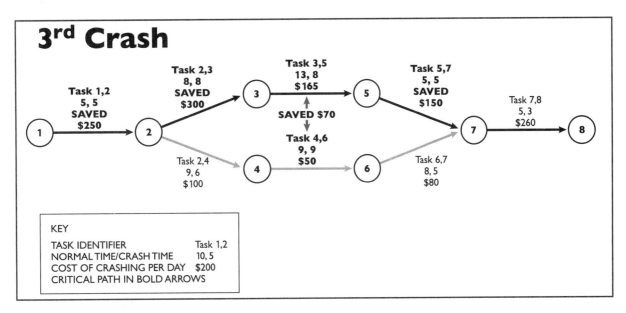

▲ FIGURE 25-4: *CPM after third crash.* We've shortened Tasks 3,5 and 4,6 by two days and saved another $70.

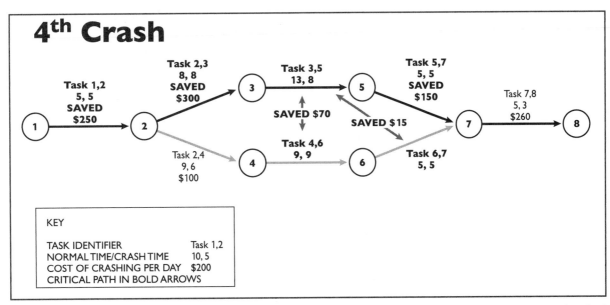

▲ FIGURE 25-5: *CPM after fourth crash.* We've shortened Tasks 3,5 and 6,7 by three days and saved another $15.

Crashing Using PDM and Gantt Chart

You can easily do the same process using your project management software. Set up the Network Diagram using PDM, and the computer will determine the critical path. Adjust the duration fields as you crash your tasks, and let the computer show you when new paths become critical. Figure 25-6 represents the "before" task plan shown in a Microsoft Project PDM-type chart while Figure 25-7 shows the "after" task plan in a Microsoft Project Gantt Chart.

Limits and Risks in CPM

The biggest risk in CPM is that spending the money on the extra resources won't save the allotted time. If you spend $175 to save $250 and then you don't save the $250, you may be in trouble. CPM works best when uncertainty is extremely low. Certain "acts of god" disasters—famine, flood, pestilence—can excuse exceeding your estimates, but ordinary estimating error isn't normally acceptable as an excuse.

Next, you won't always find smooth relationships between the cost of crashing and the time saved. It might cost you $100 to save one day on a task, but saving a second day might cost $200, or worse. Adding an extra bricklayer seems fairly straightforward, but maybe one can lay fifty bricks an hour but the second only thirty-five, and they get the same hourly rate. Maybe your option is to save one day or save six days, and nothing in between is possible, because each involves a different strategy for doing the work.

If your project is large and complex, you'll find CPM gets more and more time-consuming to apply. Just listing all the possible crashing options in a 500-task project will be a fairly daunting challenge.

Consider pursuing a "low-hanging fruit" strategy of taking advantage of obvious CPM savings and perhaps ignoring some more challenging ones. If the savings on paper are large enough, then, even allowing for the messiness of actual practice, you should end up okay.

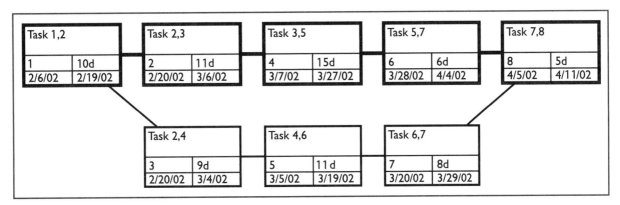

▲ FIGURE 25-6: *PDM Chart.* This PDM-type Network Diagram contains the same information as the CPM chart in Figure 25-1.

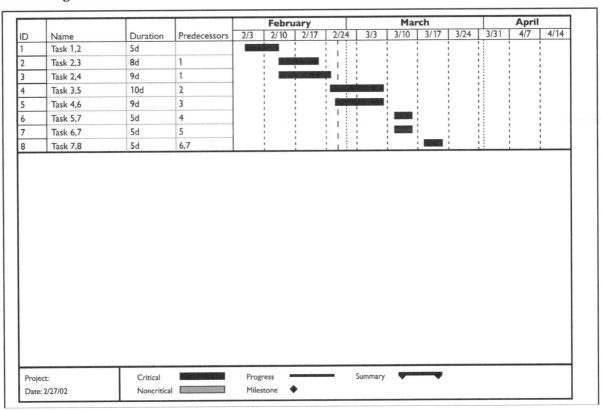

▲ FIGURE 25-7: *Gantt Chart.* This Gantt Chart contains the same information as the CPM chart in Figure 25-5.

PART VI

Executing, Tracking, and Adjusting the Project

- **How to set up a project team able to work together to get the job done**

- **How to establish clear measurements and directions for the tasks to be done, and communicate them effectively to your team**

- **How to interpret and effectively act when project variance becomes apparent**

- **What questions to ask to get the true story about your project**

- **How to establish a reporting system that people will follow**

- **How to use multiple problem-solving strategies**

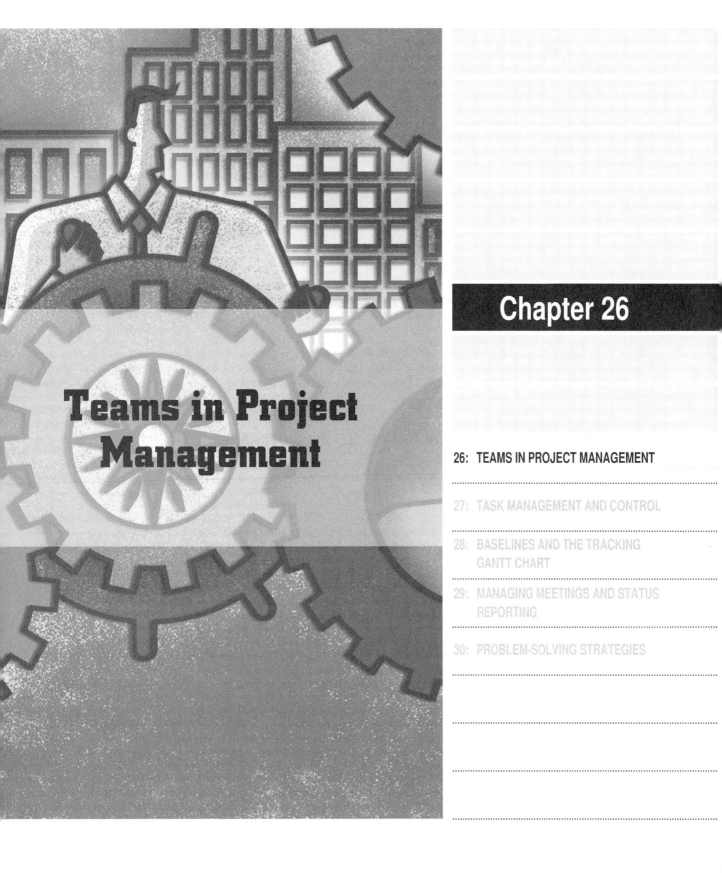

Chapter 26

Teams in Project Management

The People Side

We work with people in two ways, not only on projects but also on regular ongoing work, as individuals and as members of a team. Both roles are important; both are crucial to the success of your project. Emphasize one at the expense of the other, however, and you're likely to experience trouble.

The people side of project management is most often thought of as the "art" of project management, as opposed to the "science" of the technical analysis and structuring that makes up the planning process. We found numerous people issues in planning, and there are technical issues in teamwork as well. The "art" and "science" of project management are never as separate in practice as they seem to be in theory. You need both at every stage of the work.

Building an effective team is usually a critical requirement in achieving project success. Don't neglect it.

Recruiting the Project Team

In the ideal world of project management, you would be able to recruit your own "dream team" to do the work. In reality, you often have no choice about whom you get. Even when you have choice, it's limited. Perhaps you can only choose from existing employees, whether they possess the necessary skills or not. You may be further limited to existing employees not already assigned to other projects. The date availability of certain team members may be additionally limiting, especially of team members with very specific technical skills. For all these reasons, the idea of actually "recruiting" your project team may seem a little far-fetched.

> Even with these limitations, you should still look at the first part of building a project team as recruitment.

Even with these limitations, you should still look at the first part of building a project team as recruitment. First, you do sometimes have choices to make, and those choices likely have significant project impact. Second, you can sometimes expand the choices available through your skills in negotiation and creative thinking. Third, even when your project members are draftees, acting as if they volunteered gives you strategic advantages. Fourth, even if none of these apply, thinking of this as a "recruitment" process gives you access to some information you'd be unlikely to get otherwise.

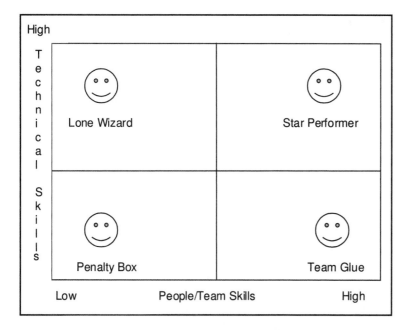

▲ FIGURE 26-1: *Characteristics of project team members.* The suitability of someone as a team member on your project is a function of both appropriate technical skill level and ability to work with others on a team.

Balancing Skills and Attitudes

While it's unusual to have complete freedom of action in recruiting a project team, you often have a pool of people from which to choose. From the project perspective, people differ in two axes: useful technical skills to do the project work and ability to work with others in a team environment (see Figure 26-1).

While in an ideal world we'd all manage teams consisting exclusively of Star Performers—people who balance strong technical skills with excellent people and teamwork skills—in practice this turns out not to be the case. Because people aren't perfect—including project managers—we normally have to work with a range of different types. Knowing who they are and how to manage them is often very helpful.

> Because people aren't perfect—including project managers—we normally have to work with a range of different types.

Star Performers

By the very nature of things, Star Performers are easy to select and easy to manage. If you have the chance to get them, by all means do so.

From an organizational perspective, however, that may not be the best thing. After all, Star Performers are a limited resource. If your project is not of the highest priority, the Star Performer could do more organizational good somewhere else. This is properly the concern of senior managers, who need to parcel out these precious resources with an eye to the bottom line.

Second, Star Performers aren't a huge advantage on work that doesn't require top technical or people skills. Given that some projects are simpler than others, you don't put your "A" team on "C" work.

Third, Star Performers are in demand, and sooner or later, they figure it out. Other project managers are casting an envious eye on your project team, and you may find suddenly that you've been robbed of the person you're counting on.

The leadership and planning challenge with Star Performers is to have a backup plan in mind. If you have Star Performers and want to keep them, make sure you're keeping an eye on the political environment.

Lone Wizards

"Who *was* that masked man?" comes the plaintive cry. The technical wizard shows up, works magic, then disappears mysteriously into the night having spoken to no one. That's the upside. The downside is that their lack of people skills can actually damage the productivity of others.

Once you've found some people with adequate technical skills to do the work on the project, it's in your best interest to change the scale and pick the one of those with the best people skills, rather than the one with the best technical skills. For one thing, people who truly are tech wizards in their topic may find it frustrating and dissatisfying to squander their skills on work that is "beneath" them.

For another, their abilities might be better used by the organization on other projects.

Finally, there is the potential damage poor people skills can do to others on the team. Poor people skills can come out in several different ways:

- Difficulty in communicating and relating, symptomized by a tendency to withdraw and avoid people contact
- Active annoyance at others who are perceived as "intellectually inferior," symptomized by attempts to either demonstrate one's own superiority or criticize and degrade those perceived as less talented or able
- Inability to share work or work on items requiring collaboration, for either of the above reasons or simply because of a lack of understanding of human dynamics, symptomized by frustration and conflict from both sides

Treat All Team Members as Prospective Hires

If you are recruiting a new employee, there are three tools you use to winnow down the stack of applicants: resumes, interviews, and reference checks. You can apply all three techniques even when your team members are assigned in advance.

Even when team members aren't your choice, treat them as if they were. Ask them for a copy of their resume, and go through it with them. You'll often be surprised with skills and experience that people possess. If they have never been called upon in the current job, you may have been missing a big part of what they can contribute.

Second, interview them. There are numerous books (including one in the *Streetwise* line) on how to plan and conduct an interview to learn what you need to know about a prospective hire.

Third, check references. Have they worked on other projects and for other project managers? Talk to others who have led them. Check with their supervisor about any areas of challenge and what has worked/not worked with them in the past.

Also with a new hire, you plan on explaining the job and your expectations. Don't forget to do that with a new team member, even if he or she has been with the organization for a while.

With improved knowledge, insight, and (in some cases) forewarning, you'll start your team process on the right footing every time!

The quicker you figure out the nature and extent of the problem, the better you will be able to handle it. That's another big reason to think of starting your team as "recruitment," even if it really isn't.

Once you know the shape of the people skill deficiencies, you can act before the problems get out of hand. It may not be practical to teach a Lone Wizard how to be a "people person," but if you can describe what you want in terms of specific behaviors, you might get it. Discipline and terminations are often not possible for a nonsupervisory project manager. However, you can still arrange positive and negative consequences in terms of writing letters to the actual supervisor, escalating unresolved problems to higher authority, or reassigning work and responsibility to someone who can work and play well with others.

Teamwork issues normally don't go away by ignoring them. The Godzilla Principle works here, too—face the issues early.

Team Glue

Someone with great technical skills and no people skills poses one challenge. The opposite situation can be challenging as well. There are some perfectly wonderful human beings who just don't have the skill set you need on a specific project. What now?

First, make sure you distinguish between a person whose technical skills are merely mediocre and someone who is actually incompetent. (The Lone Wizard is likely to maintain there is no real difference between the two.) Mediocre technical skills are perfectly adequate in performing many tasks, and in assisting and collaborating with those of higher skill on more challenging tasks.

On the other hand, if someone is simply unable to do the work at even a minimal standard, you can't very well assign work to them. If you can't get rid of them or swap them, you may have to sideline them in your planning. Look for work they *can* do that has some value; have them shadow or assist others in hopes of achieving professional growth.

In addition, many technical skills are a function of practice more than innate genius. You may deliberately be assigned people of

> First, make sure you distinguish between a person whose technical skills are merely mediocre and someone who is actually incompetent.

lower technical skill in the hopes they will get more experience. In that case, pairing them with someone possessing stronger technical talent is a secondary project objective and needs to be worked into your plan. If you know this in advance, you can add it into your plan. Extend the duration of jobs to be done by someone with lower-level tech skills. If you're considering multiple layouts for your Network Diagram, look for ways to match people with developing skills with tasks that have slack.

Penalty Box

In the same way someone can succeed in both areas, someone can be deficient in both as well—poor at the work, poor with people. And you can be stuck with them. After all, they have to work on *something*. While your first strategy should generally be to get the hot potato shifted somewhere else, that isn't always practical and sometimes isn't politic.

One interesting question to explore is why these people haven't been fired. There may be several reasons. One, they were competent at some earlier time on some earlier work. Two, they may be connected with someone else in the organization who has the clout to protect them. Three, there are reasons why we (or someone) might feel some degree of pity or responsibility to keep them employed. (This is perfectly legitimate, even if you don't like it. In the real world, not everyone enjoys employment merely because of competence, and perhaps someday we ourselves may be glad of that fact.)

A fifth reason is the commonly held belief that some people are unfireable, such as in a union situation or in the government. This, by the way, is simply false. The truth is that many supervisors are unwilling to take the time to learn the rules and document the behavior appropriately. And it's emotionally difficult to fire someone, at least for most of us.

And sixth, of course, is that very few people are in fact completely incompetent or unable. Some may have limited skills, further hampered by a lack of socially appropriate behavior, but it's your job and your challenge to look for work they *can* do and let them do it.

Human Catalysts

There are some people who function as human catalysts. They may not seem to be leaders, but somehow more work gets done when they get involved. Watch out for the tendency to evaluate people more on their input (how hard they work, how strong their knowledge) than on their output (what actually gets accomplished). It's the latter we really value, and we know that the former isn't compatible in every case with actually getting the job done.

The Ten-Penny Challenge

Your ability to influence positive behavioral change in other people is normally higher than you think. It takes patience and regular reinforcement, but it's not dependent particularly on whether you're the official supervisor or not. The strategy involves the famous management mantra, "Catch 'em doing it *right!*"

Take ten pennies and put them in your pocket. Now, go out of your office several times a day to look around. Find someone doing something right, and tell them about it, right then and there. You don't need to be flowery or overstate the accomplishment; you do need to be specific. When you finish, move a penny into another pocket. You've got to get all ten pennies moved every day. (It's not a bad idea to save a few for your home life as well.)

Initially, you'll find people resist being praised—they're not used to it. But after a while, you'll find that resistance weakening, and after that, you'll start to see change happening. Give this a couple of months to work, but at the end, you'll be amazed at how much the people around you are transformed!

When you are not the supervisor of record, you tend to have less long-term ability to influence behavioral change, but it still may be worth working on. People who've been repeatedly told about their deficiencies often find the message reinforcing in a negative way: They become more so. Try instead to find challenges they can meet. As their confidence grows, so will their ability—and your success as a team-oriented project manager!

Rewarding and Supporting the Team

Motivational strategies often assume an unwarranted degree of similarity among team members. Let's say you decide to motivate people by bringing top performers on stage in front of the company at the monthly "all-hands" meeting, giving them a certificate, and then a standing ovation from the employees. If you're extroverted and enjoy public recognition, that may sound just fine. But if your personal style is shy and you find your best reward in the work itself, a public ceremony like that may seem more like mortification than motivation.

Ten Mistaken Ideas About Motivation

1. "What motivates me motivates others."
2. "People are motivated primarily by money."
3. "Everyone loves to receive formal awards."
4. "Teams are motivated by production quotas."
5. "Good slogans and inspirational posters motivate performance."
6. "Cheerleading is a way to get the best from people."
7. "My people are professionals! They don't need 'motivating.'"
8. "I'll think about motivation when there's a problem."
9. "I treat everyone the same in all respects."
10. "Once I know the best way to motivate someone, I'll stick to it without change."

Source: Steven W. Flannes, Ph.D., and Ginger Levin, DPA, *People Skills for Project Managers*, 2001.

Chapter 27

Task Management
and Control

Difficulty in Delegating

The fundamental purpose of project execution is to get the work done on time, on budget, and to the desired standard of performance. Everything else is a method or a technique to support that goal. Teamwork matters a lot, but remember that we have teams in the work environment because we need the work to get done.

One of the chief self-diagnosed difficulties many supervisors and managers have is difficulty in delegating. "I can do it better and faster myself," goes the lament. "When I try to delegate, I get resistance and delay. I don't have people with the skill and ability I need, and as for training, who has time?" Yet delegating is the fundamental skill of supervision—it's the act of getting work done through the effort of other people.

An additional benefit of project management is that the structured tools for task management and control help you delegate,

The Crucial Importance of Delegating

There are a number of challenges in delegating, but one of the most immediate ways to improve your ability in this crucial area is to remember that there are two entirely separate reasons for you to delegate, and each requires a different approach for effectiveness.

The first and obvious reason to delegate is to get work off your desk and onto someone else's, freeing you up to do work that only you can do. Of course, that necessarily assumes that you have someone who is willing and able to accept the delegation, and that isn't always necessarily the case.

It's important to realize that the vast majority of actual training that takes place in organizations is on-the-job training (OJT), and much of that training is informal in nature. How did you learn how to do your job at your current level of skill? Some of what you know may have come from the classroom, but much of what you know has come from the act of doing it, with or without support and coaching. For most of us, some of our best insights into the work have come from the mistakes we've made. Mistakes are a great opportunity for learning, and if you aren't learning from your mistakes, you're squandering a precious resource.

So, the second reason to delegate is OJT. When you're delegating for the purpose of training, you necessarily choose someone who *can't* currently do the job. You expect that you will have to spend more of your time and energy explaining, teaching, coaching, and reviewing. You often work harder and spend more time than if you simply did the job yourself. But if you don't teach, they can't learn, and in the long run the situation stays unchanged: You have to do all the work yourself.

train, and coach, delivering not only a product at the end of the project, but also leaving team members with more skill than they had to begin with.

Negotiating Task Performance

Why would you have to negotiate task performance when you're the project manager? Should that not be expected? Unfortunately, as you've no doubt realized, your official authority and about $4 will get you a tall skim latte, extra shot—but that's about all.

Have you ever met an unmotivated person? The answer may seem obvious, but it's a trick question. Look at it this way: Have you ever met someone who spends more time dodging work than it would take to do it? Now, ask yourself, "Is this person unmotivated?" In fact, the person *is* motivated, but not in the direction you might want. Motivation is why someone is behaving in a particular way. If you don't like the behavior, a good strategy is to start by determining the motivation.

Basically, there are only three reasons why someone isn't doing what you want: they don't know, they can't do it, or they're making a choice—they *won't* do it. How you approach the issue depends on what's going on. Everybody's motivated—it's why they do what they do.

No matter how important your job assignment happens to be, it's almost never the only thing on someone else's agenda. When that person looks at your request, it naturally gets compared to the other demands, and it's not necessarily the case that yours will win.

How, then, can you negotiate? Once you know the potential problem issue on the other side, you're in a position to negotiate. If you can solve their problem, there's a good chance they'll help solve yours.

Another way to look at this is to realize that you do favors for colleagues that you aren't actually required to do. Why do you do them? It may be because they've helped you (or may in the future), because they asked nicely, because you understood why their request was important, because you're a team player, or a host of other reasons (including negative ones, such as a difficulty saying "no"). The motivations of others and your own motivations probably won't

Don't Know, Can't Do, Won't Do

This powerful analytical tool can help you learn why you aren't getting the support or cooperation you need. Always look at behavior issues in the order "don't know—can't do—won't do." You can always escalate to the next level; it's more difficult and potentially embarrassing if you have to back up.

- *Don't know.* Have you verified that the person is actually aware of what you want? Is your communication clear and precise?

- *Can't do.* Are there actual obstacles that prevent performance? These include skill/training, tools/equipment, access/authority, and improperly designed jobs.

- *Won't do.* Will the person receive a negative reward if they do what you want? Is there a positive reward for failure to perform? Does performance matter at all (from the perspective of the other person)? Look for ways to alter rewards and penalties to get the behavior you want.

PMBOK ALERT!

In the official PMBOK terminology, they use a concept similar to the Task Management Forum and refer to it officially as a "WBS Dictionary," because it provides a definition for the task name you wrote down in making your WBS. In my experience with hundreds of seminar groups, this term ends up leaving most people confused. When it's called a "Task Management Form," people quickly grasp the concept and are able to put it to immediate use. Therefore, we'll refer to it this way here.

synch 100 percent of the time, but usually at least some of what works on you will work on others, too.

The Task Management Form

One of the fundamentals of getting people to do things is to give them clear and complete information on exactly what you want. You've probably had the experience of trying to do what you heard someone say only to find out at the end that it wasn't what that someone actually wanted. In the absence of a tape recorder, we can't always be sure whether they said it badly or we heard it badly, but the outcome is the same. If you want others to do work for you and do it correctly, it's up to you to take the steps necessary to ensure understanding. A powerful and effective tool is the Task Management Form.

As you'll see in Figure 27-1, this form provides a home for all the information you need to understand what's involved in a particular task, and is therefore a very effective way to delegate. Properly done, it tends to eliminate "don't know" type difficulties with tasks.

Reducing Time Involved

If you've got a fairly large project, completing a Task Management Form for each activity can be time-consuming. To reduce the time involved, consider these two strategies:

1. Have the team members who will do the task do most of the work of preparing the form. This also achieves improved buy-in and identifies potential problems early.
2. Recycle Task Management Forms from previous projects with similar activities. Remember that templates don't always go down perfectly; expect to edit the information.

Completing the Task Management Form

While you're welcome to use this form for your own projects, you're normally better off adapting it. There may be too much fine detail in some areas and not enough in others, depending on your

TASK MANAGEMENT FORM

Task/WBS No:	Task Name:	Version No./Date

Predecessor Task(s)	Successor Tasks(s)

Specifications/Deliverables:

Resources—People/Department:

Equipment/Supplies:

Time Estimate: _____ (If PERT, add range below)

Imposed Date/Type/Reason: _____

Milestones/Dates:

PERT TIMES:

Optimistic _____ Pessimistic _____ Most Likely _____

Cost Estimate			Assigned To:	Date
	Plan	Actual		
Labor	$_____	_____		
Equipment/Supplies	$_____	_____	Completed by:	Date
Contract Costs	$_____	_____		
Overhead (___%)	$_____	_____		
			Signature:	
TOTAL	$_____	_____		

▲ FIGURE 27-1: *Task Management Form.* Use this form or your own adaptation to ensure that all task information is clear, complete, and current.

organization and the nature of your project. Form design and development is a surprisingly sophisticated activity, and a really well-done form can make a significant difference in your results.

Use Milestones

Milestones show the completion of parts of the task and help measure progress. For "Write Proposal," you might have milestones for the various sections, so that someone can start reviewing even before the entire proposal is finished. Milestones also help you manage people of lower work maturity—using more milestones gives you better control.

- *Task number*: If you use project management software, your program will automatically number your tasks. Use WBS numbers in addition if desired.
- *Task name*: Make sure the name actually gives a sense of the work. One good practice is to think of a task as an action, described with a verb followed by a noun. "Write proposal" is clearer than "Proposal" because the latter could mean writing, or typing, or mailing, or reviewing.
- *Predecessor/successor task(s)*: This information helps the person assigned the task to understand the consequences of being late.
- *Specifications/deliverables*: "Deliverables" are the physical outputs of the task. "Write proposal" means you must deliver a written proposal. Specifications involve the measurable characteristics of the task. The written proposal must contain a response to all items in the RFP, for example.
- *Resources*: The form has spaces for people as well as tools/equipment.
- *Time estimate*: You may fill in a single time or date, or you may need to complete more information. If you're using PERT time estimating, you need to indicate this on the form and also provide the three individual estimates. If there's an imposed date situation, you need to write down the date itself, the type (fixed early start, finish no later than, etc.), and the reason. If you omit the reason, you may omit the motivation to achieve the date.
- *Cost estimate*: The cost estimate may have numerous elements. Use those appropriate to your own organization.
- *Assigned to/completed by/date/signature*: Keep a record of who did what and when.

Kanban Task Management

There are immediate virtues and benefits in using a task management form system. You can increase the benefit by using a *kanban* task management technique.

A Brief History

In the late 1940s, Taiichi Ohno, an engineer (later executive vice president) of Toyota Motor Company, had a leadership role in the development of the innovative and influential Toyota Production System. One element of the system was the inventory management strategy known as "just-in-time" (JIT) inventory, using a system often called *kanban*, a Japanese term referring to printed cards.

Based on Ohno's observations of American supermarkets and the efficiencies of self-service and restock, he modeled the idea in his factories. Each production line acted as a "supermarket" for the next line, making products that the next line required, then making enough product to restock the shelves only as the product was withdrawn for the next stage.

When you needed new parts and supplies for your line, you would "purchase" them using *kanban* cards for your own line, triggering reorders up the system. Our use of *kanban* is a different idea for cards, but the term is selected with "thanx and a tip o' the hat" to Taiichi Ohno.

> Based on Ohno's observations of American supermarkets and the efficiencies of self-service and restock, he modeled the idea in his factories.

Follow the Steps

Step 1. Create a project binder that contains all the documents and printouts that your project generates. Put some notebook paper in it so that every handwritten note or meeting minute is kept together. In your project binder, put *two* copies of every Task Management Form.

Step 2. To assign a task on your project, give one copy of the Task Management Form for that activity to the person you assign. Write that person's name in the "Assigned to" space, and the date on which the work was assigned. The person who received the assignment is now accountable for it.

Step 3. During regular status meetings and other project control activities, make notes about progress on the activity on your copy of the Task Management Form. Use notebook paper placed after the form as necessary. Keep all information about the task together in your binder.

Step 4. The person performing the task is also responsible for reporting status. There are two types of status reports: regular reports that occur on the time schedule in conjunction with status reviews, and special (also known as exception) reports, which identify any unusual issues or problems experienced in doing the work.

Step 5. Problems identified in special reports and change orders generate special meetings with the project manager to resolve problems as they occur. If necessary, the task information is modified. Both project manager and task manager initial any changes and report the dates of those changes.

Step 6. The person assigned the task completes the task in line with any approved changes, verifies with checkmarks that all deliverables and specifications have been achieved, and signs the Task Management Form certifying that the task has been completed.

Step 7. The task is only considered officially complete when the signed Task Management Form is returned to the project manager.

Step 8. The Task Management Form, any notes, changes, and history become part of the paper trail of the project that is reviewed during project evaluation and "lessons learned."

You'll find with this system that people's attitudes toward the work change when the documentation and control changes. A traditional management maxim has it that "what gets measured, gets done," and this method helps ensure your tasks get the focus they require.

When You Must Interfere—And When You Must Resist

You need to get clear in your own mind for the specific project how much emphasis you need to put on the "on-the-job" training portion of your responsibility. If people need to learn how to do these tasks because they will need to do them on a fairly regular basis, giving people the opportunity to flounder around a little as they learn the job is in the long-term best interest of the organization, if not completely in the best interest of the project.

If the project is high priority and on an unbendable deadline, you might need to compromise the goal of helping people learn and turn your attention instead to how to get it done quickly and correctly, even if that violates generally applicable principles of delegation. And, if the project is so far outside the normal responsibilities of your team members that it's highly unlikely they'll need to master the skills involved, you may also choose a more active management strategy.

Don't wing this. Make up your mind at the beginning of the project what circumstances demand, tell your team members to get their expectations in the right place, and be consistent. It's often tempting to start interfering as soon as the first sign of storm clouds appear on the horizon, but if people don't work through a tempest or two, they aren't really able to learn very much.

> Make up your mind at the beginning of the project what circumstances demand.

Ensuring Quality Performance

People not only have to do the job, but do it well. Our earlier focus on quality planning comes back to the forefront in task management. We should already know what "quality" means for each specific activity and for the project as a whole. To achieve quality goals, first make sure the information is shared with the people who do the work. If they don't know the quality goals, it's highly unlikely they'll be motivated to meet them.

Second, implement measurement. While one value of measurement is that it identifies variance (especially special cause variance) in time for you to act on it, another value of measurement is that it is

Task Management

On an operational level, project management often becomes task management—you break the project into tasks, you identify and organize the tasks into a structure, you manage the team that performs the task, and then you assemble it all back together into the project goal.

That's why careful attention to the task management process is where "the rubber meets the road," the place where you have the detailed ability to make sure the project achieves its objectives.

feedback to the person performing the task. The second value is more in line with an overall commitment to progress. We identify variance not so we can come in and punish the offenders, but so the workers can learn early that there is a potential problem and solve it before the baby monster turns into a full-grown Godzilla.

Third, keep team members focused on the customer and the project goal. It's difficult sometimes for people "in the trenches" to see the big picture, and sometimes the big picture slips out of view altogether. One of your key quality objectives as project manager is to ensure that people not only know *what* they're doing, but also *why* they're doing it.

For more information on this topic, visit our Web site at www.businesstown.com

Baselines and the Tracking Gantt Chart

Chapter 28

The Importance of Baselines

In our projects, it's valuable to establish baselines—measurable elements of the project against which we can set actual performance, with the goal of determining how big and potentially how meaningful each variance we discover is.

In planning your project, we've recommended that you develop detailed schedules, budgets, and technical plans to ensure that you fully understand your own project. The payoff you get from the planning work just in those terms is normally enough to make it worth your while, but there's more value to extract. Your planning documents, once complete and accepted, become the foundation for your project tracking and monitoring system by turning into baselines. Baselines also form the foundation for project metrics, the measurable information that you will use for project management improvement.

If you want to make sure your project is on time, on budget, and to spec, you want to be able to measure your progress on those three axes. There are three primary project baselines you need to manage your project, corresponding to the Triple Constraints. The first is the schedule baseline, which is normally presented as a Tracking Gantt Chart. The second is the cost baseline, a cumulative graph showing actual versus planned expenditures to date. And the third is the technical baseline (also called the performance baseline), which is often linked to the WBS. We'll look at all three baselines and how you can use them in the next three sections.

Using the Technical Baseline

You developed the WBS to ensure that you described the scope and the deliverables in terms of tasks and activities necessary to complete them. You can use the same tool as a technical baseline to ensure good performance (see Figure 28-1).

Compare this to the form in Figure 7-2. The earlier version was an appropriate quick tracking mechanism for a smaller project. When developing your own technical baseline, you need to consider what information you need and what level of control you plan to exercise. In the first version, we simply prepared a check-off list.

Monitoring Tools

Developing your monitoring tools is a planning activity, and one of the most important of the planning stages. You need the ability to see what's going on in the overall context of the project, and unless the project is quite small, you're unlikely to be able to keep it all in your head at the requisite level of detail. The result is the need for baselines.

Remember that the presence of a variance by itself is not proof you have a problem; it's simply a data point for you to analyze. And also remember that all the information you need to interpret a project probably isn't on the page in front of you. Your judgment, your understanding, and your insight into the entirety of the project is your most valuable tool.

WBS Code	Task Name	Who Assigned	Date Assigned	Date Complete	Date Verified
1 Software Engineering					
1.1.1	Construct Game Engine	Harry	9/14/03	11/6/03	11/8/03
1.1.2	Build Level Editor	Sally	10/6/03	12/3/03	12/5/03
1.1.3	Write AI Character Routines				
1.1.4	Compile Art Files				
1.1.5	Turnover Game to Playtest				
1.1.6	Fix Program Bugs				
1.1.7	Verify Revised Game				
1 Art & Design					
1.2.1	Script Game				
1.2.2	Design Characters				
1.2.3	Build Character Animations				
1.2.4	Design Levels and Backgrounds				
1.2.5	Develop Licensing Packages				
1.2.6	Design Package Art				

▲ FIGURE 28-1: *Technical baseline.* This table was created using information from the WBS for the "Tiger Dojo" project. With it, you can track all outstanding work, when it was delegated, when it was completed, and when quality assurance validation was performed.

Here, we're tracking dates assigned as well as dates finished. With the longer time horizons on the "Tiger Dojo" project, you tend to have many more tasks outstanding, and it's harder to keep all the details in your head.

There's also a date box for validation, and that's a mechanism to link quality assurance activities directly into your project. When you receive work, the date you receive the turnover is important, but there may be some days involved in reviewing and analyzing the turnover to determine whether it's satisfactory. Measurement information should, if possible, be incorporated into the Task Management Form (Figure 27-1) so that the person responsible for the task has the power to perform quality control and improvement during the actual task.

With your technical baseline established, you record information as received and now have the ability to determine whether the project work is being completed correctly, completely, and to an adequate performance standard.

Because tracking performance involves more subjectivity than tracking cost or schedule, it's important to figure out early how you will do it and let your team know what you value most.

> Measurement information should, if possible, be incorporated into the Task Management Form.

Cost Baselines and Financial Management

There are a variety of styles for presenting your cost baseline as well. The cost baseline comes from the final approved project budget and takes the total amount available to spend and allocates those expenditures for individual activities. Depending on how you're expected to break down and report costs, such things as overhead rates may be applied against the total budget. In that case, your operating budget is your total budget less indirect cost charges. You must allocate your operating budget, not the total budget, to the tasks in your project in constructing the cost baseline, since it's the operating expenditures that you need to measure.

It's perfectly legitimate to display the information in a spreadsheet form, as we did in Figure 7-1. If you start using the Earned Value Method (details below), a spreadsheet is virtually required. In addition, cost baselines (and some Earned Value measures) work very well in graph form. Figure 28-2 is an example of a cumulative cost baseline tracking graph.

In reading the cost baseline, it's important to distinguish between delays and budget variance. Look at Weeks 5 and 11 of the chart. In both cases, the project appears to be significantly under

> Such things as overhead rates may be applied against the total budget.

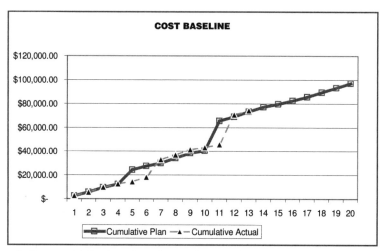

▲ Figure 28-2: *Cost baseline.* This graph compares total cumulative expenditures in the budget to actual total cumulative expenditures.

budget. Compare these weeks with Weeks 7 and 12 of the chart, where suddenly the cumulative expenditure jumps up to meet the plan line. In both cases, these are weeks in which large capital expenditures were made and charged to the project. Because the project is a little behind schedule (which the cost baseline won't show), we're behind in making some of those capital expenditures. We aren't really under budget (we're close but a slight bit over budget right now, as you can see in Week 13); rather, we've just had a delay in spending big money. Check to make sure you don't misinterpret your chart in this way.

How to Build and Interpret a Tracking Gantt Chart

The schedule baseline returns us to the Gantt Chart. The big advantage of a Tracking Gantt prepared by software is that it will automatically project the effect of schedule variances out to the end of the project. Let's take a more detailed look at this tool, so we can see how it works and how we can interpret it (see Figure 28-3).

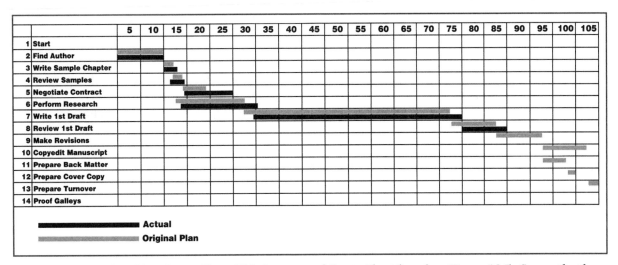

▲ FIGURE 28-3: *Tracking Gantt Chart.* This is a manual Gantt Chart based on Figure 18-5. Currently, the project is at 85 days/13 weeks of a planned 105 days/21 weeks. Is the project ahead of schedule or behind schedule? How can you tell? What can you do in the remaining weeks of the project to adjust the schedule?

Interpreting a Tracking Gantt Chart

The first potential variance we find is in Task 5 "Negotiate Contract," which seems to have taken about a week and a half longer than planned. Do we have a problem?

In this case, the parallel Task 6 "Perform Research" is the critical activity, so it looks as if we can soak up this delay. Unfortunately, we can't soak up all of it, even though a purely mathematical analysis of the schedule would suggest we could. Tasks are related to one another in a variety of ways, not all of which show on a Gantt Chart.

Here, the "Perform Research" task gets done by the writer "on spec," that is, without a guarantee of a contract and payment. Normally, schedule pressures require parties in this type of business arrangement to work on faith, and that's not a problem. But if problems with the contract begin to stretch out, faith weakens, and the writer may turn to other responsibilities, not wanting to sink too great a cost into a project that might not pan out.

That's why Task 6 takes some extra time, even after the contract is approved; it changed from being a full-time activity to being an interrupted activity, extending its duration. Because Task 6 was on the critical path, Task 7 "Write First Draft" starts late, triggering a delay of just under a week on the critical path.

Finding a Solution

What should we do about it? That depends on other project factors. If time is not the driver, a delay of less than a week may be perfectly acceptable, and so no action is required. If the deadline is strict, notice that the number of tasks that can be adjusted is quite limited: from Task 9 through Task 14.

Here's where advance warning is advantageous. If you know well enough in advance that Task 7 will finish late, you could ask for partial turnovers of manuscript sections. In effect, that would mean that Task 8 "Review First Draft" would start well before Task 7, its predecessor, is finished. This would be expressed as a Start-to-Start (SS) type dependency with a lag attached. The result can be that Task 8 will finish substantially ahead of deadline. The cost, however, is that the editor probably had other things to do, and bringing forward part of the "Review" task may force other projects off track.

On the other hand, perhaps the lateness in Task 7 wasn't detected early enough. Now, your ability to compress Task 8 is far more limited. If the manuscript is in good shape, perhaps Task 9 "Make Revisions" can be shortened. Perhaps you could negotiate with the production department to get a head start on graphics, with the idea that you might be able to delay turning over edited text without jeopardizing the final deadline.

When to Re-plan and Re-baseline Your Project

There are three basic situations that make you think about re-planning and re-baselining a project. These are imposed changes/scope creep, internal changes/variances, and circumstantial/environmental changes.

Imposed Changes/Scope Creep

The baseline of the project consists of the approved original plan plus or minus approved changes. When you have scope creep, your baseline gets modified. If the changes are relatively minor, you may not bother to update your baseline information. You can simply eyeball the baseline and interpret what it means.

If the changes are more significant, it will likely be advantageous for you to generate updated plans and new baselines. Another advantage of computer tools in project management is that automation is much easier and much quicker than updating by hand. Changes aren't completely free of effort, though, so make sure that you will get extra value from an updated plan before spending the time and effort to develop one.

Internal Changes/Variances

Changes can result from project problems and variances as well as from requested or imposed changes by people outside the project team. Again, ordinary variances don't automatically require re-planning and re-baselining. If you're a consistent week behind schedule, this is a bad thing, but the baseline will clearly show the variance, and re-baselining will add no new information to help you solve your problem.

Getting the Most Out of Your Analysis

The baseline by itself doesn't tell you everything you need to know. It serves as a picture and a tool by which you can dig farther and farther into your own project. You must normally apply all your knowledge and understanding of the project to get the most value out of your analysis. Tracking Gantt Charts are not only good for analyses, they are also good for showing people without formal project management experience what the situation looks like.

When Not to Re-plan

Because re-planning and re-baselining aren't free activities—they take time and effort you could spend elsewhere—our recommendation is not to do them lightly. If you're looking at ordinary variances and the basic direction is unchanged—the original baseline still points you in the right direction and gives you measurements you can meaningfully interpret—spend your time and energy in higher producing activities.

If, on the other hand, your project problems have gotten to a point where you have to rethink and re-plan to get from where you are now to some approximation of where you want to be, re-planning may be the only technique that will achieve your goals. The old plan no longer measures effectively.

Circumstantial/Environmental Changes

Your plan always rests upon some basic assumptions—the environmental conditions in which the work will take place. Like all assumptions, these carry certain elements of risk. If it happens that the project environment changes, the original plan and even the original destination may be overtaken by events. In that case, you have to rethink your project, and re-planning is probably not optional.

Earned Value Project Management

The Earned Value method of project management is another of the advanced tools available for you as a project manager. Most often used in the construction industry, Earned Value offers a powerful set of analytical and forecasting tools to measure, monitor, and predict cost and schedule variance.

Earned Value starts with three measurements:

1. *Planned Value (PV).* The Planned Value of the project is also known as the Budgeted Cost of Work Scheduled (BCWS). It's how much the plan says you should have spent to achieve the work that should have been done by a given date.
2. *Actual Cost (AC).* The Actual Cost of the project is also known as the Actual Cost of Work Performed (ACWP). It's how much you actually have spent by a given date to accomplish however much work you actually did by that date.
3. *Earned Value (EV).* The Earned Value of a project is also known as the Budgeted Cost of Work Performed (BCWP). It's how much you should have spent to accomplish the work you actually got done by a given date.

Various formulae based on these three items provide you with extensive tools to analyze your performance. Here are a few of the more popular tools.

- Schedule Variance (SV) = PV – EV. How much work did we get done based on how much we planned? The answer is expressed in currency units. If we should have completed $1,000 worth of work by today but have done only $800, we're $200 behind schedule.
- Cost Variance (CV) = EV – AC. In accomplishing $800 worth of work, we may have spent $900. In that case, we're also $100 over budget.
- Schedule Performance Index (SPI) = EV / PV. How are we doing against the schedule? If we've done $800 worth of work when we should have done $1,000, then our SPI is 80 percent. We're running 20 percent behind schedule.
- Cost Performance Index (CPI) = EV / AC. If we've spent $900 to do $800 worth of work, then our CPI is 89 percent. We're running 11 percent over budget.

The power of Earned Value as a forecaster can be easily seen. If we've completed 20 percent of a $5,000 project and have an SPI of 80 percent and a CPI of 89 percent, that's a disturbing trend. It suggests that the actual cost will be the budget divided by the CPI, or $5,000 / .8, or $6,250. It may be worse—if the schedule overrun keeps up, multiply the CPI times the SPI to get a factor of 71.2 percent, and divide the planned budget by that factor to get $7,022.50!

Being able to predict disaster early in a project isn't perfect, but at least it helps you and your team face the dimensions of the real problem at a time when solution may yet be possible.

> The power of Earned Value as a forecaster can be easily seen.

For more information on this topic, visit our Web site at www.businesstown.com

Chapter 29

Managing Meetings and Status Reporting

Planning Your Approach

You get some information about your project status from various objective measurements, but the majority of project status information comes from people. You ask, "How's it going? Is everything on schedule? Are there any problems?"

If you've asked these questions, you probably know the most common answers. "Everything's fine. Yes, we're on schedule. No problems." We've even heard "Yes, we're on schedule" after the deadline has passed!

When you ask people for status information, they often perceive a threat, whether you intend one or not. "How's it going?" gets interpreted as "Have you messed up?" and the answer you get has self-protection at its core.

In working with people, where egos, personal agendas, and career insecurity influence daily behavior, you have to plan your approach to get the information you require. Let's look at some proven techniques.

Why "Bad" Is the Natural State of Meetings

We've all sat through meetings that were a waste of time, yet we've also attended meetings that have actually been productive and worthwhile uses of our time. Why aren't they all like that?

As we discovered in our analysis of good luck versus bad luck, bad luck is automatic while good luck takes effort. By the same logic, it's important to realize that "bad" is the natural state of meetings. It requires no effort and no work on your part to run a bad meeting. It's the inevitable consequence of failing to take certain positive steps before the meeting and failing to exercise leadership during the meeting.

Most of us have heard many of the rules for good meetings, such as always having an agenda, a firm start and stop time, and a sense of purpose. Yet many of the meetings we attend fail to use these techniques. Why? Part of the answer may be laziness or distraction, but do remember that in certain cases people can benefit from a badly run meeting. It may make it easier for someone to dominate the conversation, or blindside the unwary, or keep a potentially unpleasant topic off the table.

As a project manager, you must run meetings and run them well, or fail to get the information and insight you need to do the rest of your job effectively. There are proven techniques available, and a few little tricks as well.

Techniques for Effective Meeting Management

Meetings qualify as projects under our definition of "temporary and unique." They take a finite amount of time and they should always be for a specific purpose and goal. Therefore, the first step in having effective meetings for your project is to decide what meetings you need and what you want them to produce. Each type of meeting tends to have its own format for best results.

Status Review Meetings

Status review meetings should give you an efficient and accurate read on where your project is right now. You want to know which tasks have been completed and which are pending. You want information on cost and performance. You need information about risks and problems. People dislike attending status meetings because they often find that someone else's problem takes control of the agenda. Everyone except those immediately concerned with the problem have to sit and wait while a few people do useful work. There's also often a sense that these meetings are more frequent than they need to be. Here are rules to make status review meetings more effective.

> Status review meetings should give you an efficient and accurate read on where your project is right now.

1. Establish the right frequency. How long does it take for the world of your project to change significantly? If tasks are measured in days, a weekly meeting may be about right. If tasks are measured in weeks, then you want to look at it biweekly. On the other hand, if tasks are measured in hours, then a daily meeting may be necessary. Also, the speed of

change may vary during your project. If you're planning a trade show, you might have monthly meetings until three months before, then biweekly for two months, then weekly, and finally daily as you go into the final week.

2. Determine the right audience. If your team size is six or fewer, then it's probably desirable for everyone to attend the status meeting. If the team divides into subteams focusing on specific task areas, then you might consider only having team leaders attend most status meetings, with others invited as needed. (You might find it politic to have the occasional "all-hands" meeting, so that people don't feel left out.)

3. Focus the meeting on essentials. The purpose of a status review meeting is to review the status of the project. That's all. If you need to follow up a status review meeting with more detailed subject-oriented meetings to get into problems or issues identified in the status review, that's fine—but do it as a separate meeting. This allows the other team members to get back to work.

4. KISS. "Keep It Short and Simple." If a meeting of this nature goes over half an hour, it's too long. Perhaps you're getting into side discussions. Perhaps people don't know to come prepared with essential information. Perhaps there are too many people attending. Establish a firm schedule; start on time and finish on time. A big clock where everyone can see it is often useful.

The output of a status review meeting should be a summary of task completions and problem responses. Update plan sections as needed after each status review and display current versions.

Risk Management Meetings

In our discussion of risk management (Chapter 21), we observed that the process of risk identification and risk response planning is ongoing. Some risks can be established at the beginning of the project; other risk information is only available later. You need to establish a regular series of risk management meetings throughout your project.

> KISS. "Keep It Short and Simple."

Who should come to these meetings? Team members who will have a role in managing the activities under discussion and people with expertise in similar projects who can offer risk management guidance are the two groups to consider.

The agenda for these meetings is based on the original risk plan and progress information to date. Go over the original risk plan, and for each item you've identified, ask the following questions:

- Is this still a risk? Is it more or less likely to occur than before?
- Are there any factors that make the risk more or less potentially damaging?
- Does the original risk response plan still work? Are there better options? Have circumstances changed the best response?

When you finish the current risk list, go through the rest of the project task by task looking for new risks. For each risk, determine probability and impact and decide whether it rises above your risk management threshold. If so, determine your risk response plan.

Keep records of all identified risks, whether above or below the threshold. Review risks that have been previously determined to be below the threshold for action to see if your decision should be reassessed.

Next, make a list of unplanned risks that have affected your project. Have there been any surprises? Any unexpected events? Did you have to use workarounds to respond to project events not in your risk management plan?

Finally, review risk responses that you have implemented. Did the previously determined strategy work as you expected? Did it do better or worse? If you could do it over again, would you use the same strategy? Were there any warning signs or triggers that you had not previously considered?

Update the risk management plan after the meeting and distribute it to the same audience that received the original plan.

Frequency of Meetings

The appropriate frequency of risk management meetings is based on the speed of change within the project and the level of risk in the project. A rule of thumb ratio would be one risk management meeting for every three status review meetings on an average-risk project, for every two on a high-risk project, and for every four on a low-risk project.

Quality Circles

At the beginning of the U.S. experience with Japanese quality management tools, quality circles were very popular. Our project management version isn't quite like a formal quality circle, but it has the same objectives of quality assurance and quality improvement.

You normally need fewer quality circle meetings than risk management meetings because there is less rapid change here. However, if you are experiencing a quality issue on the project, call a special meeting. The attendance of these meetings varies by the issues under discussion. In addition to task and topic managers (a topic manager is responsible for one of the WBS Level 2 categories on your project), operations level people who have a detailed knowledge of the work and the process are valuable assets.

While the agendas for status updates and risk management are standard, the quality circle agenda needs some advance development both on your part and on the part of your team members. Consider making the agenda a questionnaire that people organize before attending. You may want to include the following questions.

> Consider making the agenda a questionnaire that people organize before attending.

1. How have you defined "quality" for the deliverables on this project? Is the definition still relevant to current customer needs, desires, and expectations?
2. Have competitive products or services been released (or advertised) that change the benchmarks appropriate for our project?
3. How is the project performing based on the measurable quality indicators we established?
4. Have we experienced problems or setbacks outside the realm of common cause variation? What are those problems? What is the root cause of those problems? Should we establish a project or subproject to deal with the root causes?
5. Based on what we have learned so far on our project, are there any enhancements or improvements we can make to achieve a higher level of customer satisfaction without compromising our Triple Constraints performance?
6. What have we learned that we can use to improve quality on future projects?

Problem-Solving Meetings

If you shouldn't do problem solving at a status review meeting, when do you do it? Plan on calling special meetings on an as-needed basis to focus on project problems and issues as they arise. Determine who can contribute meaningfully to solving the problem; a small group tends to be easier to manage than a large one. We'll cover a variety of problem-solving strategies in the next chapter.

Periodic versus Topical Reviews

You can group all the reviews and meetings on your project into two general categories: periodic and topical reviews. Periodic reviews are reviews normally initiated and run by the project manager to track where the project is on Triple Constraints performance. We want to

How Running Good Meetings Advances Your Career

For all the project reasons we list, running good meetings is important to you and to the organization. But did you know it can help your career prospects as well?

We know that certain behaviors we exhibit at work get us considered for promotions or advancement. While project management is a career path in some organizations, in others, being assigned a project is often an audition for later managerial responsibilities. You want to succeed at your project for a number of reasons, but this is certainly one of them.

You may not realize it, but there are some behaviors you might consider quite minor that actually have a surprisingly large impact on senior management's opinion of you. And in the end, remember that it's senior management's opinion that ultimately determines when—or if—you get promoted.

Two of these seemingly minor behaviors are (1) writing good memos (and e-mails) and (2) running good meetings. Memos and e-mails may be the only work product with your name on it that senior management sees, so writing well in these ostensibly informal areas has a large impact.

Similarly, running good meetings affects your in-office reputation quite a bit more than you might think, whether senior management sits in the meetings or not. When you run a short, productive meeting, others appreciate it, and you find people are more willing to attend one of your meetings than someone else's. Word gets out, and you benefit—along with everybody else.

So take the time to prepare, and practice the leadership skills to run good meetings. It's worth it.

Be Prepared

With a topical review, you often have outside audiences, and it's appropriate to consider the best way to present the information they need. If someone plans to inspect you, it's wise to pre-inspect yourself, correct what's wrong, and tidy up the area while you're at it.

Make every topical review a task or milestone in your project schedule. Schedule preview time before each outside review, budgeting time and resources to get it done.

know if we're on time, on budget, and to spec. Status reviews and risk management meetings are both periodic reviews.

Topical reviews, as the name suggests, are about specific topics on our project. These are often (but not always) initiated by people outside the project team for their benefit. Our quality circle meetings fall into this category because they focus on only one aspect of the project, even though they are initiated by the project manager. If you're managing a grant, and the granting organization wants to audit you, that's a topical review. If the customer needs a dog-and-pony show about your prototype review, that's a topical review. If the general wants to inspect your unit, that's a topical review. If the IRS audits you, that's a topical review.

A topical review is neither better nor worse than a periodic review; it's merely different. You establish your own periodic review schedule for the project, and since you're the primary audience and beneficiary, you can alter the schedule as you see fit. Because in a periodic review you're usually simply looking for information, you can accept a less formal structure.

Getting to the Truth When People Don't Want to Share

The processes for getting project information assume that people will give you the information you need on a timely basis, even if the information could potentially make them look bad. Realistically, that's not always the case. As a project manager, you need to have a plan for getting at the real story on a timely basis in spite of potential reluctance to share.

Getting Good Information When Things Go Bad

Quite naturally, people don't want to come to you with small problems, feeling that you may conclude they can't do the job in a satisfactory manner. On the other hand, it's seriously frustrating (and sometimes catastrophic) when a large problem develops because someone didn't give you an early heads-up when it was still a small problem. To limit this happening on your project, try the following steps.

1. *Practice "Management By Wandering Around" (MBWA).* As a project manager, if you don't get out of your office and observe what's going on, it's a bad idea to assume you know what is actually going on. Being seen and visible makes you appear more involved, which will get you more information. In addition, some people find it easier to give you information informally than formally. Keep the door open.

2. *Modify the consequences.* People who are reluctant to give you information perceive they may be punished for sharing the information. "How could you be so stupid?" "You really messed up!" "You're wasting my time with small stuff you could easily handle yourself." Make sure you praise people who bring you the information. In addition, when you're late getting information about a problem you should ask why, and indicate your displeasure if they knew earlier and chose not to tell.

3. *Provide additional channels.* Sharing negative information is always difficult. Give people a variety of opportunities to make it easier for them. Formal meetings, written exception reports, status reports, walk-ins, personal visits—the more channels the better.

4. *Prepare good questions.* "Why didn't you tell me?" The classic answer is, of course, "You didn't ask." So ask. You'll see a list of questions below; develop your own and ask early and often.

Getting People to Give You Timely Information

Getting the information is important, but the timing of the information is important as well. First, problems detected early tend to be easier to solve. Second, when people have a choice between getting work done or reporting on the work that has been done, they most often choose the work. Reporting is seen as a nuisance at best.

1. *Ask for cooperation.* You may feel it's obvious that reporting matters, or feel that people should know perfectly well that it's expected. Even though that's true, you still have to make your priorities clear. Tell people that you want timely information, emphasize that it is important to you, and show appreciation.

2. *Show you use it.* Among the legitimate reasons people may be reluctant to report is the suspicion that much information is

> Getting the information is important, but the timing of the information is important as well.

collected and never used. First, make sure you don't ask for information you won't use, and second, show people how you use the information. Post updates and summary data on your project bulletin board or distribute them at meetings. When people perceive their information has value, they tend to be more willing to share.

3. *Make it easy.* It's worth some thought to see how you can simplify the collection of data. The easier it is for someone to provide reporting information, the more likely it is they will find time to do it.

> People often have very different ideas about what it means to report orally and report in writing.

Status Reports with Meaning

Status reports can sometimes obviate the need for as many status review meetings, but it's better to regard these as two separate communications channels that tend to carry different information.

People often have very different ideas about what it means to report orally and report in writing. Writing is more permanent, so there may be reluctance to divulge one's own mistakes or problems in a written report. On the other hand, writing is more distant, so someone reluctant to say something in person may find it easier to say on paper. Individuals have different reactions, but be aware of those reactions.

Forms are often more productive ways to gather information than asking for narrative reports. Narrative reports have the following disadvantages: Not everyone is able to write well, those who can write well may use their skills to bury unpleasant news so you are more likely to miss it, writing for most people is more time consuming than speech, and you'll tend to get a different format and structure from each person—that is, when there's any structure at all.

Design your own forms for reporting. You can shape the information in the way that's best for you, and at the same time lower the work burden on your team members. Here's a template of a status reporting form. It's designed to be built using a spreadsheet program because one of the most valuable parts of this form is the graphic display of actual versus plan information. Reports aren't only for you; preparing them actually provides feedback to the preparer. By setting up the format yourself, you can make it easier to produce and easier to interpret (see Figure 29-1).

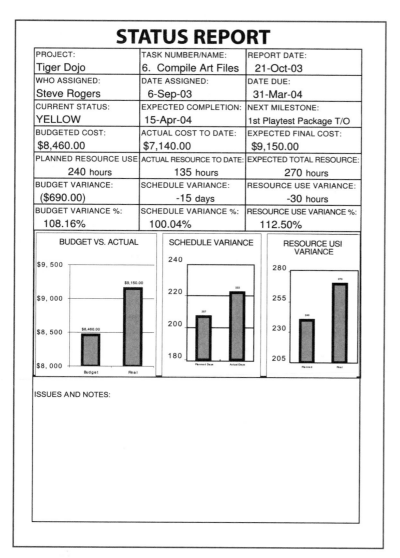

STATUS REPORT

PROJECT: Tiger Dojo	TASK NUMBER/NAME: 6. Compile Art Files	REPORT DATE: 21-Oct-03
WHO ASSIGNED: Steve Rogers	DATE ASSIGNED: 6-Sep-03	DATE DUE: 31-Mar-04
CURRENT STATUS: YELLOW	EXPECTED COMPLETION: 15-Apr-04	NEXT MILESTONE: 1st Playtest Package T/O
BUDGETED COST: $8,460.00	ACTUAL COST TO DATE: $7,140.00	EXPECTED FINAL COST: $9,150.00
PLANNED RESOURCE USE 240 hours	ACTUAL RESOURCE TO DATE: 135 hours	EXPECTED TOTAL RESOURCE: 270 hours
BUDGET VARIANCE: ($690.00)	SCHEDULE VARIANCE: -15 days	RESOURCE USE VARIANCE: -30 hours
BUDGET VARIANCE %: 108.16%	SCHEDULE VARIANCE %: 100.04%	RESOURCE USE VARIANCE %: 112.50%

ISSUES AND NOTES:

▲ FIGURE 29-1: *Status report template.* This form was built in a spreadsheet program so that the graphics will display automatically.

Important Questions to Ask

There's an important distinction in communication between a closed-ended question and an open-ended question. A closed-ended question is one that is answered with a yes or no. "Have you finished your task?" is a closed-ended question. An open-ended question, on the other hand, is one that cannot be answered with yes or no. "What did you learn about the project when you did this task?" requires a more complete answer. (Of course, you can have someone answer "Nothing," but in a way that's a revealing answer.)

When you are trying to get the full story, develop a list of questions in advance. Here are some good examples:

- What is the status of your task?
- How have you gone about doing the work?
- How has the plan helped or hindered you in doing the work?
- What has happened that wasn't in the original plan?
- What lessons should we extract if we did this task again?
- What information can you give the person who will do the successor tasks based on what you've learned in this task?

A Hidden Source of Profit

"Have you learned or discovered anything on your task or project that we could use to get extra value?"

It's a simple enough question, but one with important implications. When a major cosmetics company planned to release one of its thicker fragrances in a spray bottle form, they discovered that the viscosity of the fragrance clogged the spray nozzle after only a few squirts.

As a result, the industrial engineer in the packaging department had to design a custom Teflon-coated spray nozzle, then contract with a nozzle vendor to manufacture it. The nozzle vendor called back. "We don't have anything like this in our product line. We'd like to patent it in your name, offer it for sale in our catalog, and pay you a royalty!" While the money involved wasn't very much, it was essentially free—and free money is good.

Project management often requires creativity. You face difficult and sometimes unique problems, and work out solutions. But those solutions often have more value than just a single use. Maybe this problem crops up regularly. Maybe other people experience the same or similar problem and can use your solution. Maybe you have a new product, or at least a development or enhancement to an existing product.

From the development of the Post-It Note to the invention of vulcanized rubber, many important achievements have been essentially the accidental byproduct of other work. There may not be a fortune in the creative solution you discovered on your last project, but there may be enough value to be worth the effort.

Problem-Solving Strategies

Chapter 30

Collect Problem-Solving Tools

Project management is more about reducing uncertainty than about eliminating it. Estimates and plans are all based on our knowledge and insights into the future, which by definition includes uncertainty. While it's clear that good planning pays in fewer problems, difficulties and surprises crop up in the best-planned and best-managed projects.

That's why one of the chief tools of project managers is a robust collection of problem-solving tools. The more experienced and more capable the project manager, the wider assortment of tools he or she tends to gather. Start building your problem-solving toolbox early in your project management career, and you'll find yourself able to face most challenges and come out on top.

> The Godzilla Principle tells us that to solve a problem easily, catch it early.

The Godzilla Principle

The Godzilla Principle, as you know by now, tells us that to solve a problem easily, catch it early. The first principle of problem solving, therefore, is to keep your eyes open for trouble's leading indicators. What kind of indicators tip you off to the potential presence of a baby monster?

- *Risk identification.* The process of risk identification is the first place you can find potential problems.
- *Baseline indicators.* In a current project, the three baselines (schedule, technical, cost) provide a read on the status of the project. While you act only on significant variations, look for reasons for even small variations in case they are harbingers of a trend.
- *Macro environment.* Changes in the macro environment may wreak havoc on your project. If the CEO just got replaced, if the stock market just tanked, if your competitor just released their version of the new product you're currently designing, it's smart to focus on potential project impact.
- *History and experience.* Has the same thing happened the last three times you did a project similar to this? Preparing for it again is the course of wisdom. Learn from the experience of others—it's cheaper than making the same mistakes to get that education.

The Pop-Up Principle

Whenever you solve a problem, another one crops up, but not just in the Murphy's Law sense. Solutions are seldom perfect; they yield up problems of their own. Recognize the "pop-up" inherent in any solution to develop the best strategy for resolving it.

It might rain on our picnic. We've brainstormed three possible solutions: have it indoors, rent a tent, have a rain date. All are legitimate solutions, but each has one or more pop-ups. As with all problems, you have to recognize them before you can fix them.

> *Indoors.* The pop-ups are that it's no longer a picnic and costs might increase.

> *Tent.* The pop-ups are that it will cost more money and rain will still wash out some other activities.

> *Rain date.* The pop-ups are that attendance may drop, perishable food will have to be repurchased (driving up costs), you may pay double rental on the picnic grounds (also driving up costs), and it might rain again.

None of these is necessarily or automatically fatal, but they deserve the same attention you give to all project risks.

The best strategy is to treat the pop-ups like you treated earlier identified risks: Quantify impact and probability, and select one of the four risk strategies (avoidance, mitigation, transfer, and acceptance). For each pop-up, decide if it is worse than the original problem. Can the downside be mitigated? Can you tweak the original solution to reduce the severity of the pop-up?

The Triple Constraints Principle

Something is a problem because it threatens to make you late, threatens to drive up your costs, or threatens to degrade your performance. If the event does none of these things, then it's not a problem, but merely a happenstance.

Build Your Confidence

Attention to good process won't eliminate the stress, but it will improve your confidence that you're doing the best you can do in a situation. From that point on, your skills improve and your confidence grows, and then something very strange happens. Even though you still make decisions that cause pain when you don't have any good alternatives from which to choose, you'll find that others have more respect and sympathy for you. That, in turn, makes it more possible for you to strive to help those injured by necessary decisions, and everybody wins.

Notice that once again we're in the company of the Triple Constraints. If time is your driver, then problems that threaten to make you late are serious indeed. If it's cost, then expensive problems are the worst. If it's performance, then those issues rise to the top. The constraint hierarchy affects the seriousness of problems.

Similarly, the weak constraint becomes your ally. If you've got lots of time, then look to see how extra time could bail you out of your difficulty. If there's extra money and resources, then spend to solve problems. If performance is vaguely defined, define it in a way that gets the job done. Always take the time to think about the Triple Constraints in dealing with almost any project challenge.

> You can normally act on problems only during certain periods, known as control points.

The Control Point Principle

You can normally act on problems only during certain periods, known as control points. There are three basic potential control points available to you for any given problem. They are:

1. When you first think of it
2. When you get an early warning sign
3. When it actually happens

The Godzilla Principle reminds us we should try to get the problem at the first control point, but that's not always possible or practical. Some problems don't give off early warnings; sometimes Godzilla sneaks into Tokyo the back way. Through your risk management meetings and other project tools, discipline yourself to look carefully for warning signs, and act as soon as you can.

Eight Strategies for Effective Problem Solving

We have our four risk management strategies: avoidance, mitigation, transfer, and acceptance. There is a wide range of robust problem-solving strategies to achieve these.

Renegotiate

There was full and complete agreement on what the project should be, and you thought you could achieve it. But with severe and surprising problems (grist for the "lessons learned" mill), it turns out you can't deliver as promised. What now? Renegotiate!

You may think you're in a very weak position, but look at it this way: the money and time have been spent and there are no results. Which do you suppose your customer would prefer? Complete defeat and no extra expenditures, or the possibility of success but under a new Triple Constraints framework? While sometimes the choice is "If I can't have it all, I'll take nothing," more often you find that the customer would prefer something late and expensive to nothing on time and on budget.

Recover in a Later Step

The initial impulse is to fix the problem where it lives. But that's not always necessary or even desirable. If you're late on a critical path task, your deadline is in trouble. But if you can squeeze a later task on the path to recover the lost days, you still end up on deadline at the end. And the later task may be easier to squeeze.

Critical path matters in squeezing time, but not in cost. If you've had a cost overrun on one activity, getting another one done cheaper balances out the budget, whether the other task is critical or not.

Your performance options may be more limited because time and money are fungible in a way that performance is not, but end-of-project performance is often the cumulative effect of several interim steps. In that case, more of "B" can sometimes overcome a deficiency of "A."

Narrow Scope

Scope creeps for a variety of reasons. As long as you can handle the expanded scope, it may be desirable to accept it. But when everything is going down in either a handbasket or a bucket, it may be time to pare back the project objective to its barest essentials. Secondary goals go by the wayside, and the primary mission of the project becomes the only mission. If the Soviets speed up their

Your Best Is Your Best

Renegotiating doesn't mean that you won't get into hot water because of the original failure, or that there won't be consequences. Sometimes, in the real world, the best you can do is, after all, the best you can do—even if it's not good enough. Still, be prepared to renegotiate the objective if necessary. It may be the best choice you have available.

Moon launch, and collecting rocks is slowing you down, the rocks go overboard.

There's a cost associated with narrowing scope, and there may be a political price to pay as well. When cutting back scope overgrowth, a scalpel is sometimes a better tool than a machete. And in a practical world, you may keep elements of scope not because you're personally convinced of its essential value, but because you know who wants the scope, and what they may do if they don't get it.

> Make sure more resources will actually solve the problem.

Throw Resources at It

When there's slippage, you can sometimes correct the problem with extra resources. More bodies and more dollars can overcome some challenges. That's why many project managers act like generals and keep a strategic reserve for just this reason. You can also negotiate for extra resources when you need them.

Make sure more resources will actually solve the problem. There's actually a proof in software engineering that adding more programmers to a late project makes it later. The reasons are (1) new programmers have a learning curve that costs existing programmer time to overcome, (2) it's hard to figure out someone else's code, so finishing a job someone else started may add time, and (3) new people have new ideas, meaning inevitable redesign.

Substitute

At the beginning of a project and during planning, we start with the ideal picture. When problems rise and options shrink, it's time to review the equipment, specifications, and deliverables to ask if there are cheaper, faster alternatives that still achieve acceptable levels of performance.

Partial Delivery

If you've got to get 10,000 widgets to XYZ Corp by Wednesday, and you realize that isn't going to happen, remember that XYZ Corp probably isn't going to use all 10,000 on the first day. There is a minimum acceptable quantity that needs to be delivered on time, and it's usually possible to delay the remainder, as long as XYZ always has enough widgets on hand to meet daily needs. Stagger-shipping is a time-honored technique to balance a tough schedule.

Alternate Sources

When a vendor has you over a barrel, what are your alternatives? TQM advocates recommend a supplier partnership, in which you team with your supplier for quality results, giving them all your business in exchange for participating in ensuring good results, and that's the ideal way to go.

It takes time to set up such a relationship, and if that isn't the way your organization currently does business, you need to have a backup plan when vendors or suppliers let you down. Sometimes it's strategically savvy to split your order for a mission-critical component to make sure you have two sources if one doesn't deliver.

Re-plan

And finally, sometimes you simply have to start from where you are and develop a new map to get to some approximation of where you want and need to be. Sometimes, failure to address these problems is something for your "lessons learned" file, but some problems hit and no one is at fault or wiser for the experience. Don't spend time fretting about how things should have gone; turn your attention to how they have gone, and figure out where to go next.

Four Questions to Resolve Difficult Choices

You know you're a serious project manager the day you realize that you're not actually paid for making good decisions. Instead, you're paid to make decisions in circumstances where all the alternatives are dumpy and unpleasant. In fact, the hidden secret of serious management is that bad decision-making is harder than good! Here's why.

To make a good decision, a good alternative has to exist. Your challenge is to find it, recognize it, and implement it. Almost anybody can do that. But sometimes there aren't any good alternatives. Sometimes every alternative you can find has serious defects.

Add Today's Problems to Tomorrow's Answers

It's not necessarily wrong nor a sign of poor project management skills if you get blindsided on some project surprises that crop up. Sometimes Godzilla sneaks into Tokyo the back way, and it's not your fault you missed it.

At least that's true the first time it happens. The second, third, and fourth times are different. Keep a list of these project surprises and problems, and after the project is over and you're doing "lessons learned," go back through the tough challenges. Could the situation happen again? Given what we know is possible, could we prepare in advance to avoid or mitigate the problem? Could we have a contingency plan on hand and ready to go?

Everybody gets "learning opportunities" (a code word for "disasters") from time to time. Make sure your "learning opportunities" result in actual learning for you and your team.

In that case, decisions start moving up the chain of command. If there's a fire and you can put it out, you put it out. No need to wait around for senior management clearance. But if the fire is raging and the choice is whether it takes out Warehouse #1 or Warehouse #2, that's when we start passing the buck upstream, and quickly. By the time you're sitting in the CEO chair, there are no easy decisions left, because they've all been made by your subordinates. Now, it's your turn.

As a project manager, you'll hit this situation earlier in your career than managers in other disciplines, because of the inherent uncertainty and uniqueness of the project environment. How do you handle making a choice or a decision when you can tell there's something wrong with every alternative?

One good focusing technique is to use the following four questions. Go through each alternative to get a snapshot of your overall situation.

1. What's the best that can happen? Assuming all luck and fortune goes your way when you make this choice, what is the best outcome possible? Are there any ways you can make this outcome more probable? Are there any ways you can make this outcome more desirable? Can you quantify the probability of this event happening, even in general terms (fairly likely, highly unlikely, etc.)? Can you make this outcome more likely? Is the positive outcome in line with your organizational or project mission?

2. What's the worst that can happen? Reversing our examination, what are the negative outcomes that are possible? Even though the question asks for "the" worst, feel free to list multiple possibilities for Questions 1 and 2 alike. How serious and how negative are these outcomes? Does the damage spill over into areas outside your project, department, or purview? Are there steps you can take to reduce the negative impact? Can you quantify the probability of a bad outcome? Can you reduce the probability?

3. Is #1 worth risking #2? This is a value question, and depending on your situation you may look at answering it several different ways.

> How do you handle making a choice or a decision when you can tell there's something wrong with every alternative?

Probability-Is either #1 or #2 much more probable than the other? Because we measure risk as probability times impact, if the probability of one side is much greater or much less, that may be enough to tip our decision. Can the probability be manipulated in a way that improves your chances?

Impact-Is the outcome of #1 or #2 much greater than the other? If the upside is earning $1 million and the downside losing $1,000, then that's usually a fairly easy decision to make. If the situation is reversed, that, too, is an easy decision. Can you change the impact, either by making the good side better or the downside less?

Alternatives-You can't always quantify probability, and sometimes the impact is roughly equal—ultimate success or total disaster. But there are always at least two choices when you contemplate a decision, and the other choice is not to do what you're considering. Run both choices through these questions, and see if there's a difference. If one choice leads to certain disaster and the other choice to probable disaster, the second choice is better, even though it's not good. And, as we remember, "better is better."

4. Can I live with #2 if it happens? Some alternatives are simply not acceptable. In our expected value discussion, we discovered that gain and loss are not automatically reciprocal. If you can't live with the downside answer, you can't place the bet.

Don't Overlook Your Resources

Success expert Zig Ziglar tells the story of the young boy who went to see his father. "Dad, a tree fell down and it's blocking the path through the woods. I can't move it."

His father replied, "Son, did you use all your strength?"

The boy admitted that well, maybe not, and went out to try again. He came back. "Dad, I can't move the tree."

Again, the father asked, "Did you use all your strength?"

The boy thought harder, then said maybe not. This time he went to the garage, got a block and tackle, set it up, and tried to move the tree. Then he went back to his father. "Dad, I really can't move the tree."

"Son, did you use *all* your strength?"

The boy thought hard, and finally said, "Yes, Dad, I did."

"No, you didn't," said the father. "If you'd used *all* your strength, you would have asked for help."

You don't have to rely only on yourself to solve problems. Learn when and how—and who—to ask for help.

PART VII

Closing Out the Project

- **The mechanics of proper project closeout—finishing on time, on budget, and to spec**

- **How to develop and manage a project "lessons learned" process and use the information to improve project management effectiveness on future projects**

- **Why celebrating success is a high payoff activity for future projects**

- **How to find and use various resources for growth and further study in project management**

Finishing
the Project
the Right Way

Chapter 31

Project Closeout

Project closeout is the final phase of project management, in which you bring the project to a close, deliver the deliverables, ensure customer satisfaction, and do the administrative activities necessary to wind down the operation. Just as bringing a galleon into the harbor is no job for an amateur, closing out a project demands a high degree of focus and control.

Closing Processes

The two formal processes in project closeout are known as administrative closure and contract closeout. Administrative closure involves the technical and operational tasks necessary to deliver project outputs and shut down the work. Contract closeout is an important step on any project that has used contracts, either by issuing contracts to others, or in many cases, performing the project as a contractor. Depending on your organization's policies, contract closeout can involve numerous steps, including verification, completion of forms, negotiation of exceptions and change orders, final invoicing, and approval of invoices. Prepare a "closeout checklist" of all the activities you need to perform to close out the project, and use the checklist to speed your way through the process.

Not officially separate, but requiring a whole new world of attention, is the process of obtaining customer approvals, verifying deliverables, and ensuring overall satisfaction with the job. That can vary from being simple and straightforward to being a highly complex negotiation.

Typical Problems in Closing a Project

Problems in closing out a project fit into two overall categories: problems that arise in the process of closeout, and problems that have been ignored or missed in earlier stages of the project. Project closeout is everyone's final opportunity to ensure that we get what we want. Any needs unmet earlier are brought onto the table now.

Other problems that tend to arise during closeout that are not necessarily leftovers from problems not previously resolved include:

- *Unexpected staff turnover.* When projects near their ends, most of the technical work is done, and the pace of work tends to slow somewhat. At the same time, in most organizations, other projects are ramping up and need staff. The desire of your technical performers to seek new work and the need of other project managers for trained staff combine to make an irresistible force to raid your staff.
- *Missing documentation.* The ability to do the work and the ability to keep good records of the work done aren't particularly compatible. Documentation is often thought of as a last-minute activity that can be done in a half-hearted way, and there's a scramble at the end of the project to get it done.

- *Completion of administrative deliverables.* Your organization and your customer's organization normally have administrative requirements for projects, including processing of signoffs and approvals, completion of forms and paperwork, and delivery of resource and dollar use information to appropriate managers. It's often the case that not all the mandatory administrative requirements are listed in a single place. Just when you think you're finally done with the project, you discover an entire new set of activities!
- *Transition management.* The transition from building something to using something, or from designing something to manufacturing something, is fraught with challenges. From training to the inevitable small adjustments, from preparing documentation to overseeing the migration from old systems to new, this area requires careful planning and execution.
- *Rumors.* On large multiyear projects, people begin to worry whether they'll have a home after the project is complete. Sometimes this worry is justified. If you know there will be some layoffs or terminations at the end of the project, you need to prepare for them. If, on the other hand, people will have continued employment, make sure they know about it, or else you'll have people jumping ship prematurely.

> Just when you think you're finally done with the project, you discover an entire new set of activities!

The Output—Product, New Project, or Work?

We do a project because we want the results, but the results can lead to other activities, rather than merely be ends in themselves. If your project is to design an upgraded inventory management system, the output is a system. Feeding new information, maintaining the system, and pulling out reports are operational functions—which are work, or activities without a planned finish. If you're putting a new wall around a courtyard, the wall is a final product, finished except for occasional regular maintenance.

If you conducted a research project to uncover potential new drugs, each potential new drug you discover triggers a new project to test, refine, and obtain approval for it, which in turn triggers a new project to market it.

Determine the project output and necessary transition issues as part of your original project definition, and manage accordingly.

Determining Follow-Up Opportunities

You're only as profitable as your next client or next project. Interestingly enough, that's true from both the perspective of the project provider and the project customer. If you develop revenue-producing projects, you need an ever-increasing collection of projects to ensure growth. If you sell project expertise, you need new projects at an expanding rate for your own growth.

If your project is being done for your own organization, it normally only begins to provide revenue once it's finished. In the chart below, the organization paid to have a project performed. It finished in June, and then began to earn revenue to offset its costs. From the company's perspective, the faster the project is finished, the quicker the revenue stream begins and costs are recouped (see Figure 31-1).

From the contractor's perspective, on the other hand, the project shows up as revenue until it's completed, at which time the revenue stream stops. It doesn't get offset as does the customer's, because when it's done, it ceases to produce contractor value (see Figure 31-2).

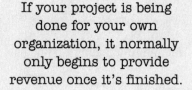

> If your project is being done for your own organization, it normally only begins to provide revenue once it's finished.

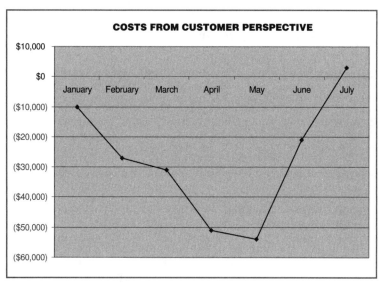

▲ FIGURE 31-1: *Costs from customer perspective.* **When you commission a project, its costs are negative until it is finished and begins to provide value.**

It's perfectly legitimate to use your presence inside an organization to look for additional business opportunities, as long as they are themselves legitimate. After all, if the company paying you makes a profit on what you do for them, finding additional opportunities for projects is in everyone's interest. If you are doing internal projects that add value, what other value can you find to add on?

The real profit opportunity is that once you have familiarity with an organization, know its problems and opportunities, and have a history of good work and trust, it becomes easier to get projects accomplished. That translates into higher and more rapid profits.

Customer Acceptance

Customer acceptance would be fairly easy to achieve if customers never changed their minds. That, alas, is not the experience of most project managers. In the Initiating phase of the project, you did everything you could to understand fully the customer's needs and objectives, and that's the first part of managing customer acceptance.

Slowing a Project

While it might look like a good idea from the contractor's perspective to slow up project completion to make more money, that strategy (although used by some) has a number of drawbacks. First, if the contract is not a fixed-price agreement, delay adds to your costs. Second, your opportunities for new business and a good reputation are diminished. Third, you pay an opportunity cost in resources tied up on the current job that can't go to new jobs.

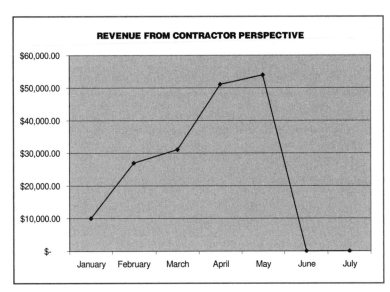

▲ FIGURE 31-2: *Costs from contractor perspective.* **The work of doing the project is a source of income; completed projects do not produce revenue.**

A Closeout Option

The skills and attitudes that help you manage a project aren't necessarily the same skills that will make you good at project closeout. As we've pointed out, closeout work is often boring for you and your team, even though it's necessary.

If you do a lot of projects that have a similar structure, and if closing out projects and filing the paperwork are an ongoing problem, consider establishing a closeout team separate from your regular project teams. This has been done in a number of organizations that have experienced this problem.

In this system, the project manager leads the project through customer acceptance and delivery, and then loads all the administrative paperwork onto the closeout team. They organize the file, prepare invoices and approve contract terms, and take care of all the paper while the project team goes on to the next project. While this work is found boring by some people, others find it satisfying to do and have the aptitude to do it very well.

Treat the Customer as Part of the Team

Throughout Planning and Executing phases, treat the customer as a member of the team. This has several advantages.

First, when the customer participates in the project, he or she naturally likes it better. Second, often customer dissatisfaction is focused on relatively small details. You may not realize which details matter most, but when the customer is on the team, you get much better feedback. Third, when you are the technical expert and the customer merely has the need, you can legitimately shape customer expectations in the direction you think is appropriate.

Final Acceptance

When the project nears closeout, the customer may get nervous. When the customer accepts the project in its final form, the ability to seek changes is dramatically diminished. If the customer is unsure of his or her needs or wants, finalizing the project is a big decision. In that case, the success of the project may well depend on the quality of your relationship with the customer, and on whether you've earned the customer's confidence.

Prepare for final acceptance. Organize the initial documents, verify that all deliverables are present and correct, identify the measurements that show how you met the original objectives and approved changes, and deliver the product or output in a formal presentation or turnover. By giving the customer a tour of the results, you do a lot to build confidence and ensure finality.

Contract Closeout

The details of contract closeout vary by organization. Not only do you have to satisfy the administrative details of turnover and ensure customer satisfaction, but you also must update all contract documentation to reflect final results, obtain necessary signatures, prepare and deliver invoices, and certify compliance with terms. Make sure you talk with your contracting and procurement professionals well in advance to ensure you do it right. Ask for someone from your contract management staff to assist you in this phase of closeout.

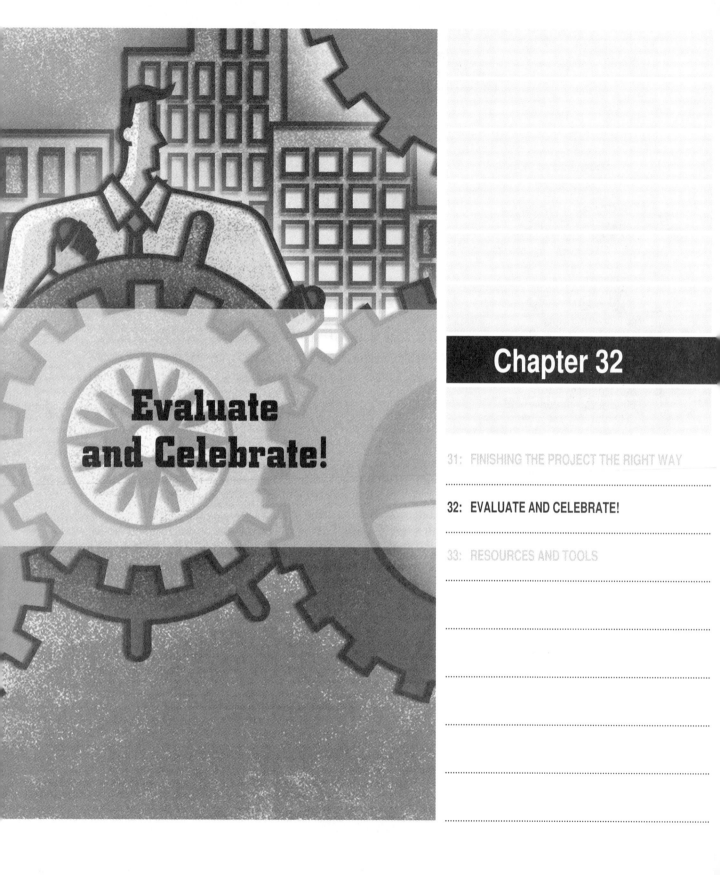

Evaluate and Celebrate!

Chapter 32

The Final Elements

At long last, our project has reached its conclusion. The deliverables are delivered, the customer is happy, and the paperwork is done. Time to move on? Almost, but not quite. There are two final elements that are part of a "best practices" approach to project management. These elements won't help the project that's just finished, but they put you on the path to better future project experiences. These steps are project evaluation and project celebration, the final elements in project closeout.

Critical Questions for Project Evaluations

We strongly recommend that you make a formal project evaluation process a fundamental step in any project. There are enormous potential benefits to be gained from relatively minor effort. After all, every project, whether successful or not, demands substantial concentration and focus, creativity in problem solving, and a wide range of practical skills. Unfortunately, unless a specific effort is made to ensure the knowledge and experience earned on one project carries forward, much of the value is lost as the team turns to the next project in line.

It's important to distinguish a "lessons learned" program from its cousin "blamestorming" (the creative process of figuring out who will be the scapegoat for any failure on this project). In both activities, you do spend time figuring out what went wrong and how it happened. In the second, once you've assigned guilt, the exercise is over. But in the first, the goal is not blame or faultfinding. For every mistake that was made by a specific individual on the team, there are usually several other people who could easily have made the same mistake. If all understand the mistake and know what to do in the future to avoid it, then we all make a profit.

Organize a "lessons learned" meeting and circulate a list of discussion questions as the agenda before the meeting. Use these questions to start your examination and build on this list:

1. What did we do right?
2. What things mattered most on this project?

3. What things surprised us on this project that weren't in our plan?
4. What things did we anticipate that turned out not to happen?
5. Where could we improve?
6. What mistakes did we successfully avoid making?
7. What should we experiment with on our next project?
8. What did we learn by doing this project?
9. What could we automate or simplify that we do over and over again?
10. What other value could we extract from the project we just completed?
11. What skills did we need that were missing on this project?
12. What skills do we anticipate we need to improve our project performance?
13. What value did we get from the formal planning or documentation?
14. What value did we not get from the formal planning or documentation that we could strive for next time?

The ability of team members to learn and grow on the job is an important reason people stay with the organization. Reduce turnover by increasing learning—and get more valuable employees out of the process!

Interview for More Information

Look for all the different ways you can get evaluation information on your project. In addition to a formal "lessons learned" meeting, interview and survey your customers, your project sponsor, and others in and outside the organization who were affected by your project. Consider interviewing key vendors and contractors as well. Their specialized expertise and insight is an oft-neglected source of information.

Documenting Lessons Learned

Complete your project by developing a "lessons learned" document in the form of a report. To the extent that any part of the document is a discussion of project mistakes, avoid naming names. Even if your intent is not to cast blame, finding one's name in print associated with an error is not comforting to most people. Focus on the future. How will the next project or projects run better, more smoothly, with fewer errors, with higher quality, and with more accurate cost and schedule performance? Start this as an organizational tradition, and watch all the projects in the organization improve!

Setting Objective Goals for Project Improvement

Striving for project management maturity is an important goal in forward-thinking organizations, because successful projects are how the organization changes and grows for the future. It's normal for organizations to start without a formal project management process and stumble through a few projects before coming to the realization that planning and organization are critical to success. Market project management success to your own top management so they know what's going on and have a chance to support you.

Promoting Project Management as a Policy

Successful organizational change always requires the participation of senior management, but it's not necessary that they be on board on Day 1. Often, one department or section in the organization starts seeing the value of formal project management methodology, and the result is more successful projects. As other departments and groups see that it works, they begin to adopt the methodology themselves. It's often best if a new management theory or policy proves itself operationally first, and then top management gets excited about it. Results matter more than theory, so start with the results and watch the theory take care of itself.

> Successful organizational change always requires the participation of senior management, but it's not necessary that they be on board on Day 1.

Get the Organization on Board

Distribute your "lessons learned" reports fairly widely so that others see the process and the outcomes, and you'll start your organization moving on the path to project management success. Offer to coach or assist other project managers on the skills you learn. As all of us who train have experienced, there's nothing like trying to teach someone else to stimulate your own learning.

Promote Objective Goals

Now that you have "lessons learned" from one project, what goals should you set for yourself and your team on your next project? The basic goals of meeting the Triple Constraints and having a happy customer at the end are always on the agenda, but what about some others?

Look for the parts of the process that have proven to be vulnerable. Is it common that your customers have trouble defining their actual requirements? Then a good goal might be to develop a questioning process to help customers pin themselves down appropriately. Have your estimates proven to be a little on the optimistic side? Decide why that's happening and work to reform the process of doing the work, or alternatively change your estimating methodology.

Establish benchmarks for quality improvement in project management based on current project performance. We can already do projects this well. How about moving the bar upward a little bit?

Celebrating the Victory . . . and the Team

Your success is ultimately given to you by the work and achievement of other people. It's appropriate for you as the project manager to accept some of the credit, because you would have had to accept all the blame. Honor and good policy demand, however, that you share that credit. Besides the demands of simple good behavior, there are a number of practical payoffs you receive when you celebrate the work and achievement of your team and of the individuals on your team.

If you ask people what they'd most like to have as a reward for outstanding performance, the overwhelming chorus is usually "money!" And money is certainly one way to reward good performance. But the project manager is often not the supervisor of all team members, and you may not have the opportunity or the power to give people financial rewards. You can recommend them for financial rewards if your organization provides them, and that's usually worth the effort, but money is frequently not an option.

> The project manager is often not the supervisor of all team members, and you may not have the opportunity or the power to give people financial rewards.

Maslow's Hierarchy

People on the higher levels of Maslow's hierarchy work more for self-esteem and self-actualization than for physical or material rewards. That means that a sincere thank-you note (copies for the personnel file and for the supervisor of record or other appropriate senior managers) or some little something that provides a personal

Be Sincere

Your souvenir may not be something with historical significance, but that's not what you need. Thoughtfulness, creativity, and a sense of shared achievement are what make tokens of recognition real and significant, and that's something within all our grasps. A simple, sincere, and honest "thank you" for the contributions of your team members is always appropriate, and surprisingly effective.

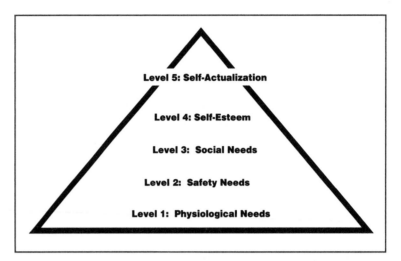

▲ FIGURE 32-1: *Maslow's hierarchy of needs.* As your needs are satisfied at a particular level, what motivates you moves up the hierarchy. Notice that most people in the organization are at Levels 3-5.

memento of the project experience has a surprisingly positive effect (see Figure 32-1). The key is sincerity—if it's clear you mean it, people will like it. If they don't think you mean it, they'll take it but it won't improve performance particularly.

Memorialization

People can find enormous satisfaction in project work, because at its end you have something to show for your effort. The best kind of memorialization and celebration is something that reminds us of that effort and applauds our performance in achieving it. At the conclusion of building the Smithsonian National Air and Space Museum, all staff received a little certificate of thanks, each hand-signed by the director. Down at the bottom there was a tiny little souvenir: a one-inch square of silver fabric (complete with dry rot) taken from the restoration of the Spirit of St. Louis. The cash value was insignificant, but the celebration and reminder of achievement was very real indeed.

Resources and Tools

Chapter 33

Starting Your Search

There is a world of resources and tools available to help you, your team, and your organization get better in project management. Because the world changes more rapidly than books get updates, the information here is a start for your own search process. There's much, much more available. Good luck, and good hunting!

The Project Management Institute (PMI)

Since its founding in 1969, the Project Management Institute (PMI) has been the leading professional body in the field. As of this writing, the organization has about 90,000 members worldwide. The purposes of PMI are to establish project management standards, provide seminars and educational programs, and offer a professional certification, the Project Management Professional (PMP) designation. It puts on regular conferences and is a publisher and distributor of books and magazines on the topic of project management. The magazine *Project Management Journal* is one of the leading publications in the field.

PMI also publishes *A Guide to the Project Management Body of Knowledge*, known as the PMBOK (pronounced "Pimm-bok") Guide. The PMBOK is a recognized American National Standard by the American National Standards Institute (ANSI). Part of becoming certified as a PMP involves getting to know the PMBOK so you can pass a test on it.

If project management is or will be a significant part of your career, there are advantages to joining PMI. You can get to know your peers and network with them, always part of a good career management strategy. You have access to a substantial amount of information on project management by project managers. You can attend conferences and seminars, work toward certification, and find companies and organizations that value the PMP designation. For more information, visit their Web site at *www.pmi.org*.

> If project management is or will be a significant part of your career, there are advantages to joining PMI.

Resources for Project Managers

There are numerous organizations that provide training and consulting to individuals in the area of project management. You can take seminars in all aspects of project management from planning to risk management from a variety of training companies. To find training companies that subscribe to PMI standards, check *www.pmirep.org* for a current list. You can also contact the author of this book or training or consulting support at *www.dobsonbooks.com*.

Consulting companies can actually provide project management leadership teams to help organizations run large, complicated projects; provide executive coaching; help organizations implement a project management improvement program; and provide other services. Start with the PMI list. To use consultants effectively, it's a good idea for you to know what you want before you ask someone to provide it for you.

Books and Periodicals

It's always wise to develop a professional library in a field you wish to master. Of course, you've already started your library with this book. You can find a variety of other overall books on project management practice, or you can go into greater depth or learn advanced techniques. A good source of titles in the area of project management can be obtained at *www.pmibookstore.org*.

There are a variety of newsletters and magazines that cover project management. These include *Successful Project Management*, the *CBP e-Advisor* (via e-mail), and others.

Even if you don't read your management books cover to cover, familiarize yourself with the index and table of contents so you can dive in when you need specific information.

> It's always wise to develop a professional library in a field you wish to master.

Academic Credentials

You can obtain a master's degree in project management, or take project management courses as part of an undergraduate or graduate degree. In a number of MBA and business Ph.D. programs, you can take a concentration in project management or at least make project management part of your overall program of study. Even if you don't plan to be a full-time project manager, you will frequently profit by having an understanding of project management processes in almost every occupation.

Before assuming you need an advanced degree, check the credentials of people who have the kind of job you want—you might waste years and money on the wrong target!

Project Management and Your Organization

In this book, we've focused primarily on how you can use project management techniques on your projects. You can normally implement much of this on your own projects simply by deciding to do so; you don't necessarily need the permission of your managers. Results speak for themselves; if project management helps you get the job done and you don't get bogged down in unnecessary detail, you'll find it pays for you.

Imagine how much better and stronger things would be if your entire organization adopted a project management philosophy and organized itself to make sure that project managers—people like you—had the resources and tools to do the job, and that others above you and below you in the organization all spoke the same language.

This approach is known by several names: Management By Projects (MBP), Managing the Organization By Projects (MOBP), Enterprise Project Management, and others. While details vary, all of these concepts have in common the idea that project management needs to be institutionalized in order to achieve the very best results. And when organizations come to the realization that projects are how they do business, many organizations have decided that a business-wide or agency-wide approach to project management is the best way to go.

The first step is for the leadership of the organization to learn enough about this concept to determine if it's right for them, and to make the necessary commitment to change. The second step is the development of metrics tools to measure success, and then the implementation of a project management improvement program.

Establishing a Project Management Improvement Program

Project management improvement does not happen overnight. A strategic plan is needed to describe the specific improvement actions to be

So Many Decisions

There are a number of decisions to make, such as how to structure the organization for maximum project effectiveness, how to coordinate such issues as shared resources, conflicts involving priorities, and development of individual project managers. This kind of initiative is practiced by some of today's cutting edge organizations, and when properly implemented, has demonstrated significant results.

pursued as a series of small projects. The plan should relate to the overall business goals of the organization and should identify the resources needed to execute the projects, the schedule, responsibilities, and measures to indicate success or failure from the improvement initiatives.

One basis for establishing a project management improvement program is understanding your organization's current location on a project management maturity scale.

In considering project management maturity, organizations must have defined business goals, established and effective project management processes, and a commitment to project management. Goals must be specific, measurable, and attainable so that projects can be completed successfully following defined processes.

Processes are critical to execute business strategies and plans. Processes need to be controlled, predicted, and improved to achieve organizational goals. The organization needs to understand the characteristics of existing processes and the factors that affect the capability of the processes; and plan, justify, and implement actions to modify processes as needed to better meet business needs.

Maturity models are used to identify where an organization's processes fall within industry-wide best practices. A project management maturity assessment can provide the framework for a project management improvement program in the organization.

As more organizations move toward management by projects, effective project management is viewed as an ingredient for success, as it promotes consistent and successful delivery of projects. It is important to assess project management maturity in order to:

- Improve the ability to complete projects successfully.
- Improve processes used for project management.
- Identify strengths and weaknesses in project management.
- Establish a baseline for improvement objectives.
- Help an organization become project-based with predictable results.

Several different maturity models have been developed to assess project management maturity using metrics. Many of these are based on similar concepts to the models developed for software by the

> Maturity models are used to identify where an organization's processes fall within industry-wide best practices.

Software Engineering Institute (SEI) at Carnegie Mellon University (*www.sei.cmu.edu*) and show goals to be achieved by levels.

Assess project management maturity by using a series of levels with key goals at each level relating to the five project management processes: Initiating, Planning, Executing, Controlling, and Closing. Maturity models use an evolutionary approach for continuously improving processes.

In addition, a metrics program can assist in the program of management improvement. Metrics can measure the status of activities under way, to take a process view and to gauge the contribution of project management to the organization. Metrics also help demonstrate to the organization its return on investment from the improved practice.

Source: Ted A. Leemann, Executive Director of Project Management, Management Concepts, Inc. Copyright © 2001 by Management Concepts, Inc. All Rights Reserved. Used with permission of Management Concepts, Inc.

> There is an art to project management, and that art requires a commitment to lifelong learning.

Developing Yourself as a Project Manager

There are subjects you can master. Once you learn them, you know them. Other subjects are part of the discipline known as "lifelong learning," the commitment to make self-development a regular and integral part of your professional career. Many of the techniques and tools of project management fit into the first category. For example, once you understand how to build a Gantt Chart, the knowledge is yours, and it's time to move on to a new intellectual challenge.

There is an art to project management, and that art requires a commitment to lifelong learning. You never completely master it; you continue to grow and develop yourself without limit. How to apply and use the Triple Constraints to understand your project environment is one example. When you read about projects in trouble, or projects that succeed, try to envision the Triple Constraints and how they shaped the project environment. How would better understanding of the constraints have helped the project manager? What types of insights can you develop by considering the project's reason for existing?

The people side of project management requires study outside the formal boundaries of the field. For example, negotiation is a core competency for most project managers because you find that you have to negotiate almost every day when you're in the project management role. The study of negotiation isn't labeled as "project management," but it's part of a project manager's course of study. The theory and practice of motivation is another area that project managers need to study. When you're not always in the role of official supervisor or manager, learning how to get people to do what you want by when you want it is a crucial art.

The End of the Road

As we finish our long journey through the world of project management, we've discovered that project management touches on every area of our work. In addition to the specific tools and techniques of the field, project managers need the full set of general management skills as well as deep knowledge of their own technical areas. It's a tall order, and no one knows it all—but we're still responsible and accountable for it.

The best way to make this work is to take on a role as a teacher, trainer, and mentor. All of us who have learned project management during the course of our own careers were taught and mentored by others. We're grateful for the training and support we have received. But at the same time we know that by training us, the project managers for whom we worked made a profit as well. They knew that for their projects to succeed, their team members needed to know the skills as well. When you train others, you not only benefit them, you frequently benefit yourself and your projects at the same time.

Your Action Plan

Develop a personal action plan for the next two years setting out what areas of project management and general management you need for your professional growth, and figure out how you will acquire those skills. Talk with your own managers about organizational support for your education. Seminars, books, classes, and conferences are an important way to grow, but don't neglect the value of learning by doing.

When you are assigned a new project, add to the project objectives your learning objectives. What will you practice this time? What skills will you work to develop? What part of project management will you focus on? Who will you teach? How will you develop the skills of your team members in project management? How will you use this project to show management the value of project management as a tool?

Your commitment and your drive for excellence in project management is a powerful asset. When you demonstrate that it is important and that it helps you succeed, you'll find that others will join in, wanting to learn what you know to make themselves, and the entire organization, more successful.

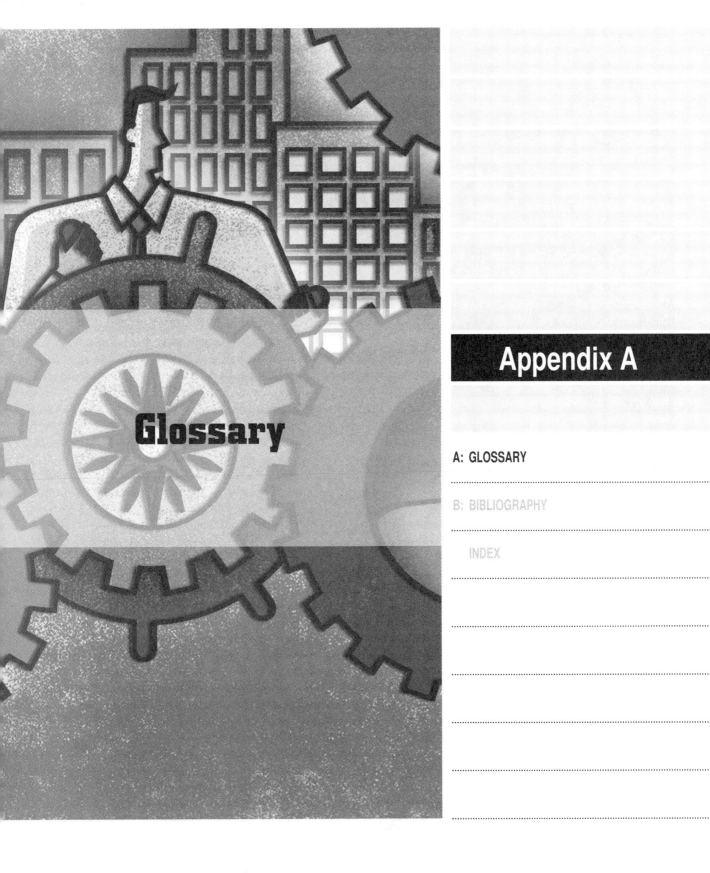

Glossary

Appendix A

Administrative Closure–The process of verifying and documenting project results, formalizing acceptance of the product or service by the customer, collecting and reviewing project records, analyzing project effectiveness, and archiving information for future use. The process can also entail reassignment or return of personnel and equipment.

Arrow Diagramming Method (ADM)–A method of network diagramming in which the work is represented by the lines.

Assumption–Something taken for granted as being true or certain without a factual basis.

Baseline–*See* Performance Baseline.

Benchmarking–A technique for identifying and measuring quality goals against an established reference point. Using benchmarking, you can compare conditions, processes, or results. By using benchmarks, you can identify potential improvements and quality goals.

Bottom-Up Estimating–Process of developing an estimate for a project by estimating each component and rolling the data up.

Budget–The proposed and/or accepted costs for a project organized by categories.

Budget Estimate–An estimate based on an analysis of a completed three-level project WBS for the purpose of job costing and/or bid preparation.

Business Risk–A risk containing the opportunity for gain as well as for loss.

Calendar Time–The number of calendar days (or other periods) necessary to complete a task or project. Includes weekends, holidays, and other nonworking days.

Change Order–A document describing a change in project scope or objectives that modifies a contract or other project authorizing documents. A change order

normally involves a cost, and normally must be approved by the person responsible for paying that cost.

Checklist–A tool used to ensure that all steps of a task are performed in order. Used in risk management to itemize risk items.

Closeout–The process of completing a project; normally includes administrative (internal) closure and contract closeout.

Common Cause Variation–Variation resulting from small causes, inherent in the system.

Conceptual/Order of Magnitude Estimate–A very rough estimate based on a general category of project with little or no available detail. Usually used to start a general discussion about a potential project.

Constraint–A factor that limits the project team's options; restrictions that affect performance, cost, and/or scheduling of the project. A project always has the Triple Constraints of time, cost, and performance, but may have additional constraints as well.

Contingency Planning–A method of active risk acceptance, in which a potential solution is drawn up but only used if a risk triggering event occurs.

Cost–The money you spend. *See* Price.

Cost Baseline–A comparison of actual costs to planned costs for the purpose of monitoring.

Cost Constraint–One of the legs of the Triple Constraints. Includes both money and resource expenditures.

Cost Estimate–An estimate of the costs that will be incurred on a project.

Cost of Quality–(1) Costs resulting from failures in quality. (2) Costs to maintain quality.

Crash Time–The shortest possible duration a task can take, given unlimited resources.

Crashing–Speeding up a task or project by spending money or resources to shorten activity durations.

Critical Path-The longest path through a schedule network. A sequence of activities from project start to finish, all of which have slack or float less than or equal to zero.

Critical Path Method (CPM)-A method of managing cost and time tradeoffs to achieve superior project performance.

Definitive Estimate-An estimate based on substantial actual work completed and detailed analysis of remaining work. Used for weekly reporting and progress measurement.

Deliverables-What you deliver: any measurable, tangible result that must be produced to complete a project. For a Web site, the deliverables include the site itself, but also specific components of the site, such as a shopping cart or tracking mechanism. In addition, deliverables might include documentation, a CD-ROM containing all the files, and a training program for users and operators. Make sure all deliverables are spelled out in the agreement to do the project, so you can ensure that each is actually done and turned over.

Delphi Method-An estimating methodology based on a written and anonymous survey of multiple experts.

Dependency-A condition in which a task cannot begin until all or some of a predecessor or successor has been completed. See Finish-to-Start, Start-to-Start, Finish-to-Finish, and Start-to-Finish Dependencies.

Direct Costs-Those costs that can be specifically identified with a particular project, program, or activity.

Driver-The driver of the project is the constraint that must be met at all costs, or else the project will be considered a failure.

Duration-The number of work days (or other periods) necessary to complete a task or project. Does not count nonworking days, such as weekends or holidays.

Early Finish (EF)-The earliest a task can finish, determined by adding the Duration to the Early Start.

Early Start (ES)-The earliest a task can start, based on the logic and duration of previous activities, as well as any imposed dates. Calculate ES as part of the forward pass.

Earned Value Method-A method for measuring project performance by comparing what was planned with what was accomplished.

Effort-The number of work hours necessary to complete a task or project. If someone is not working full time on a task or project, the level of effort will be less than the duration. If someone is working full time or overtime, or if more than one person is working full time on the task or project, the level of effort can be greater than the duration.

Estimating by Analogy-The process of building an estimate on another, similar project. Also known as "top-down estimating."

External Deliverable-A deliverable that must be approved by the project sponsor or customer.

Feasibility Estimate-A general estimate used to determine further interest in pursuing a potential project.

Final Estimate-An estimate based on a bottom-up analysis of all WBS levels, used for project cost accounting and reporting.

Finish-to-Finish (FF) Dependency-A condition in which the finish of Task 2 cannot occur until the finish of Task 1. Lead and lag may modify the relationship further.

Finish-to-Start (FS) Dependency-A condition in which the start of Task 2 cannot occur until the finish of Task 1. Lead and lag may modify the relationship further.

Fixed Costs-Expenses that must be paid regardless of the volume or level of the project.

Float-Extra time to finish a task before something is delayed. *See* Slack, *also* Free Slack/Float *and* Total Slack/Float.

Forward/Backward Pass-A procedure for calculating the critical path and identifying the presence, type, and amount of slack/float.

Free Slack/Float-The extra time available to finish a task before it delays its successor task, whether or not the project is delayed as a result.

Gantt Chart-A chart that presents multiple overlapping tasks presented over a period of time in the form of a bar chart; the easiest chart to read and understand for people not familiar with project management.

Goal-The purpose of the project, the benefit received from the project's successful completion.

Godzilla Principle-If you catch a problem early, it's easier to solve.

Hidden Agenda-An additional goal, objective, or stake someone has in the project process or outcome that is not officially stated in the project objective.

Hierarchy of Constraints-The order of driver, middle constraint, and weak constraint on an individual project.

Imposed Date-A mandatory project date that overrides normal calculations of task start/finish.

Indirect Costs-Costs necessary to the operation of the organization that cannot be readily or specifically identified with a particular project or program. Examples include depreciation, operations and maintenance, and general administrative costs. Also known as overhead.

Influence Management-The art and craft of gaining influence over others to achieve project and work goals.

Insurance Risk-A risk that only has an opportunity for loss. Also called "pure" risk.

Intact Work Team-A project team with members fully dedicated to project work and assigned to the project from start to finish.

Lag-A planned delay until you start the next activity. After we pour the concrete for the swimming pool, we need lag time for the concrete to set before we can paint it.

Late Finish (LF)-The latest a task can finish without delaying the project, based on the logic and duration of subsequent activities, plus any imposed dates. Calculate the LF as part of the backward pass.

Late Start (LS)-The latest a task can start, determined by subtracting the Duration from the Late Finish.

Lead-Overlapping one task so it starts before something else is finished. If we want the appliances to install in our new kitchen, we can order them with enough lead time so they will be here when we're ready to install.

Level of Effort-*See* Effort.

Middle Constraint-The second level of the Triple Constraints hierarchy. The middle constraint has somewhat more flexibility than the driver, but less than the weak constraint.

Milestone-A task with a Duration of zero. Milestones serve as markers for significant project events, such as starting, finishing, or completing a major phase, or for mandatory reviews or interim completions. In project management software, normally entering "0" in the Duration field turns a task into a milestone automatically.

Network Diagram-A graphic representation of how project activities relate to one another in sequence and logic. There are several types of Network Diagrams. Network Diagrams are often (incorrectly) referred to as PERT charts.

Objective-The description of the project itself, expressed in measurable terms.

Opportunity Cost-What could have been done instead with the time and resources allocated to your project.

Orange Rope-A constraint people imagine to be true that isn't.

Overhead-Name for certain indirect costs that are often billed to the project as a percentage of revenue or expenditures.

Parametric Model-An estimating tool that calculates cost and duration on the basis of variables.

Part-Time Work Team-A team in which members are also responsible for other projects and work, where few or no members are fully dedicated to the project.

Performance Baselines-The original plans of the project form the performance baselines, against which actual performance can be measured. There are normally three baselines: schedule, cost, and technical, corresponding to the Triple Constraints.

Performance Criteria-The measurable performance objectives the project must achieve to be considered acceptable. A leg of the Triple Constraints.

Periodic Reviews-Reviews initiated by the project manager to track progress on the Triple Constraints. *See also* Topical Reviews.

Power-Energy that overcomes resistance to achieve work. Applies both in engineering and in office politics.

Predecessor-A task or tasks that must be completed (or at least started) before a successor task can begin. The successor task is dependent on the predecessor(s).

Preliminary Estimate-An estimate normally developed for internal budgeting purposes, based on the Project Charter and possibly Statement of Work/Scope Statement information, but not yet on a detailed analysis of tasks.

Price-The money you charge. *See* Cost.

Program-A group of projects managed in a coordinated way. A program may include elements of ongoing operations.

Project-A temporary endeavor undertaken to create a unique product, service, or result.

Project Charter-A formal written document that states the commitment of the organization to do the project, provides a high-level summary of project objectives and goals, and assigns the project manager and defines his or her authority.

Project Management-(1) A way of thinking about projects. (2) The application of knowledge, skills, tools, and techniques to project activities in order to meet or exceed stakeholder needs and expectations from a project.

Project Management Software-Software that automates some portion of project management activities. Usually provides such tools as Gantt Charts, Network Diagrams, and progress tracking. Software options include different levels of power and different types of tracking and accounting.

Project Manager-The individual operationally responsible and accountable for managing project team members, project activities, and project goals.

Project Sponsor-The manager in the performing organization who authorizes the project, allocates cash and other resources to perform it, and has executive responsibility for the project's successful completion.

Pure Risk-A risk that only has an opportunity for loss. Also called "insurance" risk.

Quality–Exceeding the customer's expectations (Deming). Conformance to requirements (Crosby). (Additional definitions are given in Chapter 22.)

Quality Circle Meeting–A meeting to review and manage quality issues on your project.

Requirement–A need, function, feature, or attribute wanted by the customer. Also, a condition or capability required by contract, specification, or other formal document.

Requirements Allocation and Tracing–The process of linking requirements to the deliverables, actions, or processes where they are to be satisfied, and verifying that requirements have been achieved.

Requirements Analysis–The process of determining the formal or actual requirements, creating detailed specifications, and confirming understanding with the customer or users.

Resource Leveling–A process of adjusting a schedule based on resource constraints, such as maximum number of people who can be working at any one time.

Risk–Areas of uncertainty that can affect project outcomes. A risk consists of an event, the probability of occurrence of the event, and the impact of the event (usually expressed in currency units).

Risk Management–A project management process consisting of risk identification, risk quantification, risk response planning, and risk response control.

Risk Management Meeting–A periodic meeting on your project to monitor and update the risk response plan.

Scope–All of the products and services that are to be provided within the project.

Scope Creep–The observed tendency of scope to increase and expand during the project life cycle.

Scope Management Plan–A written document that identifies the scope and deliverables, and that establishes procedures to ensure scope is achieved and that changes in scope are properly approved and integrated into the project.

Scope Statement–A documented description of the project that serves to establish a common understanding among stakeholders and provides a foundation for subsequent project decisions.

Slack–Extra time to finish a task before something is delayed. *See* Float, *also* Free Slack/Float *and* Total Slack/Float.

SMART–The acronym describing the characteristics of a well-designed objective: Specific, Measurable, Agreed To, Realistic, and Time-Constrained.

Stakeholder–A stakeholder can be a person or an organization that is involved in or may be affected by project activities; someone with a vested interest in a specific outcome, or who exerts influence over a project.

Start-to-Finish (SF) Dependency–A rare condition in which the start of Task 2 cannot occur until the finish of Task 1. Lead and lag may modify the relationship further.

Start-to-Start (SS) Dependency–A condition in which the start of Task 1 cannot occur until the finish of Task 2. Lead and lag may modify the relationship further.

Statement of Work (SOW)–A narrative description of products or services to be supplied by a project.

Status Review–A periodic meeting of your project team to measure progress in achieving the Triple Constraints.

Task–A defined part of a project's work displayed in the bottom level of a Work Breakdown Structure (WBS) that accomplishes a specific project result.

Task Table–A table that organizes task, dependency, and duration information from the WBS and Network

Diagram into a form suitable for adaptation into a Gantt Chart.

Template–A pro-forma standard or sample designed to be adapted to each individual project; often a time-saver and quality enhancer in the planning process.

Time Constraint–Deadlines or other pressures to finish the project in a certain amount of time or before a specific date; a leg of the Triple Constraints.

Topical Reviews–Reviews of certain elements of your project, often initiated by customers, inspectors, funders, or others outside the project team. *See also* Periodic Reviews.

Total Quality Management (TQM)–A systems approach to quality; a group of philosophies and approaches to quality management including the work of Deming, Juran, Crosby, and others.

Total Slack/Float–The extra time available to finish a task before it results in a delay to the project.

Triple Constraints–The constraints of time, cost, and performance criteria, which limit your choices and shape the universe of your project.

Variable Costs–Costs that change depending on the volume or level of the project, such as labor.

Variance–A discrepancy between what's planned and actuals in any of the Triple Constraints areas of time, cost, and performance.

WAG–"Wild Assed Guess" or "Wildly Aimed Guess." Some more formal WAGs are called SWAG, or "Scientific Wild Assed Guess." This is a fairly common business expression, and can refer to a Conceptual/Order of Magnitude or Feasibility level estimate.

Weak Constraint–The most flexible (but not necessarily least important) member of the Hierarchy of Constraints. Exploiting the weak constraint is a powerful technique for helping to accomplish your project goals.

Work–An ongoing activity without a planned end to it.

Work Breakdown Structure (WBS)–A deliverable-oriented or activity-oriented grouping of project elements, activities, or tasks that organizes and defines the total scope of the project. The WBS can be displayed in organization chart format or in outline format.

Bibliography

Appendix B

Bennis, Warren, and Burt Nanus. *Leaders: The Strategies for Taking Charge*, New York: Harper Perennial, 1985.

Block, Peter. *The Empowered Manager: Positive Political Skills at Work*, San Francisco: Jossey-Bass Publishers, 1987.

Bramson, Robert M., Ph.D. *Coping With Difficult People*, New York: Anchor Press/Doubleday, 1981.

Caro, Robert. *The Power Broker: Robert Moses and the Fall of New York*, New York: Alfred A. Knopf, 1974.

Caroselli, Marlene, Ed.D. *Meetings That Work*, Mission, Kansas: SkillPath Publications, 1992.

Crosby, Philip B. *Quality Without Tears: The Art of Hassle-Free Management*, New York: Plume, 1985.

Dawson, Roger. *The Secrets of Power Negotiating* (audiotape), Chicago: Nightingale-Conant, 1987.

Dobson, Michael Singer, and Deborah Singer Dobson. *Coping With Supervisory Nightmares*, Mission, Kansas: SkillPath Publications, 1997 (book), 1998 (audio, video).

Dobson, Michael Singer, and Deborah Singer Dobson. *Enlightened Office Politics: Understanding, Coping With, and Winning the Game—Without Losing Your Soul*, New York: AMACOM, 2001.

Dobson, Michael Singer, and Deborah Singer Dobson. *Managing UP!: 59 Ways to Build a Career-Advancing Relationship With Your Boss*, New York: AMACOM, 2000.

Dobson, Michael Singer, and Deborah Singer Dobson. *Training Skills for Team Leaders* (video, audio), Mission, Kansas: SkillPath Publications, 1998.

Dobson, Michael S. *Exploring Personality Styles*, Mission, Kansas: SkillPath Publications, 1999.

Dobson, Michael S. *The Juggler's Guide to Managing Multiple Projects*, Newtown Square, Pennsylvania: Project Management Institute, 1999.

Dobson, Michael S. *Practical Project Management*, Mission, Kansas: SkillPath Publications, 1996.

Dobson, Michael S. *Project Management for the Technical Professional*, Newtown Square, Pennsylvania: Project Management Institute, 2001.

Dobyns, Lloyd, and Clare Crawford-Mason. *Quality or Else: The Revolution in World Business*, New York: Houghton Mifflin, 1991.

DuBrin, Andrew. *Winning Office Politics: DuBrin's Guide for the '90s*, Englewood Cliffs, New Jersey: Prentice Hall, 1990.

Fielder, Barbara. *Motivation in the Workplace*, Mission, Kansas: SkillPath Publications, 1996.

Finkler, Steven A. Ph.D., C. P. A. *The Complete Guide to Finance & Accounting for Nonfinancial Managers*, Englewood Cliffs, New Jersey: Prentice Hall, 1983.

Fisher, Roger, and William Ury. *Getting to Yes: Negotiating Agreement Without Giving In*, Middlesex, England: Penguin Books, 1981.

Flannes, Steven W., Ph.D., and Ginger Levin, DPA. *People Skills for Project Managers*, Vienna, Virginia: Management Concepts, 2001.

Fleming, Quentin W., and Joel M. Koppelman. *Earned Value Project Management* (Second Edition), Newtown Square, Pennsylvania: Project Management Institute, 2000.

Goleman, Daniel. *Emotional Intelligence*, New York: Bantam Books, 1995.

Gonick, Larry, and Woolcott Smith. *The Cartoon Guide to Statistics*, New York: HarperCollins, 1993.

Goodpasture, John C. *Managing Projects for Value (Project Management Essential Library)*, Vienna, Virginia: Management Concepts, 2002.

Haughan, Gregory T. *Effective Work Breakdown Structures (Project Management Essential*

Library), Vienna, Virginia: Management Concepts, 2002.

Humphrey, Watts S. *Managing Technical People: Innovation, Teamwork, and the Software Process*, Reading, Massachusetts: Addison-Wesley, 1997.

Imai, Masaaki. *Kaizen: The Key to Japan's Competitive Success*, New York: McGraw-Hill, 1986.

Kennedy, Marilyn Moats. *Office Politics: Seizing Power, Wielding Clout*, New York: Warner Books, 1980.

Kerzner, Harold, Ph.D. *Project Management: A Systems Approach to Planning, Scheduling, and Controlling*, Seventh Edition, New York: John Wiley & Sons, Inc., 2001.

Korda, Michael. *Power: How to Get It, How to Use It*, (audiotape), New York: Simon & Schuster Audio & Video, 1986.

Kouzes, James M., and Barry Z. Posner. *The Leadership Challenge: How to Keep Getting Extraordinary Things Done in Organizations*, San Francisco: Jossey-Bass, 1995.

Leach, Lawrence P. *Critical Chain Project Management*, Boston: Artech House, Inc., 2000.

Lewis, H. W. *Why Flip a Coin? The Art and Science of Good Decisions*, New York: John Wiley & Sons, Inc., 1997.

Machiavelli, Niccoló. *The Prince*, London: Everyman Library, 1995.

Neuendorf, Steve. *Project Measurement (Project Management Essential Library)*, Vienna, Virginia: Management Concepts, 2002.

Pachter, Barbara, and Marjorie Brody. *Climbing the Corporate Ladder: What You Need to Know and Do to Be a Promotable Person*, Mission, Kansas: SkillPath Publications, 1995.

Peters, Thomas J. and Robert H. Waterman, Jr. *In Search of Excellence*, New York: Warner Books, 1982.

Project Management Institute, *A Guide to the Project Management Body of Knowledge (PMBOK Guide)*, Newtown Square, Pennsylvania: Project Management Institute, 1999.

Project Management Institute. *Project Management Software Survey*, Newtown Square, Pennsylvania: Project Management Institute, 1999.

Rad, Parviz F. *Project Estimating and Cost Management (Project Management Essential Library)*, Vienna, Virginia: Management Concepts, 2002.

Raiffa, Howard. *The Art and Science of Negotiation: How to Resolve Conflicts and Get the Best Out of Bargaining*, Cambridge, Massachusetts: Belknap Press/Harvard University Press, 1982.

Royer, Paul S. *Project Risk Management: A Proactive Approach (Project Management Essential Library)*, Vienna, Virginia: Management Concepts, 2002.

Stein, Richard J. *Learning to Manage Technical Professionals: Crossing The Swamp*, Reading, Massachusetts: Addison-Wesley, 1993.

Tannen, Deborah, Ph.D. *Talking From 9 to 5: How Women's and Men's Conversational Styles Affect Who Gets Heard, Who Gets Credit, and What Gets Done at Work*, New York: William Morrow, 1994.

Weisbord, Marvin R. *Productive Workplaces: Organizing and Managing for Dignity, Meaning, and Community*, San Francisco: Jossey-Bass, 1987.

Wiest, Jerome D., and Ferdinand K. Levy. *A Management Guide to PERT/CPM*, Englewood Cliffs, New Jersey: Prentice-Hall, 1969.